Y0-CUP-539

*MATERIALISM
AND
THE MIND-BODY
PROBLEM*

CENTRAL ISSUES IN PHILOSOPHY SERIES

BARUCH A. BRODY
series editor

Baruch A. Brody
MORAL RULES AND PARTICULAR CIRCUMSTANCES

Hugo A. Bedau
JUSTICE AND EQUALITY

Mark Levensky
HUMAN FACTUAL KNOWLEDGE

George I. Mavrodes
THE RATIONALITY OF BELIEF IN GOD

Robert Sleigh
NECESSARY TRUTH

David M. Rosenthal
MATERIALISM AND THE MIND-BODY PROBLEM

Richard Grandy
THEORIES AND OBSERVATIONS IN SCIENCE

Gerald Dworkin
DETERMINISM, FREE WILL, AND MORAL RESPONSIBILITY

David P. Gauthier
MORALITY AND RATIONAL SELF-INTEREST

Charles Landesman
THE FOUNDATIONS OF KNOWLEDGE

Adrienne and Keith Lehrer
THEORY OF MEANING

edited by
DAVID M. ROSENTHAL
*Lehman College
of the City University of New York*

MATERIALISM AND THE MIND-BODY PROBLEM

Prentice-Hall, Inc., Englewood Cliffs, New Jersey

© 1971 by Prentice-Hall, Inc., Englewood Cliffs, N.J.

All rights reserved. No part of this book may be
reproduced in any form or by any means
without permission in writing from the publisher.

Library of Congress Catalog Card Number: 77-157186

Printed in the United States of America

C 13-560185-1
P 13-560177-0

Current Printing (last digit):
10 9 8 7 6 5 4 3 2 1

PRENTICE-HALL INTERNATIONAL, INC., London
PRENTICE-HALL OF AUSTRALIA, PTY. LTD., Sydney
PRENTICE-HALL OF CANADA, LTD., Toronto
PRENTICE-HALL OF INDIA PRIVATE LIMITED, New Delhi
PRENTICE-HALL OF JAPAN, INC., Tokyo

Foreword

~~~~~~~~~~~~~~~~~~~~~~~~~~~~~~~~~~~~~~

The Central Issues in Philosophy series is based upon the conviction that the best way to teach philosophy to introductory students is to experience or to *do* philosophy with them. The basic unit of philosophical investigation is the particular problem, and not the area or the historical figure. Therefore, this series consists of sets of readings organised around well-defined, manageable problems. All other things being equal, problems that are of interest and relevance to the student have been chosen.

Each volume contains an introduction that clearly defines the problem and sets out the alternative positions that have been taken. The selections are chosen and arranged in such a way as to take the student through the dialectic of the problem; each reading, besides presenting a particular point of view, criticizes the points of view set out earlier.

Although no attempt has been made to introduce the student in a systematic way to the history of philosophy, classical selections relevant to the development of the problem have been included. As a side benefit, the student will therefore come to see the continuity, as well as the breaks, between classical and contemporary thought. But in no case has a selection been included merely for its historical significance; clarity of expression and systematic significance are the main criteria for selection.

BARUCH A. BRODY

Contents

INTRODUCTION ... 1

part one
CLASSICAL MATERIALISM ... 19

RENÉ DESCARTES
   Selections ... 19
   from *Discourse on the Method
   of rightly directing one's Reason
   and of seeking Truth in the Sciences,* PART FIVE ... 19
   from Letter to the Marquis of Newcastle ... 21
   from Letter to Henry More ... 23
   from *Meditations on First Philosophy,*
   SIXTH MEDITATION ... 25

BENEDICT DE SPINOZA
   from *Ethics,* PARTS ONE, TWO AND THREE ... 31

THOMAS HOBBES
   Selections ... 43
   from *Leviathan,* PART I, CHAPTERS 1, 2 AND 3 ... 43
   from *De Corpore,* PART IV, CHAPTER 25 ... 47

part two
THE IDENTITY THESIS 53

J. J. C. SMART
Sensations and Brain Processes 53

JEROME SHAFFER
Mental Events and the Brain 67

JAMES W. CORNMAN
The Identity of Mind and Body 73

part three
THEORETICAL MATERIALISM 80

JAEGWON KIM
On the Psycho-Physical Identity Theory 80

THOMAS NAGEL
Physicalism 96
Postscript (November 1968) 111

KEITH GUNDERSON
Asymmetries and Mind-Body Perplexities 112

part four
FUNCTIONALISTIC MATERIALISM 128

JERRY A. FODOR
Materialism 128

HILARY PUTNAM
The Nature of Mental States 150

DAVID K. LEWIS
An Argument for the Identity Theory, with addenda (October 1969) 162

part five
ELIMINATIVE MATERIALISM — *172*

PAUL K. FEYERABEND
Mental Events and the Brain — *172*

RICHARD RORTY
Mind-Body Identity, Privacy, and Categories — *174*

RICHARD J. BERNSTEIN
The Challenge of Scientific Materialism — *200*

RICHARD RORTY
In Defense of Eliminative Materialism — *223*

BIBLIOGRAPHY — *232*

Introduction

I. BACKGROUND TO MATERIALISM

People sometimes talk about one another in terms that are just as appropriately applied to inanimate objects, and sometimes in terms that are primarily, if not exclusively, applied to human beings. For example, we talk about the size, weight, chemical composition and physical movements of ourselves and others, just as we characterize stones and houses in these ways. In addition, however, we describe the beliefs, desires and perceptions we have, and these types of characterization seem primarily reserved for application to human beings. To mark this contrast, philosophers often discriminate between two kinds of descriptions, physical and psychological.

It is clear that there is some difference between describing people (and animals) in psychological terms, and describing objects in general (including people) in physical terms. This difference reflects the fact that people are described in ways that inanimate objects are not. When we describe people in psychological terms, therefore, it seems that we are saying something about them that is not covered by any physical descriptions. It is generally conceded that this difference exists, even though no general method for classifying particular descriptions as of one sort or the other has been successful, and therefore arguments about apparent borderline cases often occur.

Just what significance this difference may have, however, is unclear. Does it follow from the fact that people are described in both psychological and physical terms that sciences such as physics and chemistry, which employ only physical terms, cannot deal exhaustively with human beings? Is psychology, understood as explaining the psychological behavior of things, a significantly different kind of science from physics or chemistry? For example, does the use of psychological descriptions in a science limit what can be accomplished by that science, or affect the nature of its methodology? Must a complete description of people contain psychological terms? And if so, does this mean that science can be given a unified foundation only at the cost of failing to deal adequately with human behavior?

One response to these questions is to claim that all the sciences, including psychology and associated human sciences, can be reduced to physics. The reduction in question would be accomplished if the terms needed for physics, and only those terms, would be sufficient to express all the claims and explanations of psychology. This view, often called "the thesis of the unity of science," has the force of a prediction about the future development of science. It is thought that when scientists have sufficient knowledge about the nature of psychological (and other peculiarly human) matters, it will be seen that psychological matters can be fully described and explained using the concepts and theoretical apparatus of physics. It is of course assumed that the concepts of physics will change with future discovery and theory construction. What is important is that whatever concepts and explanatory techniques are needed to explain the behavior of nonpsychological objects like planets, airplanes and acids will, on this view, be all that are needed to explain and account for psychological phenomena.

The difference between the two kinds of description has been a major obstacle to the acceptance of the thesis of the future unity of science, for, a complete account of human behavior cannot be expressed in physical terms if psychological descriptions say things that physical ones cannot. A defender of the unity of science might claim that even though psychological descriptions differ in nature from physical ones, psychological descriptions can nonetheless be translated into physical ones. According to this defense, if such translations were accomplished, this would show that every psychological description of something means the same as some physical description of that object. For example, any description of a person thinking, seeing or wishing could be translated into a description of the person expressed only in physical terms. And in each case, the psychological description would mean the same as the physicalistic translation. Failures to produce such translations have been attributed to our lack of detailed knowledge about human beings. For convenience we may call this defense "the translation view about psychological descriptions."

The translation view, though at one time not uncommon as a defense of the unity of science, has been almost universally abandoned. For one thing, if psychological descriptions allow us to say things about people that cannot be said by using physical descriptions, it is not clear how this could be unless the difference between them is reflected in their meaning. But then the translations required by this theory cannot be found. This is confirmed by the success contemporary philosophers have had in producing general methods for undermining the sorts of translations that have been proposed. For these reasons, defenders of the unity of science have adopted instead a second line of argument.

The second defense makes a far more modest claim than the first. On this second line, it is not only conceded that psychological descriptions differ from physical ones, but also that they differ in what they mean. It is claimed, however, that in spite of the difference in meaning between any psychological and physical descriptions, still whatever is described in psychological terms can also be described equally well (though differently) in solely physical terms. According to this defense, whenever we talk about an object, state of affairs or event in psychological terms, we can talk about the very same object, state of affairs or event in physical terms. This view is commonly known as materialism.

On this account, the things we describe psychologically are no more than physical things, material objects, or states of affairs and events involving material objects. The fact that some objects and events or states of affairs involving them can be described in psychological as well as in physical terms is not taken to show that the objects, states of affairs and events are anything other than, or more than, material in nature. For example, whenever we have a description of a person thinking, seeing or wishing, or of his thought, perception or desire, the materialist claims that what is described is simply a physical object, or a state of affairs or event involving only physical objects. In short, people (and other beings capable of psychological behavior) are thought of as no more than physical objects, of a suitably complex kind. And the thoughts, perceptions and desires that a person has are considered to be just physical states of his body, or perhaps simply states of some relevant part of that body, such as the brain or central nervous system.

There are two ways in which materialism, formulated in this way, is importantly weaker in its claims than the first defense of the unity of science, the translation view. First of all, materialism follows from the translation view, but not conversely. For if every psychological description meant the same as some physical one, it would follow that every time we talk about something in psychological terms we are talking about something material, something that could be talked about in physical terms. The translation view therefore implies materialism. But the opposite does not hold; materialism could be true and yet the translation view false. For it is in general possible that descriptions that have different meanings should nonetheless be about the same things. An example of this is that one can talk about Alaska by describing it either as the largest or as the coldest state in the union. While these two descriptions will be about the same thing, they clearly do not mean the same. Similarly, it is possible that when we describe something in solely psychological terms we might be able to talk about exactly the same thing in solely physical terms, without it implying that the two descriptions mean the same.

Materialism is also weaker than the translation view because it has seemed that the latter, unlike the former, could be established without a detailed study of psychological beings. For if descriptions expressed in psychological terms meant the same as certain ones using only physical terms, then this could be shown by examining simply what we mean by the words we use. If this were so, and the translation view were offered as a defense of the unity of science, a strange result would follow. It would then be possible to defend the unity of science, which is a claim about the results of future scientific investigation, without appealing to any such results. By contrast, offering materialism in support of the unity of science does not result in peculiarities of this sort. For materialism, like the unity of science, can only be established on the basis of results from future scientific study. That is, we shall need to have evidence that there is nothing to the psychological functioning of people that is not describable in physical terms, and that psychological states of people can be described as, and are therefore the same as, certain of the physical states of people.

In particular, suppose that a materialist holds that thoughts and other mental events or states are simply events and states of the brain. To defend this view, he would need to have detailed knowledge about the occurrence of such mental events, and of the physical events that occur simultaneously in the brain. He would also need reason to believe that the psychological events and states he studies are not just causally correlated with the physical events and states that he isolates, but that they are the same. For if causal interaction between the two kinds of states is all that could be established, this would not show that the psychological behavior of people could itself be studied in physical terms. Rather it would show only that certain causal correlates of such behavior could be studied in this way.

While materialism can be directly supported only by appealing to knowledge about physiology and psychology that we do not now have, we can still consider in advance of our having such knowledge whether the prediction made by the materialist is a likely one or not. That is, it can be argued whether future scientific research is likely to make the materialist hypothesis seem plausible. The writings collected in this volume are all examples of arguments that philosophers have advanced for and against materialism. The central issue for many is giving a correct account of the nature of psychological descriptions, and of their difference from physical descriptions; they discuss in detail the bearing that such an account has on the plausibility of materialism. Some of the selections, most noticeably the later ones, also discuss certain positive reasons for thinking that the materialist hypothesis will eventually be confirmed by scientific research. And two of the articles attempt some discussion of why we are so reluctant to accept the idea that the psychological lives of people can be explained entirely in materialistic terms.

II. CLASSICAL MATERIALISM

Philosophical interest in materialism has become especially pronounced in the last decade, in large measure stimulated by advances in such areas as neurophysiology, biophysics and computer science. With the increasing explanatory power and sophistication of these sciences, it has seemed more and more likely that science may come to explain and account for our psychological behavior without needing to describe such behavior in peculiarly psychological terms.

Similarly, dramatic advances in mechanics in the seventeenth century encouraged philosophers to explore the possibility of explaining the behavior of all objects without the use of psychological terminology. Since it was generally believed that the science of mechanics could explain the physical behavior of all objects, it was a short step to the speculation that it would be adequate to explain the psychological behavior of living things as well. And if this could be done, it was believed, it would amount to a vindication of materialism.

Commitment to the adequacy of mechanical explanation is particularly evident in the writings of Descartes. While Descartes regarded mechanical principles as sufficient for a complete explanation of the behavior of inanimate objects and nonhuman animals, he also urged that such principles did not provide a way of explaining all of the behavior of human beings. For while much of the behavior of human bodies is on a par with that of stones and animals, reflex behavior and being subject to gravity, for example, much human behavior, Descartes urged, is not. His primary example of such behavior was speech, seen as expressive of human reasoning ability. Descartes believed that in order to explain speech behavior, it is necessary to regard it as caused by states of something other than a body whose behavior is subject to mechanical laws. From these considerations Descartes concluded that every person is composed not only of a body or "extended substance," but also of a soul or "thinking substance." While all human behavior on a par with that of stones or dogs could then be explained by the application of mechanical laws to the human body, other human behavior would be explained as caused by states of the soul such as thoughts or acts of will.

In so far as Descartes used this kind of argument in support of the existence of souls, his reasoning is not unlike that often used by scientists to establish the existence of theoretical entities such as electrons. For in each case, certain objects whose existence might not be otherwise established are invoked in order to explain readily observable phenomena. And in each case it is assumed that the readily observed phenomena cannot be explained except by appeal to the causal agency of such theoretical entities, that is, entities whose existence is established theoretically. Just as tracks in cloud chambers are thought unexplainable unless they are regarded as caused by subatomic particles, so speech behavior was thought by Descartes to be unexplainable unless regarded as caused by states of nonmaterial souls such as thoughts.

Descartes uses additional arguments, however, to support his belief that souls exist, and that they are not simply material objects. The argument most often studied is based on his claim that while one can doubt the existence of any material object, including one's own body, one cannot doubt the existence of one's own soul. For in the process of doubting one is engaged in a kind of thinking, and that in itself, Descartes urges, is enough to establish that one's soul, conceived of as a thinking substance, exists. Since the existence of our bodies cannot be established with certainty though this can be done in the case of our own soul, it follows that souls must differ in nature from bodies. Descartes concludes, therefore, that a thinking part of us must exist, and that it cannot be material in nature.

This second argument for the existence of souls is more limited than the first. For while the first is a general argument that people have souls, the second can establish at best only that one's own soul exists, not that anyone else's does. Moreover, the second argument depends on the direct awareness of our own states of mind, doubting in particular. But the nature of our awareness of our own mental states is unclear, and the first argument avoids mention of this problematic matter.

Descartes advances a third argument that the thinking part of us is nonmaterial in nature. He urges that while material objects can be divided into pieces, it seems that souls cannot; therefore the two must be different in kind. This argument seems to rest on the fact that it is not clear that it makes sense to speak of dividing one's consciousness into pieces. For these reasons, Descartes concludes that people have nonmaterial parts, and that physical science will never be able to deal exhaustively with human behavior.

If, as Descartes believed, it is possible to explain some of the bodily behavior of human beings by reference to mental events, there must be suitable causal interactions between bodily and mental events. But one may wonder why particular mental events are causally connected with bodily events in the way they are. For example, why is a perception of red correlated with a bodily stimulation by a red object, and not with a bodily stimulation by an object of some other sort? Descartes' solution to this question is that the causal relations that obtain are those having the greatest survival and functional value for the body. But this kind of teleological explanation has seemed to many to be too glib. It is unclear, for example, why having noises correlated with auditory sensations and colors correlated with visual ones should be more "conducive to the welfare of the body" than if these causal correlations were reversed; nor does Descartes discuss this matter. And if survival value is proposed as an explanation, some account will be required of how this beneficial arrangement came to be. Descartes' answer to this last question, that God arranged it that way, seems unacceptable; nor does any evolutionary explanation based on the survival of the fittest seem available.

For reasons such as these, philosophers like Spinoza have attempted to conceive of the relation between a person's mind and body as more intimate than it would be if the two were simply separate objects that happen to interact causally. On Spinoza's view, minds, bodies and all other objects are properties or "modes" (i.e., "modifications") of a single substance. Conceived of as active, that is as having causal agency, this substance is God; conceived of as passive and subject to scientific laws, this substance is nature. Describing any individual object amounts to no more than describing some mode of this substance. And Spinoza claims that any mode whatever can be exhaustively described both in physical terms and in psychological terms, in his words, both "under the attribute of extension" and "under the attribute of thought." A mind, on this view, is a mode of substance conceived of under the attribute of thought, and a body is a mode conceived of under the attribute of extension.

The relation between a person's mind and his body can be described in two ways. Primarily, a mind is the idea of the human body, of the body of the person in question. But a mind is also identical with that body, for "a mode of extension and the idea of that mode are one and the same thing expressed in two different ways." (Part II, Proposition VII, Note.) It follows similarly that every individual idea, whether a thought, perception or volition, is likewise identical to some mode of substance described under the attribute of extension. So on Spinoza's view, Descartes' problem about the causal interaction between souls and bodies can be circumvented. For, on this account, the relation between mental states and objects and physical states and objects is not one of causal interaction but one of identity.

While this view clearly implies the materialist hypothesis, it has certain disadvantages as a defense of materialism. Since every individual object can be wholly described either as mental or as material, not only are all psychological things equally material ones, but all material things are equally psychological as well. So this account supports both the claims of the materialist and the opposite claim that all the behavior of all physical objects can be adequately explained solely in psychological terms. This is a strange result, for there are many physical objects that do not seem to have psychological properties. Moreover, while Spinoza's views are elegant in systematic development and contain many penetrating philosophical insights, they go far beyond what seems required to defend materialism.

Of all the seventeenth-century philosophers, perhaps Hobbes presents the purest example of materialism. On Hobbes' view, all objects of whatever sort are no more than complex collections of moving particles, and all their properties are more or less complicated motions of these component particles. Hobbes urged that sensations of living things are no more than motions in the sense organs caused by some chain of movements initiated by the object perceived. Mental events of other kinds, such as thoughts and memories, were regarded by Hobbes in a similar fashion. The relations of cause and effect that mental events have to other events are to be explained on the same mechanical principles that govern all movements of adjacent bodies. Since, like Spinoza, Hobbes denies that there is any causal interaction between a person's body and some distinct psychological substance, he can circumvent the problem of why that interaction should be as it is.

Hobbes' attempt to support materialism is limited to a schematic reconstruction of all mental events in uniformly mechanical terms. Similarly, Descartes' attempt to undermine the plausibility of an entirely mechanical treatment of human behavior suffered because of the limitations of scientific knowledge then available. In response to limitations like these, contemporary philosophers have tried to evaluate the claims of materialism largely by appeal to considerations different from those invoked by Descartes and Hobbes. In particular, they have tried to evaluate materialism in a way that is as much as possible independent of the current state of knowledge about human beings and human behavior.

III. THE IDENTITY THESIS

One view that has been widely discussed in recent philosophical writings about materialism is known as the identity thesis (hereafter abbreviated as the "IT"). According to this thesis, there are no philosophical considerations that rule out the possibility that future scientific inquiry will show that every mental state and event is identical with some material state or event. More specifically, as formulated by Smart, the IT claims that it will be shown that all experiences are identical with processes taking place in the brain. Most contemporary discussions of materialism focus on one version or another of the IT, and the contemporary selections in this volume are all devoted to this issue.

To say that one thing, a, is identical with something, b, is to claim that everything that is true of a is true of b, and conversely. But how, then, can any statement of identity be other than trivially true (if something is said to be identical with itself) or trivially false (if it is said to be identical with something else)? This puzzle can be resolved by noting that one thing can be referred to by means of different names or descriptions. A true and informative identity statement can be formulated when a thing described one way is said to be identical with that thing described another way. In such a case the two expressions said to refer to one thing need not mean the same; all that is required is that everything true of the thing referred to by one expression is true of the thing referred to by the other.

Given this understanding of identity, it is clear that the IT can be regarded as a formulation of materialism. For in effect the IT claims that everything that can be described in psychological terms can also be adequately described in physical terms, even though the two descriptions will not mean the same. And the IT, unlike Spinoza's view, does not claim that every material thing is identical with some psychological one. So although the IT does not undercut the idea that some material things are also psychological, it seems sufficiently strong as a version of materialism to support the unity of science. For it is reasonable to believe that everything can be described in physical terms with the sole possible exception of psychological objects, states and events; and the IT claims that in fact these are not exceptions.

If the IT claimed only that individual people are identical with their bodies, the thesis would not be at all startling. For the alternative to this claim seems to be the Cartesian position that our bodies are not the sort of things that can engage in mental activity. And there is little reason to think this, except for Descartes' hypothesis that nonmaterial souls must be invoked to explain speech behavior. But the IT does claim more than that people are identical with their bodies. It asserts also that psychological states, events and properties are identical with material ones. And an issue central to the formulation of the IT is just what is involved in the view that psychological states, events and properties are the same as material ones.

It is issues of this sort that lead to the central objection to the IT that Smart discusses in his article. According to this objection, even if a mental event—say an experience of a sensation—is identical with a brain event, still this single event has not only material properties but also mental ones as well. If this is so, it seems that just the identity of psychological with physical events will not be sufficient for the purposes of materialism, for the psychological properties of such events could not be treated in terms of the physical sciences. And it is argued that mental events must have peculiarly mental properties, for otherwise how could we pick out and describe such events as mental? For if sensations are the same as brain events, then it must be possible to identify such events in two ways. When we think of them as sensations we will do so in terms of their psychological features, while when we think of them as brain events we will do so in terms of their physical features.

Smart's answer is that when we describe events as psychological, the properties in terms of which we do so are neither peculiarly physical nor incompatible with being physical, that is, the words used to refer to such properties are "topic-neutral." When we identify an event as psychological, we do so in terms of some similarity the event has to certain other events, and these other events are specified, in turn, only by reference to what causes them. But we say nothing about the respect in which the similarity holds. For example, when I say I have a sensation of red, I mean no more than that something is going on like what goes on when I see something red. So I am describing my having a sensation of red only as an event which is similar (in some unspecified way) to the event of my seeing red. And the latter can be understood as the event caused in certain standard circumstances by stimulations from red objects.

Shaffer and Cornman both argue that this account is unacceptable. Shaffer's argument is that we often can report our own mental events without having noticed any physical feature they have, and that we can only talk about what kind of events they are if we have noticed some feature or another. He concludes that when we describe such events in psychological terms we are attributing properties to them that cannot be physical. For his criticism of Smart to be fully convincing, however, Shaffer must find support for his assumption that reporting our own mental events requires that we notice some features of these events.

Cornman develops an argument that seems decisive against Smart's topic-neutral account of psychological descriptions. A psychological description, Cornman urges, cannot mean the same as its topic-neutral translation if there is a sentence that implies one but not the other. But then 'I have a sensation of red.' cannot mean the same as 'Something is going on like what goes on when I see red.', for the sentence 'I have a sensation of orange.' implies the latter but not the former. This is so because when I have a sensation of orange something does happen which is similar (in some way) to what happens when I see red. And if one leaves the exact respect of similarity unspecified, and doing so is central to Smart's account, then no matter what topic-neutral translation is proposed there will always be a sentence that implies the translation but not the original psychological description. And this is sufficient to show that psychological descriptions cannot be translated into topic-neutral terms. The basis for Cornman's criticism is that a psychological description always specifies more about an event than a topic-neutral sentence does, and his argument is simply a general way of showing that this is so.

Granted that Cornman's criticism shows conclusively that Smart's topic-neutral translations fail, what does this show about the IT? It does not show that mental events are not identical with brain events, nor was it intended to. For even if mental events do have irreducibly psychological features, Cornman's argument does not try to establish that brain events could not have these very same features. In fact Cornman considers cases in scientific theories where events seem to have features normally thought to be exhibited only by events of a different type. What it does show must be stated in far more guarded terms. If we agree that psychological descriptions do not mean the same as physical ones, and that psychological descriptions of sensations and thoughts attribute psychological properties to such events, then Cornman's argument shows that one of two things must be so. Either we cannot give an entirely materialistic account of mental events, or we must first develop a topic-neutral account of psychological descriptions more successful than Smart's.

Two lines of pursuit, therefore, seem open to the materialist. The first would be to try to show that psychological descriptions of mental events do not attribute psychological properties to them. The second would be to argue that some topic-neutral account of the properties such descriptions attribute to events can succeed. Either strategy commits the materialist to the task of clarifying the nature of events in general, and the nature of the properties, if any, in terms of which events must be described. These questions are of primary concern in the articles by Kim and Nagel.[1]

IV. THEORETICAL MATERIALISM

The proponent of the IT claims that mental events can be shown by scientific research to be identical with bodily events, perhaps brain

---

[1] In addition, the two articles by Davidson listed in the bibliography are of considerable interest on exactly these points.

events. But what sorts of things are events? Ignoring refinements that distinguish their approaches, both Kim and Nagel claim that an event is an individual object's being in a certain state, or its having a certain property. In particular, a mental event is a person's having some sensation or thought, and the physical event that Nagel, though not Kim, believes will be found identical with any particular mental event is a person's body's having some property. In addition, Nagel suggests, to say that a sensation is of such-and-such a sort, for example, is a sensation of red, is simply to give a more elaborate description of the property being ascribed to the person than we do when we say merely that he has a sensation. Similarly, when we say that a bodily event is of such-and-such a sort, we are simply giving a more elaborate description of the property ascribed to a body than we do in saying simply that some event is taking place in the body.

If we adopt this last suggestion of Nagel's, we will have made some progress with the problem posed by Cornman. For the difficulty Cornman raised was that mental events themselves may have certain irreducibly psychological properties. But on Nagel's suggestion, when we seem to ascribe properties to sensations we are really just ascribing elaborate properties to people. To deal with Cornman's problem, then, we would need only to determine whether these elaborate properties of people are irreducibly psychological, and not also whether certain properties of events are as well. Because it seems clearer what people are than what events are, it seems a more straightforward matter to deal with properties of people than with properties of events.

This account of events in terms of properties of objects, however, raises problems of its own. For, on this account, the identity of events will be determined not only by whether the objects in question are identical but also by whether the properties in question are. If a sensation is identical with some bodily event, then a property of the person must be identical with a property of his body. The way identity of properties is often determined is by the meaning equivalence of the expressions referring to them. For example, it is claimed that the property of being a person is identical with the property of being a rational animal just in case 'person' and 'rational animal' mean the same. But then this account faces the difficulty that expressions which ascribe mental properties seem not to mean the same as expressions which ascribe physical ones. Both Kim and Nagel explore the possibility of resolving this difficulty by appeal to cases of event and property identity which seem clearly not to depend on meaning equivalence.

Kim and Nagel are also both concerned with how the identities projected by the IT may be similar to certain identifications based on physical theories, for example, the identification of temperature with mean molecular kinetic energy. Kim argues that such reductive identifications fail to provide an adequate model for the IT. Nagel, on the other hand, explores a way in which the kind of "identity" used in theoretical identifications may be weaker than the so-called "strict" identity discussed above in section III, and he considers the possibility that certain difficulties for the IT might be met if we formulate it as a claim involving this weaker notion.

In the last section of his paper, Nagel asks why so many people intuitively find materialism unacceptable even though they accord the physical sciences virtually unlimited explanatory power with all natural phenomena except mental ones. Nagel's suggestion is that an entirely materialistic account of the world does not allow for a way of identifying certain experiences as belonging to me. Though we can say, in materialistic terms, which experiences belong to which bodies, there seems no way to go on to say that a certain body is my body. Nagel argues that alternatives to materialism, such as Descartes', appear to get around this difficulty, but in fact do not. He concludes that this apparent failure should not be viewed as a defect of the materialist position. Gunderson, attacking the same problem, urges that our reluctance to accept a wholly physical account of the world stems from a felt asymmetry between ourselves and other natural objects. By constructing other cases in which similar asymmetries are felt which seem not to limit the possibility of explaining things solely in physical terms, Gunderson argues that this reluctance can be neutralized.

V. FUNCTIONALISTIC MATERIALISM

Even if, as on Nagel's view, there is no special problem about whether events themselves have distinctively psychological properties, we must still face the need to account for the difference between psychological and physical descriptions of events. A view, such as Smart's, that obscures or conceals this difference will to that extent be defective. If, for example, Smart's account were true, we would have no way to tell which topic-neutral descriptions were psychological and which were not. The materialist must, therefore, give an account of psychological descriptions which reflects the fact that they can be discriminated from physical ones.

One way of trying to do this is by developing an account of mental states and events in terms of the network of causal relations that each kind of state has to overt behavior, sensory stimulation and other mental states. Every thought, sensation and other mental state is seen, on this view, as definable in terms of such causal connections. For example, a person's desiring something will be defined by reference to his beliefs about the nature of that thing, his behavior in pursuing it and his satisfaction and pleasure if he obtains it, and the sensory stimulations to which he responds when he tries to get it. We can learn, therefore, what mental state someone is in by discovering what behavior and new mental states would result from various kinds of stimulation, for such states are to be identified by reference to the causal function they have in the overall behavior of a person.

On this account of mental states, psychological descriptions of people are equivalent to functional descriptions of the sort sketched above. If a functional description of a mental state makes reference to other mental states, clearly we shall be able to discriminate functional descriptions of psychological states from functional descriptions of nonpsychological ones. Functional accounts have also been proposed, however, on which functional descriptions of mental states do not refer to other mental states. In this case it is less clear whether we shall be able to discriminate psychological from nonpsychological functional descriptions. Perhaps a functional state could still be discriminated as psychological provided that it specifies causal networks connecting sensory stimulations and overt behavior of some relevant sort.

If some version of functionalism, spelled out in detail, could permit psychological descriptions to be distinguished from other sorts, would this provide an adequate basis for materialism? Fodor argues that an acceptable form of materialism would have to be based on a classification of physiological states according to their functional equivalence. To defend this functionalistic materialism, we would need to clarify the relationship between two theories, a psychological theory about states classified in functional terms, and a theory about bodily states classified physiologically. Fodor's skepticism about this view stems from his conviction that materialism defended in this way would suffer from the lack of clarity that the notion of functional equivalence exhibits.

Putnam argues that a functional account of mental states conflicts with the hypothesis that such states are identical with physical ones, and that between these two competing theories functionalism is the more credible. He believes that a psychological classification of states can be matched up with a classification of states in functional terms. But it is reasonable to expect that members of distinct psychological species, and even different people, can be in the same functional state even though there is no physiological classification of states on which the different psychological beings share any such states. Putnam concludes that since it is plausible to identify psychological states with functional ones, we cannot also identify mental states with states classified in materialist terms.

Lewis argues that a functionalist theory of mental states need not conflict with materialism, and that a clear account can be given of the notion of two states being functionally equivalent. His proposal is that mental states can be defined by reference to their causal role. Lewis suggests that this is similar to Smart's topic-neutral theory of psychological descriptions, that is, that mental states can be described by specifying the typical stimuli and responses that are associated with a state. But he also provides that these associated conditions are to be specified as causally connected to the state and not merely as accompanying it, and that the causal conditions specified may include other mental states. In this way, Lewis' account may avoid the difficulty that faced Smart's theory, that we would have no way to tell which topic-neutral descriptions are about mental states and which are not.

VI. ELIMINATIVE MATERIALISM

All of the foregoing discussions have assumed that a defense of materialism will have to preserve the distinction between psychological and physical descriptions. In fact, the attempt to meet this requirement has presented the chief obstacle to an effective defense. For this reason, it would seem fruitful to examine why defenders of materialism have insisted that this requirement be met, and also whether a plausible version of materialism might be formulated which does not attempt to preserve the distinction.

If a theory fails to capture the distinction between psychological and physical ways of talking about things, we will be unable to tell which, if any, of the claims expressed in the theory are about mental states. If we agree that mental states do exist and can be described, then we will not be able to determine whether or not such a theory succeeds in describing them. Unless we can discriminate between psychological and nonpsychological descriptions, it is argued, we would not be sure that we could still describe, predict and explain the psychological things which are part of the world. In this way it seems that if a theory has the effect of collapsing the distinction, adopting the theory will result in diminishing the descriptive power of our language in important ways.

Suppose, however, that the occurrence of various pains, perceptions, thoughts and desires could be empirically correlated with the occurrence of particular kinds of physical events. Could we not then say all we wish to about the world by talking about such physical events and never mentioning any mental ones? Granted the great inconvenience of talking about people entirely in physical terms, would we thereby lose any of the descriptive power of our present ways of talking?

The immediate reply seems obvious: we would lose our ability to talk about certain things that we think exist, mental states and events such as thoughts, sensations and so forth. But our conviction that things of any particular kind exist seems to rest on the belief that the most effective way of talking about the world includes mention of those things. If our goal is simply to talk about mental phenomena, assuming their existence, we may find that this requires us to use distinctively psychological language. But if our goal is to describe all natural phenomena whatever in the most effective way, we might perhaps discover that the best complete account of the world makes no mention of states and events that we now regard as psychological. And this discovery would undermine our conviction that such states and events exist, just as, to use Rorty's example, our discovery that the best complete account of the world makes no mention of witches has made us believe that no witches exist. This is not to say that we would come to believe that psychological descriptions do not refer to anything, any more than we now think that the women once referred to as witches did not exist. Rather, we now believe that such women existed, but that neither they nor anything else in the world is a witch. Similarly, we are supposing that we could come to think that whatever states psychological descriptions may have referred to, these states are, in fact, not psychological but physical. That is, we are considering the possibility of discoveries that would lead us to replace our present total description of the world by a better one which describes all states in solely physical terms, and nothing at all in psychological terms. And even if one insisted that we can establish that psychological, nonphysical states exist because we are directly aware of them, how could one show that the states we are directly aware of cannot be described in solely physical terms, or that they are mental as against purely physiological states?

The goal of eliminative materialism is to make the claims that such discoveries might be made seem coherent and plausible. Feyerabend urges that our current way of talking about people in both physical and psychological terms itself amounts to a theory about people. He therefore argues that the possibility of a wholly physiological account should be judged on its merits, independent of our present ways of talking. Rorty extensively develops an analogy between describing the world by reference to mental events and describing it by reference to supernatural and scientifically defunct objects, such as demons and caloric fluid. He points out that scientific discoveries have made us stop describing the world by reference to these latter kinds of things, and argues that parallel discoveries with parallel results could be made in the case of mental events. Bernstein, arguing against Rorty, claims that if we did come to use physiological descriptions in place of our current psychological ones, the former would have to come to express what is now expressed by the latter. Rorty's reply is that Bernstein's claim rests on the assumption that we know what statements describe independent of the total account we give of the world, and that this assumption is unwarranted.

VII. CONCLUDING REMARKS

The adequacy of noneliminative versions of materialism must be judged to a great extent by whether they are true to, or reckon with, the distinction between psychological and physical ways of talking about people. This is not the case with eliminative materialism, for this view urges that we need not bother to capture the distinction, and suggests instead that our goal should be a more modest one. Rather than insist on being faithful to the distinction, we should ask how psychological ways of talking help us to describe the world, and whether another way might do just as well. If eliminative materialism is correct, empirical discoveries could, in principle, lead us to supplant our distinctively psychological descriptions with equally effective ones that are entirely physical. And in this event, there would be no point to preserving the distinction between psychological and physical ways of talking about people.

The status of psychological subject matter, and its relationship to other less problematic areas of study, are questions that have received much attention. By insisting that psychological descriptions must be seen as importantly different from physical ones, the noneliminative materialist reflects a conviction that psychological subject matter differs in nature from nonpsychological subject matters. Eliminative materialism, by contrast, suggests that the distinction between psychological and physical descriptions can be evaluated on its own merits, and need not be simply taken as given. To the degree to which eliminative materialism questions the usefulness of this distinction, it also questions the warrant for thinking that psychological subject matter should be seen as a distinctive area of empirical knowledge. The eliminative materialist, therefore, is pointing out one way in which the traditional division of knowledge into subject matters should be evaluated and challenged.

part one
CLASSICAL MATERIALISM

RENÉ DESCARTES

Selections

from DISCOURSE ON THE METHOD
of rightly directing one's Reason
and of seeking Truth in the Sciences

Part V

. . . .

I specially dwelt on showing that if there were machines with the organs and appearance of a monkey, or some other irrational animal, we should have no means of telling that they were not altogether of the same nature as those animals; whereas if there were machines resembling our bodies, and imitating our actions as far as is morally possible, we should still have two means of telling that, all the same, they were not real men. First, they could never use words or other constructed signs, as we do to declare our thoughts to others. It is quite conceivable that a machine should be so made as to utter words, and even utter them in connexion with physical events that cause a change in one of its organs; so that e.g. if it is touched in one part, it asks what you want to say to it, and if touched in another, it cries out that it is hurt; but not that it should be so made as to arrange words variously in response to the meaning of what is said in its presence, as even the dullest men can do. Secondly, while they might do many things as well as any of us or better, they would infallibly fail in others, revealing that they acted not from knowledge but only from

Reprinted from *Descartes: Philosophical Writings*, translated and edited by Elizabeth Anscombe and Peter Thomas Geach, London: Thomas Nelson and Sons, Ltd., 1954, 41–44, by permission of the publishers.

the disposition of their organs. For while reason is a universal tool that may serve in all kinds of circumstances, these organs need a special arrangement for each special action; so it is morally impossible that a machine should contain so many varied arrangements as to act in all the events of life in the way reason enables us to act.

Now in just these two ways we can also recognise the difference between men and brutes. For it is a very remarkable thing that there are no men so dull and stupid, not even lunatics, that they cannot arrange various words and form a sentence to make their thoughts (*pensées*) understood; but no other animal, however perfect or well bred, can do the like. This does not come from their lacking the organs; for magpies and parrots can utter words like ourselves, and yet they cannot talk like us, that is, with any sign of being aware of (*qu'ils pensent*) what they say. Whereas men born deaf-mutes, and thus devoid of the organs that others use for speech, as much as brutes are or more so, usually invent for themselves signs by which they make themselves understood to those who are normally with them, and who thus have a chance to learn their language. This is evidence that brutes not only have a smaller degree of reason than men, but are wholly lacking in it. For it may be seen that a very small degree of reason is needed in order to be able to talk; and in view of the inequality that occurs among animals of the same species, as among men, and of the fact that some are easier to train than others, it is incredible that a monkey or parrot who was one of the most perfect members of his species should not be comparable in this regard to one of the stupidest children or at least to a child with a diseased brain, if their souls were not wholly different in nature from ours. And we must not confuse words with natural movements, the expressions of emotion, which can be imitated by machines as well as by animals. Nor must we think, like some of the ancients, that brutes talk but we cannot understand their language; for if that were true, since many of their organs are analogous to ours, they could make themselves understood to us, as well as to their fellows. It is another very remarkable thing that although several brutes exhibit more skill than we in some of their actions, they show none at all in many other circumstances; so their excelling us is no proof that they have a mind (*de l'esprit*), for in that case they would have a better one than any of us and would excel us all round; it rather shows that they have none, and that it is nature that acts in them according to the arrangements of their organs; just as we see how a clock, composed merely of wheels and springs, can reckon the hours and measure time more correctly than we can with all our wisdom.

I went on to describe the rational soul, and showed that, unlike the other things I had spoken of, it cannot be extracted from the potentiality of matter, but must be specially created; and how it is not enough for it to dwell in the human body like a pilot in his ship, which would only account for its moving the limbs of the body; in order to have in addition feelings and appetites like ours, and so make up a true man, it must be joined and united to the body more closely. Here I dwelt a little on the subject of the soul, as among the most important; for, after the error of denying God, (of which I think I have already given a sufficient refutation), there is none more likely to turn weak characters from the strait way of virtue than the supposition that the soul of brutes must be of the same nature as ours, so that after this life we have no more to hope or fear than flies or ants. Whereas, when we realise how much they really differ from us, we understand much better the arguments proving that our soul is of a nature entirely independent of the body, and thus not liable to die with it; and since we can discern no other causes that should destroy it, we are naturally led to decide that it is immortal.

from LETTER TO THE MARQUIS OF NEWCASTLE

. . . As for the understanding or thought attributed by Montaigne and others to brutes, I cannot hold their opinion; not, however, because I am doubtful of the truth of what is commonly said, that men have absolute dominion over all the other animals; for while I allow that there are some which are stronger than we are, and I believe there may be some, also, which have natural cunning capable of deceiving the most sagacious men; yet I consider that they imitate or surpass us only in those of our actions which are not directed by thought; for it often happens that we walk and that we eat without thinking at all upon what we are doing; and it is so much without the use of our reason that we repel things which harm us, and ward off blows struck at us, that, although we might fully determine not to put our hands before our heads when falling, we could not help doing so. I believe, also, that we should eat as the brutes do, without having learned how, if we had no power of thought at all; and it is said that those who walk in their sleep sometimes swim across rivers, where, had they been awake, they would have been drowned.

As for the movements of our passions, although in ourselves they are accompanied with thought, because we possess that faculty, it is, nevertheless, very evident that they do not depend upon it, because they often arise in spite of us, and, consequently, they may exist in brutes, and even be more violent than they are in the men, without

Reprinted from *The Philosophy of Descartes*, selected and translated by Henry A. P. Torrey, New York: Henry Holt and Company, 1892, 281–284.

warranting the conclusion that brutes can think; in fine there is no one of our external actions which can assure those who examine them that our body is any thing more than a machine which moves of itself, but which also has in it a mind which thinks—excepting words, or other signs made in regard to whatever subjects present themselves, without reference to any passion. I say words, or other signs, because mutes make use of signs in the same way as we do of the voice, and these signs are pertinent; but I exclude the talking of parrots, but not that of the insane, which may be apropos to the case in hand, although it is irrational; and I add that these words or signs are not to relate to any passion, in order to exclude, not only cries of joy or pain and the like, but, also, all that can be taught to any animal by art; for if a magpie be taught to say "good-morning" to its mistress when it sees her coming, it may be that the utterance of these words is associated with the excitement of some one of its passions; for instance, there will be a stir of expectation of something to eat, if it has been the custom of the mistress to give it some dainty bit when it spoke those words; and in like manner all those things which dogs, horses, and monkeys are made to do are merely motions of their fear, their hope, or their joy, so that they might do them without any thought at all.

Now, it seems to me very remarkable that language, as thus defined, belongs to man alone; for although Montaigne and Charron have said that there is more difference between one man and another than between a man and a brute, nevertheless there has never yet been found a brute so perfect that it has made use of a sign to inform other animals of something which had no relation to their passions; while there is no man so imperfect as not to use such signs; so that the deaf and dumb invent particular signs by which they express their thoughts, which seems to me a very strong argument to prove that the reason why brutes do not talk as we do is that they have no faculty of thought, and not at all that the organs for it are wanting. And it cannot be said that they talk among themselves, but we do not understand them; for, as dogs and other animals express to us their passions, they would express to us as well their thoughts, if they had them. I know, indeed, that brutes do many things better than we do, but I am not surprised at it; for that, also, goes to prove that they act by force of nature and by springs, like a clock, which tells better what the hour is than our judgment can inform us. And, doubtless, when swallows come in the spring, they act in that like clocks. All that honey-bees do is of the same nature; and the order that cranes keep in flying, or monkeys drawn up for battle, if it be true that they do observe any order, and, finally, the instinct of burying their dead is no more surprising than that of dogs and cats, which scratch the ground to bury their excrements, although they almost never do bury them, which shows that they do it by instinct only, and not by thought. It can only be said that, although the brutes do nothing which can convince us that they think, nevertheless, because their bodily organs are not very different from ours, we might conjecture that there was some faculty of thought joined to these organs, as we experience in ourselves, although theirs be much less perfect, to which I have nothing to reply, except that, if they could think as we do, they would have an immortal soul as well as we, which is not likely, because there is no reason for believing it of some animals without believing it of all, and there are many of them too imperfect to make it possible to believe it of them, such as oysters, sponges, etc.

from LETTER TO HENRY MORE, 1649

. . . But the greatest of all the prejudices we have retained from infancy is that of believing that brutes think. The source of our error comes from having observed that many of the bodily members of brutes are not very different from our own in shape and movements, and from the belief that our mind is the principle of the motions which occur in us; that it imparts motion to the body and is the cause of our thoughts. Assuming this, we find no difficulty in believing that there is in brutes a mind similar to our own; but having made the discovery, after thinking well upon it, that two different principles of our movements are to be distinguished—the one entirely mechanical and corporeal, which depends solely on the force of the animal spirits and the configuration of the bodily parts, and which may be called corporeal soul, and the other incorporeal, that is to say, mind or soul, which you may define a substance which thinks—I have inquired with great care whether the motions of animals proceed from these two principles or from one alone. Now, having clearly perceived that they can proceed from one only, I have held it demonstrated that we are not able in any manner to prove that there is in the animals a soul which thinks. I am not at all disturbed in my opinion by those doublings and cunning tricks of dogs and foxes, nor by all those things which animals do, either from fear, or to get something to eat, or just for sport. I engage to explain all that very easily, merely by the conformation of the parts of the animals. Nevertheless, although I regard it as a thing demonstrated that it cannot be proved that the brutes have thought, I do not think that it can be demonstrated that the contrary is not true, because the human mind cannot penetrate into the heart to know what goes on there; but, on examining into the probabilities of the case, I see no reason whatever to prove that brutes think, if it be not that having eyes, ears, a tongue, and other organs of sense like ours, it is

Reprinted from *The Philosophy of Descartes*, selected and translated by Henry A. P. Torrey, New York: Henry Holt and Company, 1892, 284–287.

likely that they have sensations as we do, and, as thought is involved in the sensations which we have, a similar faculty of thought must be attributed to them. Now, since this argument is within the reach of everyone's capacity, it has held possession of all minds from infancy. But there are other stronger and more numerous arguments for the opposite opinion, which do not so readily present themselves to everybody's mind; as, for example, that it is more reasonable to make earthworms, flies, caterpillars, and the rest of the animals, move as machines do, than to endow them with immortal souls.

Because it is certain that in the body of animals, as in ours, there are bones, nerves, muscles, blood, animal spirits, and other organs, disposed in such a manner that they can produce themselves, without the aid of any thought, all the movements which we observe in the animals, as appears in convulsive movements, when, in spite of the mind itself, the machine of the body moves often with greater violence, and in more various ways than it is wont to do with the aid of the will; moreover, inasmuch as it is agreeable to reason that art should imitate nature, and that men should be able to construct divers *automata* in which there is movement without any thought, nature, on her part, might produce these *automata,* and far more excellent ones, as the brutes are, than those which come from the hand of man, seeing no reason anywhere why thought is to be found wherever we perceive a conformation of bodily members like that of the animals, and that it is more surprising that there should be a soul in every human body than that there should be none at all in the brutes.

But the principal argument, to my mind, which may convince us that the brutes are devoid of reason, is that, although among those of the same species, some are more perfect than others, as among men, which is particularly noticeable in horses and dogs, some of which have more capacity than others to retain what is taught them, and although all of them make us clearly understand their natural movements of anger, of fear, of hunger, and others of like kind, either by the voice or by other bodily motions, it has never yet been observed that any animal has arrived at such a degree of perfection as to make use of a true language; that is to say, as to be able to indicate to us by the voice, or by other signs, anything which could be referred to thought alone, rather than to a movement of mere nature; for the word is the sole sign and the only certain mark of the presence of thought hidden and wrapped up in the body; now all men, the most stupid and the most foolish, those even who are deprived of the organs of speech, make use of signs, whereas the brutes never do anything of the kind; which may be taken for the true distinction between man and brute. . . . I omit, for the sake of brevity, the other arguments which deny thought to the brutes. It must, however, be observed that I speak of thought, not of life, nor of sensation; for I do not deny the life of any animal, making it to consist solely in the warmth of the heart. I do not refuse to them feeling even, in so far as it depends only on the bodily organs. Thus, my opinion is not so cruel to animals as it is favourable to men; I speak to those who are not committed to the extravagances of Pythagoras, which attached to those who ate or killed them the suspicion even of a crime. . . .

from MEDITATIONS ON FIRST PHILOSOPHY
Wherein are demonstrated the Existence of God and the Distinction of Soul from Body

Sixth Meditation

The Existence of Material Things: the Real Distinction of Mind and Body

. . . .

I will first recall to myself what kinds of things I previously thought were real, as being perceived in sensation; then I will set out my reasons for having later on called them in question; finally I will consider what to hold now.

In the first place, then: I had sensations of having a head, hands, feet, and the other members that make up the body; and I regarded the body as part of myself, or even as my whole self. I had sensations of the commerce of this body with many other bodies, which were capable of being beneficial or injurious to it in various ways; I estimated the beneficial effects by a sensation of pleasure, and the injurious, by a sensation of pain. Besides pain and pleasure, I had internal sensations of hunger, thirst, and other such appetites; and also of physical inclinations towards gladness, sadness, anger, and other like emotions. I had external sensations not only of the extension, shapes, and movements of bodies, but also of their hardness, heat, and other tangible qualities; also, sensations of light, colours, odours, flavours, and sounds. By the varieties of these qualities I distinguished from one another the sky, the earth, the seas, and all other bodies.

I certainly had some reason, in view of the ideas of these qualities that presented themselves to my consciousness (*cogitationi*), and that were the only proper and immediate object of my sensations, to think

---

Reprinted from *Descartes: Philosophical Writings*, translated and edited by Elizabeth Anscombe and Peter Thomas Geach, London: Thomas Nelson and Sons, Ltd., 1954, 111–115 and 119–123, by permission of the publishers.

that I was aware in sensation of objects quite different from my own consciousness: viz. bodies from which the ideas proceeded. For it was my experience (*experiebar*) that the ideas came to me without any consent of mine; so that I could neither have a sensation of any object, however I wished, if it were not present to the sense-organ, nor help having the sensation when the object was present. Moreover, the ideas perceived in sensation were much more vivid and prominent, and, in their own way, more distinct, than any that I myself deliberately produced in my meditations, or observed to have been impressed on my memory; and thus it seemed impossible for them to proceed from myself; and the only remaining possibility was that they came from some other objects. Now since I had no conception of these objects from any other source than the ideas themselves, it could not but occur to me that they were like the ideas. Further, I remembered that I had had the use of the senses before the use of reason; and I saw that the ideas I formed myself were less prominent than those I perceived in sensation, and mostly consisted of parts taken from sensation; I thus readily convinced myself that I had nothing in my intellect that I had not previously had in sensation.

Again, I had some reason for holding that the body I called '*my body*' by a special title really did belong to me more than any other body did. I could never separate myself entirely from it, as I could from other bodies. All the appetites and emotions I had, I felt in the body and on its account. I felt pain, and the titillations of pleasure, in parts of *this* body, not of other, external bodies. Why should a sadness of the mind follow upon a sensation of pain, and a kind of happiness upon the titillation of sense? Why should that twitching of the stomach which I call hunger tell me that I must eat; and a dryness of the throat, that I must drink; and so on? I could give no account of this except that nature taught me so; for there is no likeness at all, so far as I can see, between the twitching in the stomach and the volition to take food; or between the sensation of an object that gives me pain, and the experience (*cogitationem*) of sadness that arises from the sensation. My other judgments, too, as regards the objects of sensation seemed to have been lessons of nature; for I had convinced myself that things were so, before setting out any reasons to prove this.

Since then, however, I have had many experiences that have gradually sapped the faith I had in the senses. It sometimes happened that towers which had looked round at a distance looked square when close at hand; and that huge statues standing on the roof did not seem large to me looking up from the ground. And there were countless other cases like these, in which I found the external senses to be deceived in their judgment; and not only the external senses, but the internal senses as well. What [experience] can be more intimate than pain? Yet I had heard sometimes, from people who had had a leg or arm cut off, that they still seemed now and then to feel pain in the part of the body that they lacked; so it seemed in my own case not to be quite certain that a limb was in pain, even if I felt pain in it. And to these reasons for doubting I more recently added two more, of highly general application. First, there is no kind of sensation that I have ever thought I had in waking life, but I may also think I have some time when I am asleep; and since I do not believe that sensations I seem to have in sleep come from external objects, I did not see why I should believe this any the more about sensations I seem to have when I am awake. Secondly, I did not as yet know the Author of my being (or at least pretended I did not); so there seemed to be nothing against my being naturally so constituted as to be deceived even about what appeared to myself most true. As for the reasons of my former conviction that sensible objects are real, it was not difficult to answer them. I was, it seemed, naturally impelled to many courses from which reason dissuaded me; so I did not think I ought to put much reliance on what nature had taught me. And although sense-perceptions did not depend on my will, it must not be concluded, I thought, that they proceed from objects distinct from myself; there might perhaps be some faculty in myself, as yet unknown to me, that produced them.

But now that I am beginning to be better acquainted with myself and with the Author of my being, my view is that I must not rashly accept all the apparent data of sensation; nor, on the other hand, call them all in question.

In the first place, I know that whatever I clearly and distinctly understand can be made by God just as I understand it; so my ability to understand one thing clearly and distinctly apart from another is enough to assure me that they are distinct, because God at least can separate them. (It is irrelevant what faculty enables me to think of them as separate.) Now I know that I exist, and at the same time I observe absolutely nothing else as belonging to my nature or essence except the mere fact that I am a conscious being; and just from this I can validly infer that my essence consists simply in the fact that I am a conscious being. It is indeed possible (or rather, as I shall say later on, it is certain) that I have a body closely bound up with myself; but at the same time I have, on the one hand, a clear and distinct idea of myself taken simply as a conscious, not an extended, being; and, on the other hand, a distinct idea of body, taken simply as an extended, not a conscious, being; so it is certain that I am really distinct from my body, and could exist without it.

. . . .

I have already examined sufficiently the reason why, in spite of God's goodness, my judgments are liable to be false. But a new problem arises here about the objects that nature shows me I ought to seek or shun; and also as regards the errors I seem to have observed in internal sensations. For instance, a man is deceived by the pleasant taste of some food, and swallows the poison concealed within it. But what his nature impels him to desire is what gives the food its pleasant taste; not the poison, of which his nature knows nothing. All that can be inferred from this is that his nature is not omniscient; and this is not surprising, for a man is a finite thing and his nature has only a finite degree of perfection.

But we quite often go wrong about the things that nature does impel us towards. For instance, sick men long for drink or food that would soon be harmful to them. It might be said that they go wrong because their nature is corrupted; but this does not remove the problem. A sick man is no less God's creature than a healthy man; and it seems just as absurd that God should give him a nature that deceives him.

Now a clock built out of wheels and weights, obeys all the laws of 'nature' no less exactly when it is ill-made and does not show the right time, than when it satisfies its maker's wishes in every respect. And thus I may consider the human body as a machine fitted together and made up of bones, sinews, muscles, veins, blood, and skin in such a way that, even if there were no mind in it, it would still carry out all the operations that, as things are, do not depend on the command of the will, nor, therefore, on the mind. Now, if, for instance, the body is suffering from dropsy, it has the dryness of the throat that normally gives the mind the sensation of thirst; and this disposes its nerves and other parts to taking drink, so as to aggravate the disease. But I can easily recognise that this is just as 'natural' as it is for a body not so affected to be impelled by a similar dryness of the throat to take drink that will be beneficial to it.

Of course, if I consider my preconceived idea of the use of a clock, I may say that when it does not show the right time it is departing from its 'nature.' Similarly, if I consider the machine of the human body in relation to its normal operations, I may think it goes astray from its 'nature' if its throat is dry at a time when drink does not help to sustain it. But I see well enough that this sense of 'nature' is very different from the other. In this sense, 'nature' is a term depending on my own way of thinking (*a cogitatione mea*), on my comparison of a sick man, or an ill-made clock, to a conception of a healthy man and a well-made clock; it is something extrinsic to the object it is ascribed to. In the other sense, 'nature' is something actually found in objects; so this conception has some degree of truth.

'It may be a merely extrinsic application of a term when, considering a body that suffers from dropsy, we call its nature corrupted because it has a dry throat and yet has no need of drink. But if we consider the compound, the mind united to the body, it is not just a matter of terms; there is a real fault in its nature, for it is thirsty at a time when drink would be hurtful to it. So the question remains: how is it that the divine goodness does not prevent "nature" (in this sense) from deceiving us?'

I must begin by observing the great difference between mind and body. Body is of its nature always divisible; mind is wholly indivisible. When I consider the mind—that is, myself, in so far as I am merely a conscious being—I can distinguish no parts within myself; I understand myself to be a single and complete thing. Although the whole mind seems to be united to the whole body, yet when a foot or an arm or any other part of the body is cut off I am not aware that any subtraction has been made from the mind. Nor can the faculties of will, feeling, understanding and so on be called its parts; for it is one and the same mind that wills, feels, and understands. On the other hand, I cannot think of any corporeal or extended object without being readily able to divide it in thought and therefore conceiving of it as divisible. This would be enough to show me the total difference between mind and body, even if I did not sufficiently know this already.

Next, I observe that my mind is not directly affected by all parts of the body; but only by the brain, and perhaps only by one small part of that—the alleged seat of common sensibility. Whenever this is disposed in a given way, it gives the same indication to the mind, even if the other parts of the body are differently disposed at the time; of this there are innumerable experimental proofs, of which I need not give an account here.

I observe further that, from the nature of body, in whatever way a part of it could be moved by another part at some distance, that same part could also be moved in the same way by intermediate parts, even if the more distant part did nothing. For example, if ABCD is a cord, there is no way of moving A by pulling the end D that could not be carried out equally well if B or C in the middle were pulled and the end D were not moved at all. Now, similarly, when I feel pain in my foot, I have learnt from the science of physic that this sensation is brought about by means of nerves scattered throughout the foot; these are stretched like cords from there to the brain, and when they are pulled in the foot they transmit the pull to the inmost part of the brain, to which they are attached, and produce there a kind of disturbance which nature has decreed should give the mind a sensation of pain, as it were in the foot. But in order to reach the brain, these nerves have to pass through the leg, the thigh, the back, and the neck; so it may happen that, although it is not the part in the foot that is touched, but only some intermediate part, there is just the same disturbance produced in the brain as when the foot is injured; and so necessarily the mind will have the same sensation of pain. And the same must be believed as regards any other sensation.

Finally, I observe that, since any given disturbance in the part of the brain that directly affects the mind can produce only one kind of sensation, nothing better could be devised than that it should produce that one among all the sensations it could produce which is most conducive, and most often conducive, to the welfare of a healthy man. Now experience shows that all the sensations nature has given us are of this kind; so nothing can be found in them but evidence of God's power and goodness. For example: when the nerves of the foot are strongly and unusually disturbed, this disturbance, by way of the spinal cord, arrives at the interior of the brain; there it gives the mind the signal for it to have a certain sensation, viz. pain, as it were in the foot; and this arouses the mind to do its best to remove the cause of the pain, as being injurious to the foot. Now God might have so made human nature that this very disturbance in the brain was a sign to the mind of something else; it might have been a sign of its own occurrence in the brain; or of the disturbance in the foot, or in some intermediate place; or, in fact, of anything else whatever. But there would be no alternative equally conducive to the welfare of the body. Similarly, when we need drink, there arises a dryness of the throat, which disturbs the nerves of the throat, and by means of them the interior of the brain; and this disturbance gives the mind the sensation of thirst, because the most useful thing for us to know in this whole process is that we then need drink to keep healthy. And so in other cases.

. . . .

BENEDICT DE SPINOZA

FROM *Ethics*

PART ONE: OF GOD

Definitions

I. By cause of itself I understand that whose essence involves existence, or that whose nature cannot be conceived unless existing.

II. That thing is called finite in its own kind (*in suo genere*) which can be limited by another thing of the same nature. For example, a body is called finite because we always conceive another which is greater. So a thought is limited by another thought; but a body is not limited by a thought, nor a thought by a body.

III. By substance I understand that which is in itself and is conceived through itself; in other words, that the conception of which does not need the conception of another thing from which it must be formed.

IV. By attribute I understand that which the intellect perceives of substance as constituting its essence.

V. By mode I understand the modifications of substance, or that which is in another thing through which also it is conceived.

VI. By God I understand Being absolutely infinite, that is to say, substance consisting of infinite attributes, each one of which expresses eternal and infinite essence.

Explanation. I say absolutely infinite but not infinite in its own kind (*in suo genere*), for of whatever is infinite only in its own kind (*in suo genere*), we can deny infinite attributes; but to the essence of that

Reprinted from *Ethics*, by Benedict de Spinoza, edited by James Gutmann, New York: Hafner Publishing Company, 1957, 41–44, 63, 79–81, 83–84, 89–91, 95–96, 99–103, 130, by permission of the publishers.

which is absolutely infinite pertains whatever expresses essence and involves no negation.

Axioms

I. Everything which is, is either in itself or in another.

II. That which cannot be conceived through another must be conceived through itself.

III. From a given determinate cause an effect necessarily follows; and, on the other hand, if no determinate cause be given it is impossible that an effect can follow.

IV. The knowledge (*cognitio*) of an effect depends upon and involves the knowledge of the cause.

V. Those things which have nothing mutually in common with one another cannot through one another be mutually understood, that is to say, the conception of the one does not involve the conception of the other.

VI. A true idea must agree with that of which it is the idea (*cum suo ideato*).

VII. The essence of that thing which can be conceived as not existing does not involve existence.

Propositions

PROPOSITION I. *Substance is by its nature prior to its modifications.*
Demonstration. This is evident from Defs. 3 and 5.

PROPOSITION II. *Two substances having different attributes have nothing in common with one another.*
Demonstration. This is also evident from Def. 3. For each substance must be in itself and must be conceived through itself, that is to say, the conception of one does not involve the conception of the other.—Q.E.D.

PROPOSITION III. *If two things have nothing in common with one another, one cannot be the cause of the other.*
Demonstration. If they have nothing mutually in common with one another, they cannot (Ax. 5) through one another be mutually understood, and therefore (Ax. 4) one cannot be the cause of the other.—Q.E.D.

PROPOSITION IV. *Two or more distinct things are distinguished from one another, either by the difference of the attributes of the substances or by the difference of their modifications.*

Demonstration. Everything which is, is either in itself or in another (Ax. 1), that is to say (Defs. 3 and 5), outside the intellect there is nothing but substances and their modifications. There is nothing therefore outside the intellect by which a number of things can be distinguished one from another, but substances or (which is the same thing by Def. 4) their attributes and their modifications.—Q.E.D.

PROPOSITION V. *In nature there cannot be two or more substances of the same nature or attribute.*

Demonstration. If there were two or more distinct substances, they must be distinguished one from the other by difference of attributes or difference of modifications (Prop. 4). If they are distinguished only by difference of attributes, it will be granted that there is but one substance of the same attribute. But if they are distinguished by difference of modifications, since substance is prior by nature to its modifications (Prop. 1), the modifications therefore being placed on one side, and the substance being considered in itself, or, in other words (Def. 3 and Ax. 6), truly considered, it cannot be conceived as distinguished from another substance, that is to say (Prop. 4), there cannot be two or more substances, but only one possessing the same nature or attribute.—Q.E.D.

PROPOSITION VI. *One substance cannot be produced by another substance.*

Demonstration. There cannot in nature be two substances of the same attribute (Prop. 5), that is to say (Prop. 2), two which have anything in common with one another. And therefore (Prop. 3), one cannot be the cause of the other, that is to say, one cannot be produced by the other.—Q.E.D.

Corollary. Hence it follows that there is nothing by which substance can be produced, for in Nature there is nothing but substances and their modifications (as is evident for Ax. 1 and Defs. 3 and 5). But substance cannot be produced by substance (Prop. 6). Therefore absolutely there is nothing by which substance can be produced.—Q.E.D.

Another Demonstration. This corollary is demonstrated more easily by the *reductio ad absurdum.* For if there were anything by which substance could be produced, the knowledge of substance would be dependent upon the knowledge of its cause (Ax. 4), and therefore (Def. 3) it would not be substance.

. . . .

PROPOSITION XXV. *God is not only the efficient cause of the existence of things, but also of their essence.*

Demonstration. Suppose that God is not the cause of the essence of things, then (Ax. 4) the essence of things can be conceived without God, which (Prop. 15) is absurd. Therefore, God is the cause of the essence of things.—Q.E.D.

Note. This proposition more clearly follows from Prop. 16. For from this proposition it follows that, from the existence of the divine nature, both the essence of things and their existence must necessarily be concluded, or, in a word, in the same sense in which God is said to be the cause of Himself He must be called the cause of all things. This will appear still more clearly from the following corollary.

Corollary. Individual things are nothing but modifications or modes of God's attributes, expressing these attributes in a certain and determinate manner. This is evident from Prop. 15 and Def. 5.

* *

PART TWO: OF THE NATURE AND ORIGIN OF THE MIND

* *

Definitions

I. By body I understand a mode which expresses in a certain and determinate manner the essence of God in so far as He is considered as the thing extended. (See Corol. Prop. 25, pt. 1.)

II. I say that to the essence of anything pertains that, which being given, the thing itself is necessarily posited, and, being taken away, the thing is necessarily taken; or, in other words, that without which the thing can neither be nor be conceived, and which in its turn cannot be nor be conceived without the thing.

III. By idea I understand a conception of the mind which the mind forms because it is a thinking thing.

Explanation. I use the word "conception" rather than "perception" because the name perception seems to indicate that the mind is passive in its relation to the object. But the word conception seems to express the action of the mind.

IV. By adequate idea I understand an idea which, in so far as it is considered in itself, without reference to the object, has all the properties or internal signs (*denominationes intrinsecas*) of a true idea.

Explanation. I say internal, so as to exclude that which is external, the agreement, namely, of the idea with its object.

V. Duration is the indefinite continuation of existence.

Explanation. I call it indefinite because it cannot be determined by the nature itself of the existing thing nor by the efficient cause, which necessarily posits the existence of the thing but does not take it away.

VI. By reality and perfection I understand the same thing.

VII. By individual things I understand things which are finite and which have a determinate existence; and if a number of individuals so unite in one action that they are all simultaneously the cause of one effect, I consider them all, so far, as a one individual thing.

Axioms

I. The essence of man does not involve necessary existence; that is to say, the existence as well as the non-existence of this or that man may or may not follow from the order of nature.
II. Man thinks.
III. Modes of thought, such as love, desire, or the emotions of the mind, by whatever name they may be called, do not exist unless in the same individual exists the idea of a thing loved, desired, etc. But the idea may exist although no other mode of thinking exist.
IV. We perceive that a certain body is affected in many ways.
V. No individual things are felt or perceived by us except bodies and modes of thought.
The postulates will be found after Proposition 13.

Propositions

PROPOSITION I. *Thought is an attribute of God, or God is a thinking thing.*
Demonstration. Individual thoughts, or this and that thought, are modes which express the nature of God in a certain and determinate manner (Corol. Prop. 25, pt. 1). God therefore possesses an attribute (Def. 5, pt. 1) the conception of which is involved in all individual thoughts, and through which they are conceived. Thought, therefore, is one of the infinite attributes of God which expresses the eternal and infinite essence of God (Def. 6, pt. 1), or, in other words, God is a thinking thing.—Q.E.D.
Note. This proposition is plain from the fact that we can conceive an infinite thinking Being. For the more things a thinking being can think, the more reality or perfection we conceive it to possess, and therefore the being which can think an infinitude of things in infinite ways is necessarily infinite by his power of thinking. Since, therefore, we can conceive an infinite Being by attending to thought alone, thought is necessarily one of the infinite attributes of God (Defs. 4 and 6, pt. 1), which is the proposition we wished to prove.

PROPOSITION II. *Extension is an attribute of God, or God is an extended thing.*

Demonstration. The demonstration of this proposition is of the same character as that of the last.

• •

PROPOSITION VI. *The modes of any attribute have God for a cause only in so far as He is considered under that attribute of which they are modes, and not in so far as He is considered under any other attribute.*

Demonstration. Each attribute is conceived by itself and without any other (Prop. 10, pt. 1). Therefore the modes of any attribute involve the conception of that attribute and of no other, and therefore (Ax. 4, pt. 1) have God for a cause in so far as He is considered under that attribute of which they are modes, and not so far as He is considered under any other attribute.—Q.E.D.

Corollary. Hence it follows that the formal being of things which are not modes of thought does not follow from the divine nature because of His prior knowledge of these things, but, as we have shown, just as ideas follow from the attribute of thought, in the same manner and with the same necessity the objects of ideas follow and are concluded from their attributes.

PROPOSITION VII. *The order and connection of ideas is the same as the order and connection of things.*

This is evident from Ax. 4, pt. 1. For the idea of anything caused depends upon a knowledge of the cause of which the thing caused is the effect.

Corollary. Hence it follows that God's power of thinking is equal to His actual power of acting, that is to say, whatever follows *formally* from the infinite nature of God, follows from the idea of God [*idea Dei*], in the same order and in the same connection *objectively* in God.

Note. Before we go any further, we must here recall to our memory what we have already demonstrated—that everything which can be perceived by the infinite intellect as constituting the essence of substance pertains entirely to the one sole substance only, and consequently that substance thinking and substance extended are one and the same substance, which is now comprehended under this attribute and now under that. Thus, also, a mode of extension and the idea of that mode are one and the same thing expressed in two different ways—a truth which some of the Hebrews appear to have seen as if through a cloud, since they say that God, the intellect of God, and the things which are the objects of that intellect are one and the same thing. For example, the circle existing in Nature and the idea that is in God of an existing circle are one and the same thing which is manifested through different attributes; and, therefore, whether we think of Nature under the attribute of extension or under the attribute of thought or under any other attribute whatever, we shall discover one and the same order or one and the same connection of causes, that is to say, in every case the same sequence of things. Nor have I had any other reason for saying that God is the cause of the idea, for example, of the circle in so far only as He is a thinking thing, and of the circle itself in so far as He is an extended thing, but this, that the formal being of the idea of a circle can only be perceived through another mode of thought, as its proximate cause, and this again must be perceived through another, and so on *ad infinitum*. So that when things are considered as modes of thought we must explain the order of the whole of Nature or the connection of causes by the attribute of thought alone, and when things are considered as modes of extension, the order of the whole of Nature must be explained through the attribute of extension alone, and so with other attributes. Therefore, God is in truth the cause of things as they are in themselves, in so far as He consists of infinite attributes, nor for the present can I explain the matter more clearly.

• •

> PROPOSITION XII. *Whatever happens in the object of the idea constituting the human mind must be perceived by the human mind; or, in other words, an idea of that thing will necessarily exist in the human mind. That is to say, if the object of the idea constituting the human mind be a body, nothing can happen in that body which is not perceived by the mind.*

Demonstration. The knowledge of everything which happens in the object of any idea necessarily exists in God (Corol. Prop. 9, pt. 2), in so far as He is considered as affected with the idea of that object; that is to say (Prop. 11, pt. 2), in so far as He forms the mind of any being. The knowledge, therefore, necessarily exists in God of everything which happens in the object of the idea constituting the human mind, that is to say, it exists in Him in so far as He forms the nature of the human mind; or, in other words (Corol. Prop. 11, pt. 2), the knowledge of this thing will necessarily be in the mind, or the mind perceives it. —Q.E.D.

Note. This proposition is plainly deducible and more easily to be understood from Note, Prop. 7, pt. 2, to which the reader is referred.

> PROPOSITION XIII. *The object of the idea constituting the human mind is a body, or a certain mode of extension actually existing, and nothing else.*

Demonstration. For if the body were not the object of the human mind, the ideas of the modifications of the body would not be in God (Corol. Prop. 9, pt. 2) in so far as He has formed our mind, but would be in Him in so far as He has formed the mind of another thing; that is to say (Corol. Prop. 11, pt. 2), the ideas of the modifications of the body would not be in our mind. But (Ax. 4, pt. 2) we have ideas of the modifications of a body, therefore, the object of the idea constituting the human mind is a body, and that, too, (Prop. 11, pt. 2) actually existing. Again, if there were also any other object of the mind besides a body, since nothing exists from which some effect does not follow (Prop. 36, pt. 1), the idea of some effect produced by this object would necessarily exist in our mind (Prop. 11, pt. 2). But (Ax. 5, pt. 2) there is no such idea, and therefore the object of our mind is a body existing, and nothing else.—Q.E.D.

Corollary. Hence it follows that man is composed of mind and body, and that the human body exists as we perceive it.

Note. Hence we see not only that the human mind is united to the body, but also what is to be understood by the union of the mind and body. But no one can understand it adequately or distinctly without knowing adequately beforehand the nature of our body; for those things which we have proved hitherto are altogether general, nor do they refer more to man than to other individuals, all of which are animate, although in different degrees. For of everything there necessarily exists in God an idea of which He is the cause, in the same way as the idea of the human body exists in Him; and therefore everything that we have said of the idea of the human body is necessarily true of the idea of any other thing. We cannot, however, deny that ideas, like objects themselves, differ from one another, and that one is more excellent and contains more reality than another, just as the object of one idea is more excellent and contains more reality than another. Therefore, in order to determine the difference between the human mind and other things and its superiority over them, we must first know, as we have said, the nature of its object, that is to say, the nature of the human body. I am not able to explain it here, nor is such an explanation necessary for what I wish to demonstrate.

Thus much, nevertheless, I will say generally—that in proportion as one body is better adapted than another to do or suffer many things, in the same proportion will the mind at the same time be better adapted to perceive many things, and the more the actions of a body depend upon itself alone, and the less other bodies co-operate with it in action, the better adapted will the mind be for distinctly understanding. We can thus determine the superiority of one mind to another; we can also see the reason why we have only a very confused knowledge of our body, together with many other things which I shall deduce in what follows. For this reason I have thought it worth while more accurately to explain and demonstrate the truths just mentioned, to which end it is necessary for me to say beforehand a few words upon the nature of bodies.

PROPOSITION XV. *The idea which constitutes the formal being of the human mind is not simple, but is composed of a number of ideas.*

Demonstration. The idea which constitutes the formal being of the human mind is the idea of a body (Prop. 13, pt. 2) which (Post. 1) is composed of a number of individuals composite to a high degree. But an idea of each individual composing the body must necessarily exist in God (Corol. Prop. 8, pt. 2); therefore (Prop. 7, pt. 2) the idea of the human body is composed of these several ideas of the component parts. —Q.E.D.

PROPOSITION XVI. *The idea of every way in which the human body is affected by external bodies must involve the nature of the human body, and at the same time the nature of the external body.*

Demonstration. All ways in which any body is affected follow at the same time from the nature of the affected body and from the nature of the affecting body (Ax. 1, following Corol. Lem. 3); therefore, the idea of these modifications (Ax. 4, pt. 1) necessarily involves the nature of each body, and therefore the idea of each way in which the human body is affected by an external body involves the nature of the human body and of the external body.—Q.E.D.

Corollary 1. Hence it follows, in the first place, that the human mind perceives the nature of many bodies together with that of its own body.

Corollary 2. It follows, secondly, that the ideas we have of external bodies indicate the constitution of our own body rather than the nature of external bodies. This I have explained in the Appendix of the First Part by many examples.

. . . .

PROPOSITION XIX. *The human mind does not know the human body itself, nor does it know that the body exists except through ideas of modifications by which the body is affected.*

Demonstration. The human mind is the idea itself or the knowledge of the human body (Prop. 13, pt. 2). This knowledge (Prop. 9, pt. 2) is in God in so far as He is considered as affected by another idea of an individual thing. But because (Post. 4) the human body needs a number of bodies by which it is, as it were, continually regenerated, and because the order and connection of ideas is the same as the order and connection of causes (Prop. 7, pt. 2), this idea will be in God in so far as He is considered as affected by the ideas of a multitude of individual things.

God, therefore, has the idea of the human body or knows the human body in so far as He is affected by a multitude of other ideas, and not in so far as He forms the nature of the human mind; that is to say (Corol. Prop. 11, pt. 2), the human mind does not know the human body. But the ideas of the modifications of the body are in God in so far as He forms the nature of the human mind; that is to say (Prop. 12, pt. 2), the human mind perceives these modifications and, consequently (Prop. 16, pt. 2), the human body itself actually existing (Prop. 17, pt. 2). The human mind, therefore, perceives the human body, etc.—Q.E.D.

PROPOSITION XX. *There exists in God the idea or knowledge of the human mind, which follows in Him and is related to Him in the same way as the idea or knowledge of the human body.*

Demonstration. Thought is an attribute of God (Prop. 1, pt. 2), and therefore there must necessarily exist in God an idea of Himself (Prop. 3, pt. 2), together with an idea of all His modifications, and consequently (Prop. 11, pt. 2) an idea of the human mind. Moreover, this idea or knowledge of the mind does not exist in God in so far as He is infinite, but in so far as He is affected by another idea of an individual thing (Prop. 9, pt. 2). But the order and connection of ideas is the same as the order and connection of causes (Prop. 7, pt. 2). This idea or knowledge of the mind, therefore, follows in God, and is related to God in the same manner as the idea or knowledge of the body.—Q.E.D.

PROPOSITION XXI. *This idea of the mind is united to the mind in the same way as the mind itself is united to the body.*

Demonstration. We have shown that the mind is united to the body because the body is the object of the mind (Props. 12 and 13, pt. 2), therefore, by the same reasoning, the idea of the mind must be united with its object, the mind itself, in the same way as the mind itself is united to the body.—Q.E.D.

Note. This proposition is to be understood much more clearly from what has been said in the Note to Prop. 7, pt. 2, for we have there shown that the idea of the body and the body, that is to say (Prop. 13, pt. 2), the mind and the body, are one and the same individual which at one time is considered under the attribute of thought, and at another under that of extension: the idea of the mind, therefore, and the mind itself are one and the same thing, which is considered under one and the same attribute, that of thought. It follows, I say, that the idea of the mind and the mind itself exist in God from the same necessity and from the same power of thought. For, indeed, the idea of the mind, that is to say, the idea of the idea, is nothing but the form of the idea in so far as this is considered as a mode of thought and without relation to the object, just as a person who knows anything by that very fact knows that he knows, and knows that he knows that he knows, and so on *ad infinitum*. But more on this subject afterwards.

PROPOSITION XXII. *The human mind not only perceives the modifications of the body, but also the ideas of these modifications.*

Demonstration. The ideas of the ideas of modifications follow in God and are related to God in the same way as the ideas themselves of modifications. This is demonstrated like Prop. 20, pt. 2. But the ideas of the modifications of the body are in the human mind (Prop. 12, pt. 2), that is to say, in God (Corol. Prop. 11, pt. 2), in so far as He constitutes the essence of the human mind; therefore, the ideas of these ideas will be in God in so far as He has the knowledge or idea of the human mind; that is to say (Prop. 21, pt. 2), they will be in the human mind itself, which, therefore, not only perceives the modifications of the body, but also the ideas of these modifications.—Q.E.D.

PROPOSITION XXIII. *The mind does not know itself except in so far as it perceives the ideas of the modifications of the body.*

Demonstration. The idea or knowledge of the mind (Prop. 20, pt. 2) follows in God and is related to God in the same way as the idea or knowledge of the body. But since (Prop. 19, pt. 2) the human mind does not know the human body itself, that is to say (Corol. Prop. 11, pt. 2), since the knowledge of the human body is not related to God in so far as He constitutes the nature of the human mind, therefore the knowledge of the mind is not related to God in so far as He constitutes the essence of the human mind; and therefore (Corol. Prop. 11, pt. 2) the human mind so far does not know itself. Moreover, the ideas of the modifications by which the body is affected involve the nature of the human body itself (Prop. 16, pt. 2), that is to say (Prop. 13, pt. 2), they agree with the nature of the mind; therefore, a knowledge of these ideas will necessarily involve a knowledge of the mind. But (Prop. 22, pt. 2) the knowledge of these ideas is in the human mind itself, and therefore the human mind so far only has a knowledge of itself.—Q.E.D.

. . . .

PROPOSITION XXVI. *The human mind perceives no external body as actually existing unless through the ideas of the modifications of its body.*

Demonstration. If the human body is in no way affected by any external body, then (Prop. 7, pt. 2) the idea of the human body, that is to say (Prop. 13, pt. 2), the human mind, is not affected in any way by the idea of the existence of that body, nor does it in any way perceive the existence of that external body. But in so far as the human body is affected in any way by any external body, so far (Prop. 16, pt. 2, with its Corol.) does it perceive the external body.—Q.E.D.

Corollary. In so far as the human mind imagines an external body, so far it has not an adequate knowledge of it.

Demonstration. When the human mind through the ideas of the modifications of its body contemplates external bodies, we say that it then imagines (Note, Prop. 17, pt. 2), nor can the mind (Prop. 26, pt. 2) in any other way imagine external bodies as actually existing. Therefore (Prop. 25, pt. 2) in so far as the mind imagines external bodies it does not possess an adequate knowledge of them.—Q.E.D.

• •

PART THREE: ON THE ORIGIN AND NATURE OF THE EMOTIONS

• •

PROPOSITION II. *The body cannot determine the mind to thought, neither can the mind determine the body to motion nor rest, nor to anything else if there be anything else.*

Demonstration. All modes of thought have God for a cause in so far as He is a thinking thing, and not in so far as He is manifested by any other attribute (Prop. 6, pt. 2). That which determines the mind to thought, therefore, is a mode of thought and not of extension, that is to say (Def. 1, pt. 2), it is not the body. This is the first thing which was to be proved. Again, the motion and rest of the body must be derived from some other body, which has also been determined to motion or rest by another, and, absolutely, whatever arises in the body must arise from God, in so far as He is considered as affected by some mode of extension, and not in so far as He is considered as affected by any mode of thought (Prop. 6, pt. 2), that is to say, whatever arises in the body cannot arise from the mind, which is a mode of thought (Prop. 11, pt. 2). This is the second thing which was to be proved. Therefore, the body cannot determine, etc.—Q.E.D.

Note. This proposition will be better understood from what has been said in the Note of Prop. 7, pt. 2, that is to say, that the mind and the body are one and the same thing, conceived at one time under the attribute of thought, and at another under that of extension. For this reason, the order or concatenation of things is one, whether Nature be conceived under this or under that attribute, and consequently the order of the state of activity and passivity of our body is coincident in Nature with the order of the state of activity and passivity of the mind. This is also plain from the manner in which we have demonstrated Prop. 12, pt. 2.

• •

THOMAS HOBBES

Selections

from LEVIATHAN

Chapter 1: Of Sense

Sense. Concerning the thoughts of man, I will consider them first singly, and afterwards in train, or dependence upon one another. Singly, they are every one a *representation* or *appearance,* of some quality, or other accident of a body without us, which is commonly called an *object.* Which object worketh on the eyes, ears, and other parts of a man's body; and by diversity of working, produceth diversity of appearances.

The original of them all, is that which we call SENSE, for there is no conception in a man's mind, which hath not at first, totally, or by parts, been begotten upon the organs of sense. The rest are derived from that original.

To know the natural cause of sense, is not very necessary to the business now in hand; and I have elsewhere written of the same at large. Nevertheless, to fill each part of my present method, I will briefly deliver the same in this place.

The cause of sense, is the external body, or object, which presseth the organ proper to each sense, either immediately, as in the taste and touch; or mediately, as in seeing, hearing, and smelling; which pressure, by the mediation of the nerves, and other strings and membranes of the body, continued inwards to the brain and heart, causeth there a resistance, or counter-pressure, or endeavour of the heart to deliver

---

Reprinted from *The English Works of Thomas Hobbes of Malmesbury,* collected and edited by Sir William Molesworth, Bart., London: John Bohn, 1839, Vol. III, Part I, 1–6 and 11–13.

itself, which endeavour, because *outward,* seemeth to be some matter without. And this *seeming,* or *fancy,* is that which men call *sense;* and consisteth, as to the eye, in a *light,* or *colour figured;* to the ear, in a *sound;* to the nostril, in an *odour;* to the tongue and palate, in a *savour;* and to the rest of the body, in *heat, cold, hardness, softness,* and such other qualities as we discern by *feeling.* All which qualities, called *sensible,* are in the object, that causeth them, but so many several motions of the matter, by which it presseth our organs diversely. Neither in us that are pressed, are they any thing else, but divers motions; for motion produceth nothing but motion. But their appearance to us is fancy, the same waking, that dreaming. And as pressing, rubbing, or striking the eye, makes us fancy a light; and pressing the ear, produceth a din; so do the bodies also we see, or hear, produce the same by their strong, though unobserved action. For if these colours and sounds were in the bodies, or objects that cause them, they could not be severed from them, as by glasses, and in echoes by reflection, we see they are; where we know the thing we see is in one place, the appearance in another. And though at some certain distance, the real and very object seem invested with the fancy it begets in us; yet the object is one thing, the image or fancy is another. So that sense, in all cases, is nothing else but original fancy, caused, as I have said, by the pressure, that is, by the motion, of external things upon our eyes, ears, and other organs thereunto ordained.

But the philosophy-schools, through all the universities of Christendom, grounded upon certain texts of Aristotle, teach another doctrine, and say, for the cause of *vision,* that the thing seen, sendeth forth on every side a *visible species,* in English, a *visible show, apparition,* or *aspect,* or *a being seen;* the receiving whereof into the eye, is *seeing.* And for the cause of *hearing,* that the thing heard, sendeth forth an *audible species,* that is an *audible aspect,* or *audible being seen;* which entering at the ear, maketh *hearing.* Nay, for the cause of *understanding* also, they say the thing understood, sendeth forth an *intelligible species,* that is, an *intelligible being seen;* which, coming into the understanding, makes us understand. I say not this, as disproving the use of universities; but because I am to speak hereafter of their office in a commonwealth, I must let you see on all occasions by the way, what things would be amended in them; amongst which the frequency of insignificant speech is one.

Chapter 2: Of Imagination

Imagination. That when a thing lies still, unless somewhat else stir it, it will lie still for ever, is a truth that no man doubts of. But that when a thing is in motion, it will eternally be in motion, unless somewhat else stay it, though the reason be the same, namely, that nothing can change itself, is not so easily assented to. For men measure, not only other men, but all other things, by themselves; and because they find themselves subject after motion to pain, and lassitude, think every thing else grows weary of motion, and seeks repose of its own accord; little considering, whether it be not some other motion, wherein that desire of rest they find in themselves, consisteth. From hence it is, that the schools say, heavy bodies fall downwards, out of an appetite to rest, and to conserve their nature in that place which is most proper for them; ascribing appetite, and knowledge of what is good for their conservation, which is more than man has, to things inanimate, absurdly.

When a body is once in motion, it moveth, unless something else hinder it, eternally; and whatsoever hindreth it, cannot in an instant, but in time, and by degrees, quite extinguish it; and as we see in the water, though the wind cease, the waves give not over rolling for a long time after: so also it happeneth in that motion, which is made in the internal parts of a man, then, when he sees, dreams, &c. For after the object is removed, or the eye shut, we still retain an image of the thing seen, though more obscure than when we see it. And this is it, the Latins call *imagination,* from the image made in seeing; and apply the same, though improperly, to all the other senses. But the Greeks call it *fancy;* which signifies *appearance,* and is as proper to one sense, as to another. IMAGINATION therefore is nothing but *decaying sense;* and is found in men, and many other living creatures, as well sleeping, as waking.

The decay of sense in men waking, is not the decay of the motion made in sense; but an obscuring of it, in such manner as the light of the sun obscureth the light of the stars; which stars do no less exercise their virtue, by which they are visible, in the day than in the night. But because amongst many strokes, which our eyes, ears, and other organs receive from external bodies, the predominant only is sensible; therefore, the light of the sun being predominant, we are not affected with the action of the stars. And any object being removed from our eyes, though the impression it made in us remain, yet other objects more present succeeding, and working on us, the imagination of the past is obscured, and made weak, as the voice of a man is in the noise of the day. From whence it followeth, that the longer the time is, after the sight or sense of any object, the weaker is the imagination. For the continual change of man's body destroys in time the parts which in sense were moved: so that distance of time, and of place, hath one and the same effect in us. For as at a great distance of place, that which we look at appears dim, and without distinction of the smaller parts; and as voices grow weak, and inarticulate; so also, after great distance of time, our imagination of the past is weak; and we lose, for example, of cities we have seen, many particular streets, and of actions, many particular circumstances. This *decaying sense,* when we would express the thing itself, I mean *fancy* itself, we call *imagination,* as I said before: but when we would express the decay, and signify that the sense is fading, old, and past, it is called *memory.* So that imagination and memory are but one thing, which for divers considerations hath divers names.

. . . .

Chapter 3: Of the Consequence or Train of Imaginations

By *Consequence,* or TRAIN of thoughts, I understand that succession of one thought to another, which is called, to distinguish it from discourse in words, *mental discourse.*

When a man thinketh on any thing whatsoever, his next thought after, is not altogether so casual as it seems to be. Not every thought to every thought succeeds indifferently. But as we have no imagination, whereof we have not formerly had sense, in whole, or in parts; so we have no transition from one imagination to another, whereof we never had the like before in our senses. The reason whereof is this. All fancies are motions within us, relics of those made in the sense: and those motions that immediately succeeded one another in the sense, continue also together after sense: insomuch as the former coming again to take place, and be predominant, the latter followeth, by coherence of the matter moved, in such manner, as water upon a plane table is drawn which way any one part of it is guided by the finger. But because in sense, to one and the same thing perceived, sometimes one thing, sometimes another succeedeth, it comes to pass in time, that in the imagining of any thing, there is no certainty what we shall imagine next; only this is certain, it shall be something that succeeded the same before, at one time or another.

Train of thoughts unguided. This train of thoughts, or mental discourse, is of two sorts. The first is *unguided, without design,* and inconstant; wherein there is no passionate thought, to govern and direct those that follow, to itself, as the end and scope of some desire, or other passion: in which case the thoughts are said to wander, and seem impertinent one to another, as in a dream. Such are commonly the thoughts of men, that are not only without company, but also without care of any thing; though even then their thoughts are as busy as at other times, but without harmony; as the sound which a lute out of tune would yield to any man; or in tune, to one that could not play. And yet in this wild ranging of the mind, a man may oft-times perceive the way of it, and the dependence of one thought upon another. For in a discourse of our present civil war, what could seem more impertinent, than to ask, as one did, what was the value of a Roman penny? Yet the coherence to me was manifest enough. For the thought of the war, introduced the thought of the delivering up the king to his enemies; the thought of that, brought in the thought of the delivering up of Christ; and that again the thought of the thirty pence, which was the price of that treason; and thence easily followed that malicious question, and all this in a moment of time; for thought is quick.

Train of thoughts regulated. The second is more constant; as being *regulated* by some desire, and design. For the impression made by such things as we desire, or fear, is strong, and permanent, or, if it cease for a time, of quick return: so strong it is sometimes, as to hinder and break our sleep. From desire, ariseth the thought of some means we have seen produce the like of that which we aim at; and from the thought of that, the thought of means to that mean; and so continually, till we come to some beginning within our own power. And because the end, by the greatness of the impression, comes often to mind, in case our thoughts begin to wander, they are quickly again reduced into the way: which observed by one of the seven wise men, made him give men this precept, which is now worn out, *Respice finem;* that is to say, in all your actions, look often upon what you would have, as the thing that directs all your thoughts in the way to attain it.

. . . .

from DE CORPORE

Chapter 25: Of Sense and Animal Motion

. . . .

2. *The investigation of the nature of sense, and the definition of sense.* Now that all mutation or alteration is motion or endeavour (and endeavour also is motion) in the internal parts of the thing that is altered, hath been proved (in art. 9, chap. 8) from this, that whilst even the least parts of any body remain in the same situation in respect of one another, it cannot be said that any alteration, unless perhaps that the whole body together hath been moved, hath happened to it; but that

---

Reprinted from *The English Works of Thomas Hobbes of Malmesbury*, collected and edited by Sir William Molesworth, Bart., London: John Bohn, 1839, Vol. I, Part IV, 389–394 and 396–399.

it both appeareth and is the same it appeared and was before. Sense, therefore, in the sentient, can be nothing else but motion in some of the internal parts of the sentient; and the parts so moved are parts of the organs of sense. For the parts of our body, by which we perceive any thing, are those we commonly call the organs of sense. And so we find what is the subject of our sense, namely, that in which are the phantasms; and partly also we have discovered the nature of sense, namely, that it is some internal motion in the sentient.

I have shown besides (in chap. 9, art. 7) that no motion is generated but by a body contiguous and moved: from whence it is manifest, that the immediate cause of sense or perception consists in this, that the first organ of sense is touched and pressed. For when the uttermost part of the organ is pressed, it no sooner yields, but the part next within it is pressed also; and, in this manner, the pressure or motion is propagated through all the parts of the organ to the innermost. And thus also the pressure of the uttermost part proceeds from the pressure of some more remote body, and so continually, till we come to that from which, as from its fountain, we derive the phantasm or idea that is made in us by our sense. And this, whatsoever it be, is that we commonly call *the object*. Sense, therefore, is some internal motion in the sentient, generated by some internal motion of the parts of the object, and propagated through all the media to the innermost part of the organ. By which words I have almost defined what sense is.

Moreover, I have shown (art. 2, chap. 15) that all resistance is endeavour opposite to another endeavour, that is to say, reaction. Seeing, therefore, there is in the whole organ, by reason of its own internal natural motion, some resistance or reaction against the motion which is propagated from the object to the innermost part of the organ, there is also in the same organ an endeavour opposite to the endeavour which proceeds from the object; so that when that endeavour inwards is the last action in the act of sense, then from the reaction, how little soever the duration of it be, a phantasm or idea hath its being, which, by reason that the endeavour is now outwards, doth always appear as something situate without the organ. So that now I shall give you the whole definition of sense, as it is drawn from the explication of the causes thereof and the order of its generation, thus: SENSE *is a phantasm, made by the reaction and endeavour outwards in the organ of sense, caused by an endeavour inwards from the object, remaining for some time more or less.*

3. *The subject and object of sense.* The *subject* of sense is the *sentient* itself, namely, some living creature; and we speak more correctly, when we say a living creature seeth, than when we say the eye seeth. The object is the thing received; and it is more accurately said, that we see the sun, than that we see the light. For light and colour,

and heat and sound, and other qualities which are commonly called sensible, are not objects, but phantasms in the sentients. For a phantasm is the act of sense, and differs no otherwise from sense than *fieri,* that is, being a doing, differs from *factum esse,* that is, being done; which difference, in things that are done in an instant, is none at all; and a phantasm is made in an instant. For in all motion which proceeds by perpetual propagation, the first part being moved moves the second, the second the third, and so on to the last, and that to any distance, how great soever. And in what point of time the first or foremost part proceeded to the place of the second, which is thrust on, in the same point of time the last save one proceeded into the place of the last yielding part; which by reaction, in the same instant, if the reaction be strong enough, makes a phantasm; and a phantasm being made, perception is made together with it.

4. *The organs of sense.* The *organs* of sense, which are in the sentient, are such parts thereof, that if they be hurt, the very generation of phantasms is thereby destroyed, though all the rest of the parts remain entire. Now these parts in the most of living creatures are found to be certain spirits and membranes, which, proceeding from the *pia mater,* involve the brain and all the nerves; also the brain itself, and the arteries which are in the brain; and such other parts, as being stirred, the heart also, which is the fountain of all sense, is stirred together with them. For whensoever the action of the object reacheth the body of the sentient, that action is by some nerve propagated to the brain; and if the nerve leading thither be so hurt or obstructed, that the motion can be propagated no further, no sense follows. Also if the motion be intercepted between the brain and the heart by the defect of the organ by which the action is propagated, there will be no perception of the object.

5. *All bodies are not endued with sense.* But though all sense, as I have said, be made by reaction, nevertheless it is not necessary that every thing that reacteth should have sense. I know there have been philosophers, and those learned men, who have maintained that all bodies are endued with sense. Nor do I see how they can be refuted, if the nature of sense be placed in reaction only. And, though by the reaction of bodies inanimate a phantasm might be made, it would nevertheless cease, as soon as ever the object were removed. For unless those bodies had organs, as living creatures have, fit for the retaining of such motion as is made in them, their sense would be such, as that they should never remember the same. And therefore this hath nothing to do with that sense which is the subject of my discourse. For by sense, we commonly understand the judgment we make of objects by their phantasms; namely, by comparing and distinguishing those phantasms; which we could never do, if that motion in the organ, by

which the phantasm is made, did not remain there for some time, and make the same phantasm return. Wherefore sense, as I here understand it, and which is commonly so called, hath necessarily some memory adhering to it, by which former and later phantasms may be compared together, and distinguished from one another.

Sense, therefore, properly so called, must necessarily have in it a perpetual variety of phantasms, that they may be discerned one from another. For if we should suppose a man to be made with clear eyes, and all the rest of his organs of sight well disposed, but endued with no other sense; and that he should look only upon one thing, which is always of the same colour and figure, without the least appearance of variety, he would seem to me, whatsoever others may say, to see, no more than I seem to myself to feel the bones of my own limbs by my organs of feeling; and yet those bones are always and on all sides touched by a most sensible membrane. I might perhaps say he were astonished, and looked upon it; but I should not say he saw it; it being almost all one for a man to be always sensible of one and the same thing, and not to be sensible at all of any thing.

. . . .

7. *Imagination, the remains of past sense; which also is memory. Of sleep.* But the motion of the organ, by which a phantasm is made, is not commonly called sense, except the object be present. And the phantasm remaining after the object is removed or past by, is called *fancy,* and in Latin *imaginatio;* which word, because all phantasms are not images, doth not fully answer the signification of the word *fancy* in its general acceptation. Nevertheless I may use it safely enough, by understanding it for the Greek Φαντασία.

IMAGINATION therefore is nothing else but *sense decaying,* or *weakened,* by the absence of the object. But what may be the cause of this decay or weakening? Is the motion the weaker, because the object is taken away? If it were, then phantasms would always and necessarily be less clear in the imagination, than they are in sense; which is not true. For in dreams, which are the imaginations of those that sleep, they are no less clear than in sense itself. But the reason why in men waking the phantasms of things past are more obscure than those of things present, is this, that their organs being at the same time moved by other present objects, those phantasms are the less predominant. Whereas in sleep, the passages being shut up, external action doth not at all disturb or hinder internal motion.

If this be true, the next thing to be considered, will be, whether any cause may be found out, from the supposition whereof it will follow, that the passage is shut up from the external objects of sense to the internal organ. I suppose, therefore, that by the continual action of objects, to which a reaction of the organ, and more especially of the spirits, is necessarily consequent, the organ is wearied, that is, its parts are no longer moved by the spirits without some pain; and consequently the nerves being abandoned and grown slack, they retire to their fountain, which is the cavity either of the brain or of the heart; by which means the action which proceeded by the nerves is necessarily intercepted. For action upon a patient, that retires from it, makes but little impression at the first; and at last, when the nerves are by little and little slackened, none at all. And therefore there is no more reaction, that is, no more sense, till the organ being refreshed by rest, and by a supply of new spirits recovering strength and motion, the sentient awaketh. And thus it seems to be always, unless some other preternatural cause intervene; as heat in the internal parts from lassitude, or from some disease stirring the spirits and other parts of the organ in some extraordinary manner.

8. *How phantasms succeed one another.* Now it is not without cause, nor so casual a thing as many perhaps think it, that phantasms in this their great variety proceed from one another; and that the same phantasms sometimes bring into the mind other phantasms like themselves, and at other times extremely unlike. For in the motion of any continued body, one part follows another by cohesion; and therefore, whilst we turn our eyes and other organs successively to many objects, the motion which was made by every one of them remaining, the phantasms are renewed as often as any one of those motions comes to be predominant above the rest; and they become predominant in the same order in which at any time formerly they were generated by sense. So that when by length of time very many phantasms have been generated within us by sense, then almost any thought may arise from any other thought; insomuch that it may seem to be a thing indifferent and casual, which thought shall follow which. But for the most part this is not so uncertain a thing to waking as to sleeping men. For the thought or phantasm of the desired end brings in all the phantasms, that are means conducing to that end, and that in order backwards from the last to the first, and again forwards from the beginning to the end. But this supposes both appetite, and judgment to discern what means conduce to the end, which is gotten by experience; and experience is store of phantasms, arising from the sense of very many things. For $\varphi\alpha\nu\tau\alpha\zeta\epsilon\sigma\theta\alpha\iota$ and *meminisse, fancy* and *memory,* differ only in this, that memory supposeth the time past, which fancy doth not. In memory, the phantasms we consider are as if they were worn out with time; but in our fancy we consider them as they are; which distinction is not of the things themselves, but of the considerations of the sentient. For there is in memory something like that which happens in looking upon things at a great distance; in which as the small

parts of the object are not discerned, by reason of their remoteness; so in memory, many accidents and places and parts of things, which were formerly perceived by sense, are by length of time decayed and lost.

The perpetual arising of phantasms, both in sense and imagination, is that which we commonly call discourse of the mind, and is common to men with other living creatures. For he that thinketh, compareth the phantasms that pass, that is, taketh notice of their likeness or unlikeness to one another. And as he that observes readily the likenesses of things of different natures, or that are very remote from one another, is said to have a good fancy; so he is said to have a good judgment, that finds out the unlikenesses or differences of things that are like one another. Now this observation of differences is not perception made by a common organ of sense, distinct from sense or perception properly so called, but is memory of the differences of particular phantasms remaining for some time; as the distinction between hot and lucid, is nothing else but the memory both of a heating, and of an enlightening object.

. . . .

part two
THE IDENTITY THESIS

J. J. C. SMART

Sensations and Brain Processes

This paper[1] takes its departure from arguments to be found in U. T. Place's "Is Consciousness a Brain Process?"[2] I have had the benefit of discussing Place's thesis in a good many universities in the United States and Australia, and I hope that the present paper answers objections to his thesis which Place has not considered and that it presents his thesis in a more nearly unobjectionable form. This paper is meant also to supplement the paper "The 'Mental' and the 'Physical,'" by H. Feigl,[3] which in part argues for a similar thesis to Place's.

Suppose that I report that I have at this moment a roundish, blurry-edged after-image which is yellowish towards its edge and is orange towards its center. What is it that I am reporting? One answer to this question might be that I am not reporting anything, that when I say that it looks to me as though there is a roundish yellowy-orange patch of light on the wall I am expressing some sort of *temptation*, the temptation to say that there *is* a roundish yellowy-orange patch on the

---

Reprinted from *The Philosophy of Mind*, edited by V. C. Chappell, Englewood Cliffs: Prentice-Hall, Inc., 1962, 160-172, by permission of the publishers, J. J. C. Smart and *The Philosophical Review*.

[1] This is a very slightly revised version of a paper which was first published in the *Philosophical Review*, LXVIII (1959), 141-56. Since that date there have been criticisms of my paper by J. T. Stevenson, *Philosophical Review*, LXIX (1960), 505-10, to which I have replied in *Philosophical Review*, LXX (1961), 406-7, and by G. Pitcher and by W. D. Joske, *Australasian Journal of Philosophy*, XXXVIII (1960), 150-60, to which I have replied in the same volume of that journal, pp. 252-54.

[2] *British Journal of Psychology*, XLVII (1956), 44-50; reprinted in *The Philosophy of Mind*, ed. V. C. Chappell, Englewood Cliffs: Prentice-Hall, Inc., 1962, 101-109. (Page references are to the reprint in that volume.)

[3] *Minnesota Studies in the Philosophy of Science*, Vol. II (Minneapolis: University of Minnesota Press, 1958), pp. 370-497.

wall (though I may know that there is not such a patch on the wall). This is perhaps Wittgenstein's view in the *Philosophical Investigations* (see §§ 367, 370). Similarly, when I "report" a pain, I am not really reporting anything (or, if you like, I am reporting in a queer sense of "reporting"), but am doing a sophisticated sort of wince. (See § 244: "The verbal expression of pain replaces crying and does not describe it." Nor does it describe anything else?)[4] I prefer most of the time to discuss an after-image rather than a pain, because the word "pain" brings in something which is irrelevant to my purpose: the notion of "distress." I think that "he is in pain" entails "he is in distress," that is, that he is in a certain agitation-condition.[5] Similarly, to say "I am in pain" may be to do more than "replace pain behavior": it may be partly to report something, though this something is quite nonmysterious, being an agitation-condition, and so susceptible of behavioristic analysis. The suggestion I wish if possible to avoid is a different one, namely that "I am in pain" is a genuine report, and that what it reports is an irreducibly psychical something. And similarly the suggestion I wish to resist is also that to say "I have a yellowish-orange after-image" is to report something irreducibly psychical.

Why do I wish to resist this suggestion? Mainly because of Occam's razor. It seems to me that science is increasingly giving us a viewpoint whereby organisms are able to be seen as physicochemical mechanisms:[6] it seems that even the behavior of man himself will one day be explicable in mechanistic terms. There does seem to be, so far as science is concerned, nothing in the world but increasingly complex arrangements of physical constituents. All except for one place: in consciousness. That is, for a full description of what is going on in a man you would have to mention not only the physical processes in his tissues, glands, nervous system, and so forth, but also his states of consciousness: his visual, auditory, and tactual sensations, his aches and pains. That these should be *correlated* with brain processes does not help, for to say that they are *correlated* is to say that they are something "over and above." You cannot correlate something with itself. You correlate footprints with burglars, but not Bill Sikes the burglar

[4] Some philosophers of my acquaintance, who have the advantage over me in having known Wittgenstein, would say that this interpretation of him is too behavioristic. However, it seems to me a very natural interpretation of his printed words, and whether or not it is Wittgenstein's real view it is certainly an interesting and important one. I wish to consider it here as a possible rival both to the "brain-process" thesis and to straight-out old-fashioned dualism.

[5] See Ryle, *The Concept of Mind* (London: Hutchinson's University Library, 1949), p. 93.

[6] On this point see Paul Oppenheim and Hilary Putnam, "Unity of Science as a Working Hypothesis," in *Minnesota Studies in the Philosophy of Science*, Vol. II (Minneapolis: University of Minnesota Press, 1958), pp. 3–36.

with Bill Sikes the burglar. So sensations, states of consciousness, do seem to be the one sort of thing left outside the physicalist picture, and for various reasons I just cannot believe that this can be so. That everything should be explicable in terms of physics (together of course with descriptions of the ways in which the parts are put together— roughly, biology is to physics as radio-engineering is to electromagnetism) except the occurrence of sensations seems to me to be frankly unbelievable. Such sensations would be "nomological danglers," to use Feigl's expression.[7] It is not often realized how odd would be the laws whereby these nomological danglers would dangle. It is sometimes asked, "Why can't there be psychophysical laws which are of a novel sort, just as the laws of electricity and magnetism were novelties from the standpoint of Newtonian mechanics?" Certainly we are pretty sure in the future to come across new ultimate laws of a novel type, but I expect them to relate simple constituents: for example, whatever ultimate particles are then in vogue. I cannot believe that ultimate laws of nature could relate simple constituents to configurations consisting of perhaps billions of neurons (and goodness knows how many billion billions of ultimate particles) all put together for all the world as though their main purpose in life was to be a negative feedback mechanism of a complicated sort. Such ultimate laws would be like nothing so far known in science. They have a queer "smell" to them. I am just unable to believe in the nomological danglers themselves, or in the laws whereby they would dangle. If any philosophical arguments seemed to compel us to believe in such things, I would suspect a catch in the argument. In any case it is the object of this paper to show that there are no philosophical arguments which compel us to be dualists.

The above is largely a confession of faith, but it explains why I find Wittgenstein's position (as I construe it) so congenial. For on this view there are, in a sense, no sensations. A man is a vast arrangement of physical particles, but there are not, over and above this, sensations or states of consciousness. There are just behavioral facts about this vast mechanism, such as that it expresses a temptation (behavior disposition) to say "there is a yellowish-red patch on the wall" or that it goes through a sophisticated sort of wince, that is, says "I am in pain." Admittedly Wittgenstein says that though the sensation "is not a something," it is nevertheless "not a nothing either" (§ 304), but this need only mean that the word "ache" has a use. An ache is a thing, but only in the innocuous sense in which the plain man, in the first paragraph

---

[7] Feigl, *op. cit.,* p. 428. Feigl uses the expression "nomological danglers" for the laws whereby the entities dangle: I have used the expression to refer to the dangling entities themselves.

of Frege's *Foundations of Arithmetic*, answers the question "What is the number one?" by "a thing." It should be noted that when I assert that to say "I have a yellowish-orange after-image" is to express a temptation to assert the physical-object statement "There is a yellowish-orange patch on the wall," I mean that saying "I have a yellowish-orange after-image" is (partly) the exercise of the disposition[8] which is the temptation. It is not to *report* that I have the temptation, any more than is "I love you" normally a report that I love someone. Saying "I love you" is just part of the behavior which is the exercise of the disposition of loving someone.

Though for the reasons given above, I am very receptive to the above "expressive" account of sensation statements, I do not feel that it will quite do the trick. Maybe this is because I have not thought it out sufficiently, but it does seem to me as though, when a person says "I have an after-image," he *is* making a genuine report, and that when he says "I have a pain," he *is* doing more than "replace pain-behavior," and that "this more" is not just to say that he is in distress. I am not so sure, however, that to admit this is to admit that there are non-physical correlates of brain processes. Why should not sensations just be brain processes of a certain sort? There are, of course, well-known (as well as lesser-known) philosophical objections to the view that reports of sensations are reports of brain-processes, but I shall try to argue that these arguments are by no means as cogent as is commonly thought to be the case.

Let me first try to state more accurately the thesis that sensations are brain-processes. It is not the thesis that, for example, "after-image" or "ache" means the same as "brain process of sort X" (where "X" is replaced by a description of a certain sort of brain process). It is that, in so far as "after-image" or "ache" is a report of a process, it is a report of a process that *happens to be* a brain process. It follows that the thesis does not claim that sensation statements can be *translated* into statements about brain processes.[9] Nor does it claim that the logic of a sensation statement is the same as that of a brain-process statement. All it claims is that in so far as a sensation statement is a report of something, that something is in fact a brain process. Sensations are nothing over and above brain processes. Nations are nothing "over and above" citizens, but this does not prevent the logic of nation

---

[8] Wittgenstein did not like the word "disposition." I am using it to put in a nutshell (and perhaps inaccurately) the view which I am attributing to Wittgenstein. I should like to repeat that I do not wish to claim that my interpretation of Wittgenstein is correct. Some of those who knew him do not interpret him in this way. It is merely a view which I find myself extracting from his printed words and which I think is important and worth discussing for its own sake.

[9] See Place, *op. cit.*, p. 102, and Feigl, *op. cit.*, p. 390, near top.

statements being very different from the logic of citizen statements, nor does it insure the translatability of nation statements into citizen statements. (I do not, however, wish to assert that the relation of sensation statements to brain-process statements is very like that of nation statements to citizen statements. Nations do not just *happen to be* nothing over and above citizens, for example. I bring in the "nations" example merely to make a negative point: that the fact that the logic of A-statements is different from that of B-statements does not insure that A's are anything over and above B's.)

Remarks on Identity

When I say that a sensation is a brain process or that lightning is an electric discharge, I am using "is" in the sense of strict identity. (Just as in the—in this case necessary—proposition "7 is identical with the smallest prime number greater than 5.") When I say that a sensation is a brain process or that lightning is an electric discharge I do not mean just that the sensation is somehow spatially or temporally continuous with the brain process or that the lightning is just spatially or temporally continuous with the discharge. When on the other hand I say that the successful general is the same person as the small boy who stole the apples I mean only that the successful general I see before me is a time slice[10] of the same four-dimensional object of which the small boy stealing apples is an earlier time slice. However, the four-dimensional object which has the general-I-see-before-me for its late time slice is identical in the strict sense with the four-dimensional object which has the small-boy-stealing-apples for an early time slice. I distinguish these two senses of "is identical with" because I wish to make it clear that the brain-process doctrine asserts identity in the *strict* sense.

I shall now discuss various possible objections to the view that the processes reported in sensation statements are in fact processes in the brain. Most of us have met some of these objections in our first year as philosophy students. All the more reason to take a good look at them. Others of the objections will be more recondite and subtle.

Objection 1. Any illiterate peasant can talk perfectly well about his after-images, or how things look or feel to him, or about his aches and pains, and yet he may know nothing whatever about neurophysiology.

---

[10] See J. H. Woodger, *Theory Construction*, International Encyclopedia of Unified Science, II, No. 5 (Chicago: University of Chicago Press, 1939), 38. I here permit myself to speak loosely. For warnings against possible ways of going wrong with this sort of talk, see my note "Spatialising Time," *Mind*, LXIV (1955), 239–41.

A man may, like Aristotle, believe that the brain is an organ for cooling the body without any impairment of his ability to make true statements about his sensations. Hence the things we are talking about when we describe our sensations cannot be processes in the brain.

Reply. You might as well say that a nation of slugabeds, who never saw the Morning Star or knew of its existence, or who had never thought of the expression "the Morning Star," but who used the expression "the Evening Star" perfectly well, could not use this expression to refer to the same entity as we refer to (and describe as) "the Morning Star." [11]

You may object that the Morning Star is in a sense not the very same thing as the Evening Star, but only something spatiotemporally continuous with it. That is, you may say that the Morning Star is not the Evening Star in the strict sense of "identity" that I distinguished earlier.

There is, however, a more plausible example. Consider lightning.[12] Modern physical science tells us that lightning is a certain kind of electrical discharge due to ionization of clouds of water vapor in the atmosphere. This, it is now believed, is what the true nature of lightning is. Note that there are not two things: a flash of lightning and an electrical discharge. There is one thing, a flash of lightning, which is described scientifically as an electrical discharge to the earth from a cloud of ionized water molecules. The case is not at all like that of explaining a footprint by reference to a burglar. We say that what lightning really is, what its true nature as revealed by science is, is an electrical discharge. (It is not the true nature of a footprint to be a burglar.)

To forestall irrelevant objections, I should like to make it clear that by "lightning" I mean the publicly observable physical object, lightning, not a visual sense-datum of lightning. I say that the publicly observable physical object lightning is in fact the electrical discharge, not just a correlate of it. The sense-datum, or rather the having of the sense-datum, the "look" of lightning, may well in my view be a correlate of the electrical discharge. For in my view it is a brain state *caused* by the lightning. But we should no more confuse sensations of lightning with lightning than we confuse sensations of a table with the table.

In short, the reply to Objection 1 is that there can be contingent statements of the form "A is identical with B," and a person may well know that something is an A without knowing that it is a B. An

---

[11] Cf. Feigl, *op. cit.*, p. 439.
[12] See Place, *op. cit.*, p. 106; also Feigl, *op. cit.*, p. 438.

illiterate peasant might well be able to talk about his sensations without knowing about his brain processes, just as he can talk about lightning though he knows nothing of electricity.

Objection 2. It is only a contingent fact (if it is a fact) that when we have a certain kind of sensation there is a certain kind of process in our brain. Indeed it is possible, though perhaps in the highest degree unlikely, that our present physiological theories will be as out of date as the ancient theory connecting mental processes with goings on in the heart. It follows that when we report a sensation we are not reporting a brain-process.

Reply. The objection certainly proves that when we say "I have an after-image" we cannot *mean* something of the form "I have such and such a brain-process." But this does not show that what we report (having an after-image) is not *in fact* a brain process. "I see lightning" does not *mean* "I see an electrical discharge." Indeed, it is logically possible (though highly unlikely) that the electrical discharge account of lightning might one day be given up. Again, "I see the Evening Star" does not *mean* the same as "I see the Morning Star," and yet "The Evening Star and the Morning Star are one and the same thing" is a contingent proposition. Possibly Objection 2 derives some of its apparent strength from a "Fido"–Fido theory of meaning. If the meaning of an expression were what the expression named, then of course it *would* follow from the fact that "sensation" and "brain-process" have different meanings that they cannot name one and the same thing.

Objection 3.[13] Even if Objections 1 and 2 do not prove that sensations are something over and above brain-processes, they do prove that the qualities of sensations are something over and above the qualities of brain-processes. That is, it may be possible to get out of asserting the existence of irreducibly psychic processes, but not out of asserting the existence of irreducibly psychic *properties*. For suppose we identify the Morning Star with the Evening Star. Then there must be some properties which logically imply that of being the Morning Star, and quite distinct properties which entail that of being the Evening Star. Again, there must be some properties (for example, that of being a yellow flash) which are logically distinct from those in the physicalist story.

---

[13] I think this objection was first put to me by Professor Max Black. I think it is the most subtle of any of those I have considered, and the one which I am least confident of having satisfactorily met. [See Jerome Shaffer, "Mental Events and the Brain," reprinted in this volume, pp. 67–72; and James W. Cornman, "The Identity of Mind and Body," reprinted in this volume, pp. 73–79.]

Indeed, it might be thought that the objection succeeds at one jump. For consider the property of "being a yellow flash." It might seem that this property lies inevitably outside the physicalist framework within which I am trying to work (either by "yellow" being an objective emergent property of physical objects, or else by being a power to produce yellow sense-data, where "yellow," in this second instantiation of the word, refers to a purely phenomenal or introspectible quality). I must therefore digress for a moment and indicate how I deal with secondary qualities. I shall concentrate on color.

First of all, let me introduce the concept of a normal percipient. One person is more a normal percipient than another if he can make color discriminations that the other cannot. For example, if A can pick a lettuce leaf out of a heap of cabbage leaves, whereas B cannot though he can pick a lettuce leaf out of a heap of beetroot leaves, then A is more normal than B. (I am assuming that A and B are not given time to distinguish the leaves by their slight difference in shape, and so forth.) From the concept of "more normal than" it is easy to see how we can introduce the concept of "normal." Of course, Eskimos may make the finest discriminations at the blue end of the spectrum, Hottentots at the red end. In this case the concept of a normal percipient is a slightly idealized one, rather like that of "the mean sun" in astronomical chronology. There is no need to go into such subtleties now. I say that "This is red" means something roughly like "A normal percipient would not easily pick this out of a clump of geranium petals though he would pick it out of a clump of lettuce leaves." Of course it does not exactly mean this: a person might know the meaning of "red" without knowing anything about geraniums, or even about normal percipients. But the point is that a person can be *trained* to say "This is red" of objects which would not easily be picked out of geranium petals by a normal percipient, and so on. (Note that even a color-blind person can reasonably assert that something is red, though of course he needs to use another human being, not just himself, as his "color meter.") This account of secondary qualities explains their unimportance in physics. For obviously the discriminations and lack of discriminations made by a very complex neurophysiological mechanism are hardly likely to correspond to simple and nonarbitrary distinctions in nature.

I therefore elucidate colors as powers, in Locke's sense, to evoke certain sorts of discriminatory responses in human beings. They are also, of course, powers to cause sensations in human beings (an account still nearer Locke's). But these sensations, I am arguing, are identifiable with brain processes.

Now how do I get over the objection that a sensation can be identified with a brain process only if it has some phenomenal property, not possessed by brain processes, whereby one-half of the identification may be, so to speak, pinned down?

Reply. My suggestion is as follows. When a person says, "I see a yellowish-orange after-image," he is saying something like this: "*There is something going on which is like what is going on when* I have my eyes open, am awake, and there is an orange illuminated in good light in front of me, that is, when I really see an orange." (And there is no reason why a person should not say the same thing when he is having a veridical sense-datum, so long as we construe "like" in the last sentence in such a sense that something can be like itself.) Notice that the italicized words, namely "there is something going on which is like what is going on when," are all quasilogical or topic-neutral words. This explains why the ancient Greek peasant's reports about his sensations can be neutral between dualistic metaphysics or my materialistic metaphysics. It explains how sensations can be brain-processes and yet how a man who reports them need know nothing about brain-processes. For he reports them only very abstractly as "something going on which is like what is going on when. . . ." Similarly, a person may say "someone is in the room," thus reporting truly that the doctor is in the room, even though he has never heard of doctors. (There are not two people in the room: "someone" *and* the doctor.) This account of sensation statements also explains the singular elusiveness of "raw feels"—why no one seems to be able to pin any properties on them.[14] Raw feels, in my view, are colorless for the very same reason that *something* is colorless. This does not mean that sensations do not have plenty of properties, for if they are brain-processes they certainly have lots of neurological properties. It only means that in speaking of them as being like or unlike one another we need not know or mention these properties.

This, then, is how I would reply to Objection 3. The strength of my reply depends on the possibility of our being able to report that one thing is like another without being able to state the respect in which it is like. I do not see why this should not be so. If we think cybernetically about the nervous system we can envisage it as able to respond to certain likenesses of its internal processes without being able to do more. It would be easier to build a machine which would tell us, say on a punched tape, whether or not two objects were similar, than it would be to build a machine which would report wherein the similarities consisted.

---

[14] See B. A. Farrell, "Experience," *Mind*, LIX (1950), 170–98; reprinted in *The Philosophy of Mind*, ed. V. C. Chappell, Englewood Cliffs: Prentice-Hall, Inc., 1962, pp. 23–48; see especially p. 27 of that volume [p. 174 of the original].

Objection 4. The after-image is not in physical space. The brain-process is. So the after-image is not a brain process.

Reply. This is an *ignoratio elenchi*. I am not arguing that the after-image is a brain-process, but that the experience of having an after-image is a brain-process. It is the *experience* which is reported in the introspective report. Similarly, if it is objected that the after-image is yellowy-orange, my reply is that it is the experience of seeing yellowy-orange that is being described, and this experience is not a yellowy-orange something. So to say that a brain-process cannot be yellowy-orange is not to say that a brain-process cannot in fact be the experience of having a yellowy-orange after-image. There is, in a sense, no such thing as an after-image or a sense-datum, though there is such a thing as the experience of having an image, and this experience is described indirectly in material object language, not in phenomenal language, for there is no such thing.[15] We describe the experience by saying, in effect, that it is like the experience we have when, for example, we really see a yellowy-orange patch on the wall. Trees and wallpaper can be green, but not the experience of seeing or imagining a tree or wallpaper. (Or if they are described as green or yellow this can only be in a derived sense.)

Objection 5. It would make sense to say of a molecular movement in the brain that it is swift or slow, straight or circular, but it makes no sense to say this of the experience of seeing something yellow.

Reply. So far we have not given sense to talk of experiences as swift or slow, straight or circular. But I am not claiming that "experience" and "brain-process" mean the same or even that they have the same logic. "Somebody" and "the doctor" do not have the same logic, but this does not lead us to suppose that talking about somebody telephoning is talking about someone over and above, say, the doctor. The ordinary man when he reports an experience is reporting that something is going on, but he leaves it open as to what sort of thing is going on, whether in a material solid medium or perhaps in some sort of gaseous medium, or even perhaps in some sort of nonspatial medium (if this makes sense). All that I am saying is that "experience" and "brain-process" may in fact refer to the same thing, and if so we may

[15] Dr. J. R. Smythies claims that a sense-datum language could be taught independently of the material object language ("A Note on the Fallacy of the 'Phenomenological Fallacy,'" *British Journal of Psychology*, XLVIII [1957], 141–44). I am not so sure of this: there must be some public criteria for a person having got a rule wrong before we can teach him the rule. I suppose someone might *accidentally* learn color words by Dr. Smythies' procedure. I am not, of course, denying that we can learn a sense-datum language in the sense that we can learn to report our experience. Nor would Place deny it.

easily adopt a convention (which is not a change in our present rules for the use of experience words but an addition to them) whereby it would make sense to talk of an experience in terms appropriate to physical processes.

Objection 6. Sensations are private, brain processes are *public*. If I sincerely say, "I see a yellowish-orange after-image," and I am not making a verbal mistake, then I cannot be wrong. But I can be wrong about a brain-process. The scientist looking into my brain might be having an illusion. Moreover, it makes sense to say that two or more people are observing the same brain-process but not that two or more people are reporting the same inner experience.

Reply. This shows that the language of introspective reports has a different logic from the language of material processes. It is obvious that until the brain-process theory is much improved and widely accepted there will be no *criteria* for saying "Smith has an experience of such-and-such a sort" *except* Smith's introspective reports. So we have adopted a rule of language that (normally) what Smith says goes.

Objection 7. I can imagine myself turned to stone and yet having images, aches, pains, and so on.

Reply. I can imagine that the electrical theory of lightning is false, that lightning is some sort of purely optical phenomenon. I can imagine that lightning is not an electrical discharge. I can imagine that the Evening Star is not the Morning Star. But it is. All the objection shows is that "experience" and "brain-process" do not have the same meaning. It does not show that an experience is not in fact a brain process.

This objection is perhaps much the same as one which can be summed up by the slogan: "What can be composed of nothing cannot be composed of anything." [16] The argument goes as follows: on the brain-process thesis the identity between the brain-process and the experience is a contingent one. So it is logically possible that there should be no brain-process, and no process of any other sort either (no heart process, no kidney process, no liver process). There would be the experience but no "corresponding" physiological process with which we might be able to identify it empirically.

I suspect that the objector is thinking of the experience as a ghostly entity. So it is composed of something, not of nothing, after all. On his view it is composed of ghost stuff, and on mine it is composed of brain stuff. Perhaps the counter-reply will be[17] that the experience is

[16] I owe this objection to Dr. C. B. Martin. I gather that he no longer wishes to maintain this objection, at any rate in its present form.

[17] Martin did not make this reply, but one of his students did.

simple and uncompounded, and so it is not composed of anything after all. This seems to be a quibble, for, if it were taken seriously, the remark "What can be composed of nothing cannot be composed of anything" could be recast as an a priori argument against Democritus and atomism and for Descartes and infinite divisibility. And it seems odd that a question of this sort could be settled a priori. We must therefore construe the word "composed" in a very weak sense, which would allow us to say that even an indivisible atom is composed of something (namely, itself). The dualist cannot really say that an experience can be composed of nothing. For he holds that experiences are something over and above material processes, that is, that they are a sort of ghost stuff. (Or perhaps ripples in an underlying ghost stuff.) I say that the dualist's hypothesis is a perfectly intelligible one. But I say that experiences are not to be identified with ghost stuff but with brain stuff. This is another hypothesis, and in my view a very plausible one. The present argument cannot knock it down a priori.

Objection 8. The "beetle in the box" objection (see Wittgenstein, *Philosophical Investigations,* § 293). How could descriptions of experiences, if these are genuine reports, get a foothold in language? For any rule of language must have public criteria for its correct application.

Reply. The change from describing how things are to describing how we feel is just a change from uninhibitedly saying "this is so" to saying "this looks so." That is, when the naïve person might be tempted to say, "There is a patch of light on the wall which moves whenever I move my eyes" or "A pin is being stuck into me," we have learned how to resist this temptation and say "It *looks as though* there is a patch of light on the wallpaper" or "It *feels as though* someone were sticking a pin into me." The introspective account tells us about the individual's state of consciousness in the same way as does "I see a patch of light" or "I feel a pin being stuck into me": it differs from the corresponding perception statement in so far as it withdraws any claim about what is actually going on in the external world. From the point of view of the psychologist, the change from talking about the environment to talking about one's perceptual sensations is simply a matter of disinhibiting certain reactions. These are reactions which one normally suppresses because one has learned that in the prevailing circumstances they are unlikely to provide a good indication of the state of the environment.[18] To say that something looks green to me is simply to say that my experience is like the experience I get when I see something that really is green. In my reply to Objection 3, I pointed out

---

[18] I owe this point to Place, in correspondence.

the extreme openness or generality of statements which report experiences. This explains why there is no language of private qualities. (Just as "someone," unlike "the doctor," is a colorless word.)[19]

If it is asked what is the difference between those brain processes which, in my view, are experiences and those brain processes which are not, I can only reply that it is at present unknown. I have been tempted to conjecture that the difference may in part be that between perception and reception (in D. M. MacKay's terminology) and that the type of brain process which is an experience might be identifiable with MacKay's active "matching response." [20] This, however, cannot be the whole story, because sometimes I can perceive something unconsciously, as when I take a handkerchief out of a drawer without being aware that I am doing so. But at the very least, we can classify the brain processes which are experiences as those brain processes which are, or might have been, causal conditions of those pieces of verbal behavior which we call reports of immediate experience.

I have now considered a number of objections to the brain-process thesis. I wish now to conclude with some remarks on the logical status of the thesis itself. U. T. Place seems to hold that it is a straight-out scientific hypothesis.[21] If so, he is partly right and partly wrong. If the issue is between (say) a brain-process thesis and a heart thesis, or a liver thesis, or a kidney thesis, then the issue is a purely empirical one, and the verdict is overwhelmingly in favor of the brain. The right sorts of things don't go on in the heart, liver, or kidney, nor do these organs possess the right sort of complexity of structure. On the other hand, if the issue is between a brain-or-liver-or-kidney thesis (that is, some form of materialism) on the one hand and epiphenomenalism on the other hand, then the issue is not an empirical one. For there is no conceivable experiment which could decide between materialism and epiphenomenalism. This latter issue is not like the average straight-out empirical issue in science, but like the issue between the nineteenth-century English naturalist Philip Gosse[22] and the orthodox geologists

[19] The "beetle in the box" objection is, *if it is sound,* an objection to *any* view, and in particular the Cartesian one, that introspective reports are genuine reports. So it is no objection to a weaker thesis that I would be concerned to uphold, namely, that if introspective reports of "experiences" are genuinely reports, then the things they are reports of are in fact brain processes.

[20] See his article "Towards an Information-Flow Model of Human Behaviour," *British Journal of Psychology,* XLVII (1956), 30–43.

[21] *Op. cit.* For a further discussion of this, in reply to the original version of the present paper, see Place's note "Materialism as a Scientific Hypothesis," *Philosophical Review,* LXIX (1960), 101–4.

[22] See the entertaining account of Gosse's book *Omphalos* by Martin Gardner in *Fads and Fallacies in the Name of Science,* 2nd ed. (New York: Dover, 1957), pp. 124–27.

and paleontologists of his day. According to Gosse, the earth was created about 4000 B.C. exactly as described in *Genesis,* with twisted rock strata, "evidence" of erosion, and so forth, and all sorts of fossils, all in their appropriate strata, just as if the usual evolutionist story had been true. Clearly this theory is in a sense irrefutable: no evidence can possibly tell against it. Let us ignore the theological setting in which Philip Gosse's hypothesis had been placed, thus ruling out objections of a theological kind, such as "what a queer God who would go to such elaborate lengths to deceive us." Let us suppose that it is held that the universe just *began* in 4004 B.C. with the initial conditions just everywhere as they were in 4004 B.C., and in particular that our own planet began with sediment in the rivers, eroded cliffs, fossils in the rocks, and so on. No scientist would ever entertain this as a serious hypothesis, consistent though it is with all possible evidence. The hypothesis offends against the principles of parsimony and simplicity. There would be far too many brute and inexplicable facts. Why are pterodactyl bones just as they are? No explanation in terms of the evolution of pterodactyls from earlier forms of life would any longer be possible. We would have millions of facts about the world as it was in 4004 B.C. that just have to be *accepted.*

The issue between the brain-process theory and epiphenomenalism seems to be of the above sort. (Assuming that a behavioristic reduction of introspective reports is not possible.) If it be agreed that there are no cogent philosophical arguments which force us into accepting dualism, and if the brain-process theory and dualism are equally consistent with the facts, then the principles of parsimony and simplicity seem to me to decide overwhelmingly in favor of the brain-process theory. As I pointed out earlier, dualism involves a large number of irreducible psychophysical laws (whereby the "nomological danglers" dangle) of a queer sort, that just have to be taken on trust, and are just as difficult to swallow as the irreducible facts about the paleontology of the earth with which we are faced on Philip Gosse's theory.

JEROME SHAFFER

Mental Events and the Brain

When J. J. C. Smart propounded his version of the Identity Theory,[1] he confessed that he found the most powerful objection to his theory to be as follows. Even if we can establish the *de facto* identity of mental events and neural events, do we not still have to admit the existence of mental features (to pin down one side of the *de facto* identity)? Are we not then still committed to something irreducibly mental? If so, we have the "nomological danglers" which are incompatible with the thorough-going materialism Smart wishes to establish. Smart's attempt to deal with this objection has been criticized by me[2] and by others,[3] and Smart has replied to some of these criticisms.[4] I wish to reconsider

Reprinted from *The Journal of Philosophy*, LX, 6 (March 14, 1963), 160–166, by permission of the editor and Jerome Shaffer.

[1] "Sensations and Brain Processes," *The Philosophical Review*, 68 (1959). [Reprinted in this volume, pp. 53–66. References below are to the occurrence in this volume.]

[2] "Could Mental States be Brain Processes?," *The Journal of Philosophy*, 58, 26 (Dec. 21, 1961), 813.

[3] George Pitcher, "Sensations and Brain Processes: A Reply to Professor Smart," *Australasian Journal of Philosophy*, 38, 2 (August, 1960): 150; J. T. Stevenson, "Sensations and Brain Processes: A Reply to J. J. C. Smart," *The Philosophical Review*, 69, 4 (October, 1960): 505; Kurt Baier, "Smart on Sensations," *Australasian Journal of Philosophy*, 40, 1 (May, 1962): 56; James W. Cornman, "The Identity of Mind and Body," *The Journal of Philosophy*, 59, 18 (Aug. 30, 1962): 486 [reprinted in this volume, pp. 73–79; references below are to the occurrence in this volume].

[4] "Sensations and Brain Processes: A Rejoinder to Dr. Pitcher and Mr. Joske," *Australasian Journal of Philosophy*, 38, 3 (December, 1960): 252; "Further Remarks on Sensations and Brain Processes," *The Philosophical Review*, 70 (1961): 406; "Brain Processes and Incorrigibility," *Australasian Journal of Philosophy*, 40, 1 (May, 1962): 68.

this objection to Smart's theory, especially in the light of some recent criticisms[5] of my own paper.

On the Identity Theory, the having of an after-image, the feeling of a pain, or the occurrence of a thought is claimed to be identical, as a matter of empirical fact, with some event occurring in the brain. The two occurrences are held to be identical in the same sense that a flash of lightning is held to be identical with a particular sort of electrical discharge, i.e., not that the terms referring to them are synonymous but that the terms happen to pick out, refer to, or denote one and the same event.

Now there are serious problems concerning whether mental and brain events *could* be identical. I shall return to this issue at the end of this discussion. But assuming it could be shown that they are identical, there still is a problem here for Smart's materialism. For if it is an *empirical* identity, then how we identify mental events will have to be different from how we identify brain events; if they were identified in the same way, then they would not be logically independent. Now suppose we identified mental events by noticing the occurrence of some peculiarly *mental* feature. Then we would still be left with some irreducibly nonphysical aspects, and this Smart would find objectionable.

So the new task, for Smart, is to give some account, in nonmentalistic terms, of what we report when we report the having of a thought or after-image or pain. According to Smart, all such reports are of the following form: there is now occurring an internal process, x, such that x is like what goes on when a particular physical stimulus affects me. Thus to report an orange after-image is to report "something going on which is like what is going on when I have my eyes open, am awake, and there is an orange illuminated in good light in front of me, that is, when I really see an orange." [6] In this definition there appear only physicalistic terms and logical terms; there are no peculiarly mental terms in it. But there are no terms describing brain events either. So it can turn out to be the case that the "something going on" which is reported is factually identical with a particular brain event. Whatever will be found to be common to such situations will be, of course, for science to determine, if it can; that the common internal process is a brain process is merely an empirical conjecture. This is the way Smart replies to the charge that he is still left with an irreducibly mental feature.[7]

[5] Cornman, *op. cit.*; Robert C. Coburn, "Shaffer on the Identity of Mental States and Brain Processes," *The Journal of Philosophy*, 60, 4 (Feb. 14, 1963): 89.

[6] Smart, "Sensations and Brain Processes," 61.

[7] This is clearly pointed out in Cornman's article (*op. cit.*, 76) as well as in some recent replies by Smart (cited above).

At the heart, then, of Smart's Identity Theory is the suggestion that mental events are definable as the concomitants or products of certain physical stimulus conditions or anything that is just like those concomitants or products. Now there are some very serious difficulties in this view. In the first place, I am inclined to think the definition could not be completed. Indefinitely many factors would be relevant in stating the causally sufficient conditions for, say, seeing an orange, to use the example of the after-image cited above. Any one of these could prevent the final brain event from occurring. We would have to mention "normal" conditions and "normal" subjects, or speak of "all other things being equal," and that would be to admit that we could not actually complete the translation. Secondly, even if the translation could be completed in theory, it would be so filled with complicated assertions about propagation of energy, media, nerves, etc., that it is unbelievable that such things would be part of what the ordinary man *means* when he reports a mental event (or even what the neurophysiologist means).

What leads Smart to think that mental events can be defined in terms of the stimulus conditions that are their causes? His reason is that "sensation talk must be learned by reference to some environmental stimulus situation or another."[8] But while this latter claim seems sensible enough, it does not follow that *what* is learned in some environmental stimulus situation is definable in terms of that environmental stimulus situation. We might learn what the expression, 'seeing stars', means by being hit on the head, but to know how the expression is learned is not to know the meaning; a blind man might know how the meaning of the expression is learned, but still not know the meaning. Smart's purported analyses of the meanings of mental terms are, at best, instructions for coming to learn the meanings of these terms, rules for the obtaining of examples to be used in ostensive definitions.

I have shown that Smart's account of the meaning of reports of sensations is defective. I now wish to give a general argument why no such materialistic maneuvering can succeed, showing that we cannot avoid admitting at the least the existence of *nonphysical properties or features,* even if we give up nonphysical *events* as a different class from physical *events.*

Let us take the case where a person reports the having of some mental event, the having of an after-image, a thought, or a sensation of pain. Now such a person has surely noticed that *something* has occurred, and he has surely noticed that this something has *some* features (or how could he report it was an after-image rather than a sensation

---

[8] Smart, "Brain Processes and Incorrigibility," 69.

of pain?). Now it seems to me obvious that, in many cases at least, the person does not notice any *physical* features—he does not notice that his brain is in some particular state, nor does he notice any external physical stimulus, nor any physical event between the stimulus and the neurological response. Yet he does notice *some* feature. Hence he must notice something other than a physical feature. The noticing of some nonphysical feature is the only way to explain how anything is noticed at all.

In my earlier discussion of Smart's views (*op. cit.*), I had put this point ambiguously by saying that we could have information about our own mental events without having information about our physical events. Cornman claims that I beg the question here against the Identity Theory; he says, "If, as Smart believes, all mental states are indeed brain processes, then when we have information about mental states we thereby have information about brain processes" (Cornman, 488–89).† I think Cornman is right here. That is why I now wish to put the point in terms of *noticing*. I may have noticed a person at a party, but from the fact that the person turns out to be the best dressed woman in America it does not follow that I noticed this feature of the person. Similarly, from the fact that the event I notice turns out to be a brain event (if the Identity Theory is correct) it does not follow that I noticed a neurological feature, nor a physical feature of any sort. Hence when I claim that a person may notice the occurrence of a mental event without noticing the occurrence of anything physical, I cannot be accused of begging the question against the Identity Theory.

If my argument is correct, Smart must conclude that when a person reports the having of some mental event, the person must have noticed the occurrence of some nonphysical feature. In some of Smart's recent replies, he suggests two ways he might try to avoid this conclusion. (1) He construes the reporter of a mental event to be noticing a similarity between two brain events, but says that the person may not notice the respect in which the events are similar.[9] My point is that it is most implausible to think that, at least in most cases of reporting mental events, the person notices anything at all about his brain. (2) He sometimes hints that the report of a mental event is merely a behavioral response and therefore not a case of noticing at all. Thus, at one point, in discussing how a person might report a similarity without being able to say in what respect they are similar, Smart says, "Thinking cybernetically it is indeed easier to envisage the nervous system as being able to react to likenesses of its internal processes without being

† [Page 75 in this volume.]
[9] "Sensations and Brain Processes," 150; "Rejoinder to Dr. Pitcher and Mr. Joske," 253.

able to issue descriptions of these likenesses." [10] And at another point, in trying to describe the difference between those brain events which are identical with mental events and those which are not, he says, "We can distinguish the ones which are sensations as those which can in suitable circumstances be the specific causal conditions of those behavior reactions which are sensation reports." [11] Although he admits to being "very receptive" to this view of the report as a mere expression or reaction, he cannot accept it.[12] And surely he is right in rejecting it, for such a view cannot account for the obvious fact that 'I now have an orange after-image' can be used to make true or false statements and, therefore, can be used to make a genuine report.

If the above remarks are sound, then we must admit, at the very least, the existence of nonphysical properties or nonphysical features. Are they "irreducibly different" from physical properties, the "nomological danglers" that Smart is so fearful of? Not necessarily. Suppose we are able to discover psychological laws that govern mental phenomena. And suppose we are able to deduce these and other psychological laws from neurophysiological laws, via the empirically determined correspondences of the mental and neural. Furthermore, suppose we are able to predict the occurrence of further mental states not included in our original empirically determined correspondences on the basis of the occurrence of neural states. Will we not then be in a position to give a complete explanation of psychological phenomena and psychological laws in terms of the physical? And if we now adopt conventions that will allow us to speak of mental events as having location in the brain, then we will indeed have shown that psychology is reducible to physiology and the mental reducible to the physical. The properties would still be different properties, but they would no longer be *irreducibly* different.[13]

So far in this discussion I have assumed it could turn out that mental events and brain events are identical. I wish to consider this assumption now with respect to a recent criticism that has been made by Coburn (*op. cit.*). I had argued that the Identity Theory must be rejected on a priori grounds. If mental and brain events were identical, they would have to occur in the same place. But it makes no sense to say of some mental event, a thought for example, that it occurred in some particular part of the brain. Hence the identity cannot hold. However, I further suggested that we could adopt a convention for

---

[10] "Rejoinder to Dr. Pitcher and Mr. Joske," 253.
[11] "Further Remarks," 407. [See also page 61 in this volume.]
[12] "Sensations and Brain Processes," 56.
[13] This sort of empirical reduction is discussed at length by Ernest Nagel, *The Structure of Science*, chs. 11 and 12; cf. esp. p. 366.

the locating of mental events in the brain which would rule out this a priori objection. The consequence of adopting this convention would be to change our concept of a mental event, but, I claimed, there was nothing in our present concept that ruled out the adoption of such a convention.

Coburn argues that such a convention could not be adopted. If we take mental events to be locatable in space, then they would be " 'public' entities in the sense that no person would be in any better position essentially than any other for determining with certainty whether such an experience was occurring" (91). If Coburn is right in saying that mental events would then become *"public"* in this sense, I would agree that a convention for locating them in space could not be adopted. But why should one think that they would become "public"? Coburn's reason is that "the idea that something should be going on in such and such a place and yet that one person should occupy an intrinsically privileged epistemological position vis-à-vis that occurrence is *prima facie* absurd" (91). But is that true? Mental events can occur at such and such a *time* and still be private. Why is *temporal* location possible but not *spatial* location? I see no absurdity in adopting such a convention.

As I pointed out in the paper Coburn discusses (820), mental events will have certain public aspects if we accept the Identity Theory. Brain events are public events, and if mental events are identical with them then there will be a respect in which mental events are public too. And conversely, of course, there will be a respect in which brain events are private. That is to say, there will be this class of events which will be known to occur either on the basis of neurological observations or by introspection. There will still be privileged access to these events, but there will also be public access to them. The event I know to have occurred on the basis of introspection will turn out to be one and the same as the event you know to have occurred by neurological observation. This is possible because one and the same event will have both physical and nonphysical features. Therefore there will be physiological criteria for its occurring; in addition the person concerned will be in a position to report its occurrence without appeal to these physiological criteria.

But suppose there is a conflict between neurological observation and introspection? Then we will have an *empirical* refutation of the Identity Theory.[14]

[14] Cf. Smart, "Brain Processes and Incorrigibility," 68.

JAMES W. CORNMAN

The Identity of Mind and Body

"Could mental states be brain processes?" This is the title question of an article by Jerome Shaffer.* Before attempting to answer this question we should first consider what kind of question it is. That is, what kind of approach is required in order to arrive at a satisfactory answer? Is it, for example, an empirical question? That is, is arriving at a satisfactory answer an empirical matter? Shaffer seems to think that it is and also claims that those who hold the Identity Theory, i.e., the theory that mental states are identical with certain physical processes such as brain processes, consider the problem expressed by the question to be a matter of empirical fact. But let us see whether it is or not.

One necessary condition of the identity of mental phenomena with some kind of physical phenomena is that there be, using Feigl's terminology, a one-to-one "simultaneity-correspondence between the mental and the physical." However, this one-to-one correspondence need not be between each mental phenomenon and some one physical phenomenon. It might be between each mental phenomenon and some group of physical phenomena or between each of a kind of physical phenomena and some group of mental phenomena. Thus, for example, it might be that each mental phenomenon is in a one-to-one simultaneity-correspondence with some particular group of brain processes. Assuming that we are interested in a version of the Identity Theory that postulates a one-to-one simultaneity-correspondence between mental phenomena and brain processes, how could we discover whether or not the above-mentioned necessary condition has been met?

Reprinted from *The Journal of Philosophy*, LIX, 18 (August 30, 1962), 486–492, by permission of the editor and James W. Cornman.

* "Could Mental States be Brain Processes?," *The Journal of Philosophy*, 58 (1961), 26: 813. Unless otherwise noted, all page references will be to this article.

Certainly we should do so by an empirical investigation in which we tried to correlate the different brain processes of persons with the different mental phenomena they described themselves as experiencing. Thus, this much of the question concerning the correctness of the Identity Theory is a matter of empirical fact. But this would decide the issue only with regard to one necessary condition of the theory's correctness. The rest of the answer is not an empirical matter.

To show this let me point out that there is at least one other proposed solution to the mind-body problem that has as a necessary condition the above one-to-one simultaneity-correspondence. This kind of correspondence is a necessary condition not only of the Identity Theory, but also of Psycho-Physical Parallelism, which is the theory that although mental phenomena are distinct from and causally independent of physical phenomena, there is nevertheless some kind of a one-to-one simultaneity-correspondence between the mental and the physical. Thus one necessary condition of Parallelism is the same kind of one-to-one correspondence that is a necessary condition of the Identity Theory.

Given that the required one-to-one correspondence has been empirically established, what further must we do to decide between the Identity Theory and Parallelism? We exhaust all the empirical means available in deciding upon the truth of the above-mentioned necessary condition. It might for that reason be suggested that this is the perfect place to employ Occam's razor as a means of justifying the Identity Theory. However, aside from the question of when Occam's razor is applicable, there are certain conceptual difficulties involved in the Identity Theory which at least delay the application of the razor.

The central conceptual problem for the Identity Theory arises, I believe, from the fact that mental phenomena seem to have properties inappropriate to physical phenomena, and physical phenomena seem to have properties inappropriate to mental phenomena. However, the particular way in which the problem arises depends upon which version of the Identity Theory is at issue. Shaffer, I believe, holds one species of the materialistic version, i.e., the view that mental phenomena are not only identical with brain processes but are in some important sense reducible to brain processes. J. J. C. Smart, who also holds this view, has considered the objection that raises the problem for the materialistic version. As Smart puts it, the objection grants that "it may be possible to get out of asserting the existence of irreducibly psychic processes, but not out of asserting the existence of irreducibly psychic *properties*." [1] Thus, the objection goes, although

---

[1] J. J. C. Smart, "Sensations and Brain Processes," *The Philosophical Review*, 68 (1959): 148. [Reprinted in a slightly revised version in this volume, pp. 53-66.]

sensations may be identical with brain processes and thus there would be no irreducibly psychic processes, nevertheless these brain processes would have two quite different sorts of properties, physical and psychic. Thus even assuming, for example, that the sentence 'I see a yellowish-orange after-image' is a report about some brain process, that brain process would have the property of "being a yellowish-orange after-image." If this is a property it is certainly a psychic property, that is, a property that lies outside a materialistic framework.

Smart, however, thinks that he has a way of doing away with psychic properties. What he proposes is that, although a sentence such as 'I see a yellowish-orange after-image' is a report about some brain process, it does not, as some others think, attribute some psychic property to the brain process. To show that it does not Smart provides what I take to be a rough translation of the sentence. Thus the adequacy of Smart's claim rests upon the adequacy of translations such as he provides. He claims that when "a person says, 'I see a yellowish-orange after-image', he is saying something like this: *'There is something going on which is like what is going on when* I have my eyes open, am awake, and there is an orange illuminated in good light in front of me, that is, when I really see an orange'" (Smart, 149).†

Will this translation solve the problem? Shaffer thinks not. He has two reasons. He says, first,

> The difficulty with such a definition is that it leaves no room for the fact that we are sometimes justified in the reports we make about our own [mental states] although we have no information at all about [physical processes], not even indefinite information (819).

This objection assumes that we can have information about our own mental states without having any information about any physical process. However, this is where it goes wrong. For if, as Smart believes, all mental states are indeed brain processes, then when we have information about mental states we thereby have information about brain processes. We do not have, of course, the information one finds in physiology, but still information, albeit of a different kind, about brain processes.

Shaffer's second objection to Smart's translation is:

> In general, it is hopeless to expect to be able to define psychic properties in terms of physical properties and still hold, as Identity theorists do, that it is a factual discovery that [mental states] and [brain processes] are identical (819).

† [Page 61 in this volume.]

Shaffer here, I take it, is accusing Smart of holding two inconsistent theses: that the verification of his version of the Identity Theory is an empirical matter, and that psychic properties are definable in terms of physical properties. Surely it is true that psychic properties are not definable in terms of the physiological properties of brain processes, because it is a factual, i.e., empirical, discovery whether or not there is some variety of a one-to-one simultaneity-correspondence between mental phenomena and brain processes. But there is nothing inconsistent in the twofold claim that an empirical discovery is a necessary condition of the justification of the theory that mental phenomena and brain processes are identical, and that psychic properties are definable within a physicalistic framework, *unless* the definitions are in terms of physiological properties of brain processes. However, as Smart states, his translation is not in terms of any physical properties. That is, it attributes neither a psychic nor a physical property to the appropriate brain process because it does not attribute any specified kind of property at all. The sentence as translated merely refers to something going on that is *in some unspecified way* like other things that go on under certain conditions. Thus, if Smart is correct, he can consistently assert both his translation and that the Identity Theory involves an empirical discovery. Thus, I think, Smart can avoid Shaffer's objections.

However, there are objections he cannot avoid. To see this, let us examine his translation of 'I see a yellowish-orange after-image'. Whereas the original sentence, call it P_1, seems to specify in some respect what is going on, the translation, call it M, does not. The consequence of this is that, although P_1 is a sufficient condition of M, it is not a necessary condition, because there is a sentence that implies M but does not imply P_1. Such a sentence is P_2: 'I see a roughly spherical shape'. Thus M does not mean P_1. To avoid this problem we might try to translate P_1 into M', which would refer not merely to an orange but to some n number of things that have only one thing in common, their yellowish-orange color. Thus, since not all of the n things would be spherical or any other one specific shape, then P_2 would be eliminated. However, we would have a related problem because there is a sentence such as 'I see a colored after-image' (P_3) which implies M' but does not imply P_1. Thus M' does not mean P_1. I believe that any other emendations of M would fail in a similar manner because the crucial part of M: "there is something going on," is just too general. Psychic properties cannot be eliminated by this kind of translation, nor, I believe, by any other.

But even if the Identity Theorist is faced with the ineliminability of psychic properties, does he have an insoluble problem, as Smart seems to think? Shaffer thinks not. He claims that the Identity Theorist "should not be disconcerted by admitting that psychic properties are different from physical properties" (820). However, I am not sure what his reasons are. Surely, if the Identity Theorist wishes to work within a physicalistic framework as Smart does, there is a problem concerning those psychic properties which at least seems to lie outside a physicalistic framework. And if no translation of psychological expressions that would show them to be within such a framework succeeds, then a materialistic version of the Identity Theory such as Smart's would seem to fail.

However, not all versions of the Identity Theory are materialistic. Neither a Double Aspect version nor an Idealistic version is faced with Smart's problem, and both, so far as I can see, are as compatible with the requirements of science as the Materialistic version is. Have we then the right to conclude that at least some versions of the Identity Theory can be justified by application of Occam's razor? Not yet, I think, because there remains a conceptual problem facing any version of the Identity Theory.

In general we accept the principle of the identity of indiscernibles as the criterion of identity. That is, we say that two nonsynonymous names or descriptions refer to the same thing if and only if a predicate is truly predicated of one if and only if it is also truly predicated of the other. Let us apply this to predicates that are relevant to the Identity Theory. For example, we can talk about intense, unbearable, nagging, or throbbing pains. And yellow, dim, fading, or circular after-images. And dogmatic, false, profound, or unconscious beliefs. On the other hand we can also discuss publicly observable, spatially located, swift, irreversible physical processes. Thus if the Identity Theory is correct, it seems that we should sometimes be able to say truthfully that physical processes such as brain processes are dim or fading or nagging or false, and that mental phenomena such as after-images are publicly observable or physical or spatially located or swift.

However, there surely is some doubt about whether these expressions can be truthfully used. They seem to be in some sense meaningless. Utilizing Gilbert Ryle's concept of a category mistake, we can say that the above expressions are meaningless in the sense that they commit a category mistake; i.e., in forming these expressions we have predicated predicates, appropriate to one logical category, of expressions that belong to a different logical category. This is surely a conceptual mistake. Consequently, because what would appear to be a necessary condition of the truth of the Identity Theory involves a category mistake, the Identity Theory, unlike the competing dualistic theories, seems to be in serious conceptual difficulty. Thus we cannot, it would seem, arrive at the Identity Theory via Occam's razor. Shaffer suggests that we need only adopt a new rule of language, one which prescribes that a mental state is "located in that place where its corresponding [brain] process is located" (816). If this one new rule were adopted, Shaffer believes that the identity of mental states and brain processes could then be empirically established, because the criterion of identity, he claims, is that brain processes and mental states be identical if and only if they exist at the same time and same place, and each is an empirically necessary condition for the presence of the other. Given the new rule, and since the other two conditions of identity can be empirically established, the Identity Theory can be either verified or falsified empirically.

But if, as assumed above, the identity of indiscernibles is the ultimate criterion of identity, then Shaffer would seem to have no right to adopt a convention that would make it possible for brain processes and mental states to be identical, because if, as argued above, each has properties not truly attributable to the other, then, by Leibniz's principle, they are not identical. The conclusion, then, is that the adoption of merely this one rule, as Shaffer suggests, is surely not enough.

But, perhaps, to avoid this problem we could adopt rules that would eliminate all the category mistakes involved in the Identity Theory. This would surely be legitimate if, as Smart seems to think, all that is required is that we adopt new rules for the application of the appropriate expressions without changing the present rules (Smart, 152).‡ That is, if the situation is such that there are no rules for the application of these expressions which in any way forbid the required addition, then no change in existing rules is needed. However, if the formation of the relevant expressions involves category mistakes—a statement which, to be sure, has been no more than intuitively justified—then what is needed is not merely the addition of new rules but the change of old ones, because category mistakes are violations of rules for application of expressions. And this kind of conceptual change in order to justify a philosophical theory is surely not legitimate.

Have we then reached the point at which we must conclude that the Identity Theory, no matter which version, is doomed to failure because of insoluble conceptual difficulties? There is, I think, one possible way to avoid this conclusion. The above attempts to save the Identity Theory fail because they proceed on the assumption that the theory is mistaken if it fails to meet the requirements of the principle of the identity of indiscernibles. However, this assumption may not be warranted. An equivalent way to express this principle is that, for any x and y, x and y are *not* identical if and only if some property ϕ is such that 'ϕx' is true and 'ϕy' is false, or, conversely, 'ϕx' is false and

‡ [Pages 62–63 in this volume.]

'ϕy' is true. From this we can see that one necessary condition of applying this principle to some x and y is that both 'ϕx' and 'ϕy' have a truth-value. But this necessary condition cannot be met if either 'ϕx' or 'ϕy' involves a category mistake. In such cases, then, the principle does not apply. Another way to show this is that, if we apply this principle in such a case, then whatever the expressions in question refer to would fail to be identical and also fail to be not identical, which is surely mistaken. Because the principle does not apply in such cases, it is at least possible that if two terms are in different logical categories they both refer to the same thing.

To show that this kind of identity, which I shall call "cross-category identity," is not unusual, let me cite what seems to be a widely accepted case of cross-category identity. We talk of the temperature of a gas as being identical with the mean kinetic energy of the gas molecules. But although we can say that the temperature of a certain gas is 80° centigrade, it is surely in some sense a mistake to say that the mean kinetic energy of the gas molecules is 80° centigrade. If this mistake is what I have called a category mistake, then this is a case of cross-category identity. If it is also a category mistake to talk of a fading or dim brain process, then we have some grounds for thinking that the identity of mind and body would be a cross-category identity, and, therefore, that the Identity Theory need not involve conceptual difficulties. The next project, then, for an Identity Theorist might well be to develop further the concept of a category and to work out further in what cases the application of the concept of cross-category identity is justified.

part three
THEORETICAL MATERIALISM

JAEGWON KIM

On the Psycho-Physical Identity Theory

This paper aims at an interpretation and evaluation of the so-called Psycho-Physical Identity Theory of mind. In Part I, I examine one group of arguments often offered in support of the theory. These arguments share the characteristic of being based upon considerations of theoretical simplicity in science; roughly, they contend that the Identity Theory leads to a simpler and more fruitful structure of scientific theory than its rival theories. Thus, these arguments can be called "arguments from scientific simplicity." I dispute the cogency and strength of these arguments. In Part II, I raise some questions concerning the interpretation of the Identity Theory—in particular, questions concerning the notion of identity of events and states—and suggest some tentative answers. I then examine another type of argument offered in support of the theory to the effect that it leads to a simpler scheme of entities than its rival theories. An argument of this type can be called "an argument from ontological simplicity."

I

1. The Psycho-Physical Identity Theory asserts that the so-called mental states, such as feelings of pain and the having of an after image, are just states of the brain. Pain, for example, is taken to be just some not as yet completely understood state or process in the brain. Let us refer to this brain state allegedly identical with pain as "brain state B." The identity in question is explained as the "strict identity" of reference, and this notion is illustrated by examples such as the identity

Reprinted from the *American Philosophical Quarterly*, III, 3 (July 1966), 227–235, by permission of the editor and Jaegwon Kim.

of the Morning Star and the Evening Star. Thus, the two expressions "pain" and "brain state B" are said to refer to or denote the same event or state, just as the expressions "the Morning Star" and "the Evening Star" refer to the same planet. Further, the pain-brain state B identity is said to be an empirical fact subject to factual confirmation and not something that can be ascertained *a priori*.

If pain is identical with brain state B, there must be a concomitance between occurrences of pain and occurrences of brain state B—and presumably not between occurrences of pain in me and occurrences of brain state B in someone else, but between my pains and my brain states B. Thus, a necessary condition of the pain-brain state B identity is that the two expressions "being in pain" and "being in brain state B" have the same extension; namely, the following equivalence must hold: "For every x, x is in pain at time t if and only if x is in brain state B at time t." An equivalence statement of a similar sort will correspond to each particular psycho-physical identity statement. I shall refer to a statement of this kind as "a psycho-physical correlation statement."

It is clear that a psycho-physical correlation statement does not entail the corresponding identity statement—at least, the identity must be understood in such a way that it is not entailed by a mere correlation. For otherwise the Identity Theory would fail to be a significant thesis distinguishable from other theories of mind such as some forms of Interactionism and the Double-Aspect Theory. It is perhaps clearer that the identity entails the corresponding correlation, and at least to this extent, the identity statement has a factual component. Further, the correlation is the *only* factual component of the identity; the factual content of the identity statement is exhausted by the corresponding correlation statement.

It is often emphasized that a particular psycho-physical identity (e.g., pain and brain state B) is a factual identity. From this some philosophers seem to infer that the Identity Theory is an empirical theory refutable or confirmable by experience. This is misleading, however. To begin with, a particular psycho-physical identity statement is not confirmable or refutable *qua* identity statement; it is confirmable or refutable insofar as, and only insofar as, the corresponding correlation statement entailed by it is confirmable or refutable by observation and experiment. There is no conceivable observation that would confirm or refute the identity but not the associated correlation. Moreover, not only the psycho-physical identity statement, but also the corresponding "psycho-physical interaction statement," the corresponding "psycho-physical double-aspect statement," and so on, are all confirmable or refutable by fact. And the very same evidence will confirm all of them or none of them; the very same evidence will refute all of them or none of them. Thus, the pain-brain state B identity statement is not an empirical hypothesis vis-à-vis the corresponding correlation, interaction, and double-aspect statements.

An essentially similar comment is in order for the claim that the Identity Theory itself is an empirical theory. It is asserted [1] that the Identity Theory would be "empirically false" if there were mental states not associated with the brain, namely "disembodied" mental states. This is true, although how the existence of such states could be ascertained *empirically* is a mystery. However, what is often not noticed is that the existence of disembodied mental states would refute not only the Identity Theory but also the Double-Aspect Theory, Parallelism, Epiphenomenalism, and some forms of Interactionism; for it would contradict the general hypothesis of psycho-physical correlation, a fact assumed, and to be explained, by philosophical theories of mind and body. If there were no correlation at all between mental and physical events, there would be no need for a theory of mind-body relation. So, within the context of philosophical discussion, it is of no significance that the Identity Theory is a factually refutable theory: it is not an empirical hypothesis vis-à-vis its rival theories.

2. The proponents of the Identity Theory, however, will be quick to point out that the foregoing considerations issue from an excessively narrow conception of "factual support." They will probably concede that an identity statement has no more direct observational consequences than the corresponding correlation statement. But it may be that the inclusion of such statements within a scientific theory will effect significant simplification of the structure of the theory and lead to new laws and theories, new explanations and predictions. If these conjectures turn out to be true, it would be proper to claim a broad factual support for the Identity Theory. Arguments of this kind have been offered by most adherents of the theory; even some critics of the theory have argued that certain developments and discoveries in science would increase the plausibility of the theory.

In "Minds and Machines," [2] Hilary Putnam offers an argument of this nature. He cites two advantages for identifying the mental and the physical:

(1) "It would be possible . . . to derive from physical theory the classical laws (or low-level generalizations) of common-sense 'mentalistic' psychology, such as: 'People tend to avoid things with which they have had painful experiences.'

---

[1] See Jerome A. Shaffer, "Recent Work on the Mind-Body Problem," *American Philosophical Quarterly*, vol. 2 (1965), pp. 81–104, especially pp. 93–94.

[2] In S. Hook (ed.), *Dimensions of Mind* (New York, New York University Press, 1960).

(2) "It would be possible to predict the cases (and they are legion) in which common-sense 'mentalistic' psychology fails." [3]

Briefly, the argument is that we ought to identify—or, at least, we are permitted to identify—the mental with the physical to make possible the reduction of mentalistic psychology to some physical theory of the body, presumably neurophysiology. Such a reduction is claimed to have two benefits: to unify and simplify scientific theory, and to make new predictions possible. The benefits of theoretical reduction in science cannot be questioned; in particular, the reduction of mentalistic psychology to a physical theory of the body, if carried out, would be a major scientific achievement. The question, however, is whether or not such a reduction presupposes the identification of the mental with the physical.

The reduction of one scientific theory to another involves the derivation of the laws of the reduced theory from the laws of the theory to which it is reduced.[4] If the reduction is to be genuinely intertheoretic, the reduced theory will contain concepts not included in the vocabulary of the reducing theory, and these concepts will occur essentially in the laws of the reduced theory. Hence, if these laws are to be derived from the laws of the reducing theory in which those concepts do not occur, we shall need, as auxiliary premises of derivation, certain statements in which concepts of both theories occur. We may refer to these statements as "connecting principles." Thus, the reduction of mentalistic psychology to neurophysiology will require connecting principles in which both mentalistic and neurophysiological concepts occur; they will enable us to move from neurophysiological premises to mentalistic conclusions.

Putnam's claim, then, may plausibly be taken as asserting that psycho-physical identity statements can serve as such connecting principles, just as statements like "Gas is a collection of molecules" and "Temperature is the mean kinetic energy of molecules" serve as connecting principles in the reduction of classical thermodynamics to statistical mechanics. This is plausible enough, but it alone does not support the psycho-physical identification. What needs to be shown is that *unless* the identification is made, the derivation of mentalistic laws from neurophysiological laws is impossible. That is, it has to be shown that nothing less than psycho-physical identity statements will do as psycho-physical connecting principles. But it is dubious that this

---

[3] *Ibid.*, pp. 170–171.
[4] For an illuminating discussion of the problem of reduction in science, see Ernest Nagel, *The Structure of Science* (New York, Harcourt, Brace & World, Inc., 1961), chap. 11.

can be shown; in fact, psycho-physical correlation statements seem sufficiently strong to function as the requisite connecting principles.

Consider a simple example: the usual derivation of the Boyle-Charles law of the gas from certain statistical-mechanical assumptions about gas. Essential to this derivation is the assertion that the temperature of a body of gas is a constant times the mean translational kinetic energy of the molecules of the gas—that is, $(1/2)M\bar{v}^2 = (3/2)RT$. Now, in order to derive the Boyle-Charles law, it is sufficient to interpret this equation as asserting a mere correlation between the temperature and the mean kinetic energy of a gas, namely to the effect that whenever a gas has such-and-such temperature, it has such-and-such mean kinetic energy, and conversely. It is not necessary to interpret the equation to the effect that temperature *is* mean kinetic energy. The equation clearly does not assert this; it only asserts that the *value* of temperature is the same as the *value* of mean kinetic energy.

Similarly, it is plausible to suppose that, without identifying the mental with the physical, mentalistic psychology can be reduced to physical theory in the sense that given a suitable set of psycho-physical correlation statements, laws of mentalistic psychology can be derived from physical theory. If psycho-physical identity statements are sufficient for such derivation, the corresponding psycho-physical correlation statements will do just as well. It is not easy to demonstrate this conclusively for the reason that it is not clear exactly what an identity statement asserts over and above the corresponding correlation statement. In Part II of this paper I shall claim that an identity statement involves the identification of properties; for example, the pain-brain state *B* identity involves the identification of the property of being in pain with the property of being in brain state *B*. On the other hand, I shall claim that the corresponding correlation statement involves only extensional identity of the two properties. If this construal is correct, it is evident that the correlation statement can do everything that the identity statement does on the further reasonable assumption that there are no "intensional" contexts in neurophysiology.

3. Herbert Feigl and J. J. C. Smart have offered a somewhat different reason for identifying the mental with the physical.[5] They have argued that by such identification we are able to eliminate what they call "nomological danglers," irreducible and unexplainable psycho-

---

[5] H. Feigl, "The 'Mental' and the 'Physical'" in H. Feigl, M. Scriven, and G. Maxwell (eds.), *Minnesota Studies in the Philosophy of Science,* vol. 2 (Minneapolis, University of Minnesota Press, 1958); J. J. C. Smart, "Sensations and Brain Processes," *The Philosophical Review,* vol. 68 (1959), pp. 141–156 [reprinted in a slightly revised version in this volume, pp. 53–66; the reference below is to the occurrence in this volume]; J. J. C. Smart, *Philosophy and Scientific Realism* (London, Routledge & Kegan Paul, 1963).

physical laws. It is argued that the identification of pain with a brain process is justified by some kind of methodological principle of "parsimony" or "simplicity" in science. The reasoning behind this argument seems to be as follows.

A correlation statement cries out for an explanation: Why is it that whenever and wherever there is water, there is H_2O? Why is it that whenever and only whenever a person has pain he is in some specific brain state? Now, according to this line of reasoning, we can answer these questions if, and perhaps only if, we accept the corresponding identity statements. That is, we shall answer: Because water *is* H_2O, because pain *is* brain state B, and so on. But how can we explain these facts of identity? The answer is that they are not in need of explanation, that they cannot be explained—not because we lack relevant factual or theoretical information, but because they are not the sort of thing that can be explained. It is nonsense to ask for an explanation of why Cicero *is* Tully, or why the Evening Star *is* the Morning Star; it is equally nonsensical to ask for an explanation of why water *is* H_2O, or why pain *is* brain state B. Water just is H_2O, and pain just is brain state B. Generally, most identity statements do not seem to be capable of functioning as the explananda of scientific explanations; and psycho-physical identity statements are not in need of any explanation at all. On the other hand, psycho-physical laws, not being identity statements, must either be explained by deduction from higher laws or be taken as fundamental, unexplainable laws of nature. And if they are to be deduced from higher laws, then at least some of these higher laws in turn must be psycho-physical statements, and so in any case we are left with fundamental and irreducible psycho-physical laws.

Thus, it turns out that by moving from correlation statements to identity statements we do not explain facts that were previously unexplained; rather, we make them "non-explainable." Now, the question is this: In what sense does this achieve scientific or theoretical simplicity of the sort desired in science? In what respect does it contribute to the unity and fruitfulness of the system of scientific laws and theories?

I think that the simplicity thus achieved is rather trivial and of minimal significance from a scientific point of view. To begin with, the explanation of a correlation by an identity—"Why is pain correlated with brain state B?" "Because pain *is* brain state B"—is trivial. The factual cash value of the identity is simply the correlation, and in terms of factual information we are simply repeating in the explanans what is supposed to be explained. This is a far cry from the usual kind of scientific explanation in which a fact or a regularity is explained by invoking more general and more comprehensive laws and theoretical principles far richer in factual implication and theoretical power than the explanandum. But further, the introduction of these identity statements does not produce simplicity in a theoretically meaningful sense. The essential import of reduction in science lies in that it achieves a more parsimonious set of primitive concepts and primitive assumptions. When optics is reduced to electromagnetic theory, we thereby reduce the number of independent factual commitments about the world; the reduction of thermodynamics to statistical mechanics yields the same kind of simplification. Previously we had two theories, each with its own postulates; now we have one.

But merely to replace correlation statements by identity statements does not effect this sort of simplicity. First, such replacement does not reduce the number of primitive concepts, for mentalistic concepts remain nonsynonymous with physicalistic concepts. Second, it does not reduce the number of independent primitive assumptions, for factual identity statements simply replace the corresponding factual correlation statements. It yields neither economy of concepts nor economy of assumptions.

4. If the foregoing considerations are correct, why should we, it might be asked, accept such apparently noncontroversial identity statements as "Water is H_2O" and "Temperature is the mean kinetic energy of molecules"? Should we not in these cases, too, stop short of identification and be satisfied with correlation? I would claim that the water-H_2O identity is, indeed, disanalogous with the pain-brain state B case, and that the temperature-energy case is rather like the pain-brain state B case.

"Water" and "H_2O" (in the sense of "substance whose molecular structure is H_2O") are both substantive expressions referring to physical things and not to properties, events, states, or the like. Any bit of water has a decomposition into H_2O molecules; the two occupy the same spatio-temporal volume. The reduction of macro-chemistry to micro-chemistry, which is in part based on such identities as that of water and H_2O, is an example of micro-reduction:[6] the things in the domain of the reduced theory have a decomposition into proper parts that belong in the domain of the reducing theory. In this sense, water has a decomposition into H_2O molecules; gas a decomposition into molecules and atoms. The net effect of micro-reduction is the explanation of the properties of some entity on the basis of the properties of the parts of the entity. So, water is literally made up of H_2O molecules, and a body of gas, of molecules and atoms.

Temperature, however, is unlike water and gas. Temperature is not

---

[6] See P. Oppenheim and H. Putnam, "Unity of Science as a Working Hypothesis" in H. Feigl, M. Scriven, and G. Maxwell, *op. cit.*

a thing that is made up of certain parts; we cannot pick out a bit of temperature or an instance of it and say that it is made up of mean kinetic energy. The domain of classical thermodynamics does not contain temperature in the way the domain of macro-chemistry contains water; rather, it contains gas, or bodies of gas, and temperature is a state variable whose values are used to characterize the thermodynamic states of a system—in other words, it is a property of the things in the domain. But it in itself is not a thing: it has no decomposition into mean kinetic energy.

Take pain: again, pain is not a thing. It is supposed to be an event or state; and we may take it as a property of living organisms. A pain has no parts—it has no decomposition into parts of the brain or into neurons. It only has a "participant," the person (or the biological organism) who has the pain. This person has a decomposition into parts of his body, organs, tissues, cells, and so on. So, there is almost an exact analogy between the temperature-energy case and the pain-brain state case. A physical thing, such as a body of gas, has temperature, and temperature itself is not a thing. The physical thing having temperature has a decomposition into molecules, and these molecules collectively have a certain property, namely a certain value of mean kinetic energy. And there is a definite correlation between this property of the molecules and the property temperature of the physical thing. A biological organism, such as a man, has pain, and pain itself is not a thing. The biological organism having the pain has a decomposition into organs, tissues, and so on—and, in particular, into the brain and the nervous system as a whole. The brain and the nervous system have a certain property, say some patterns of electric pulses ("brain state B"), and there is a definite correlation between the two properties, the property of being in pain and the property of being in this kind of brain state.

Thus, on this view, micro-reduction is still possible, and the unification of the domains of various scientific disciplines is also possible by repeated micro-reduction of one discipline to another. What should be noticed here is that the micro-reduction of one theory to another does not require—nor does it sanction—the reduction of properties in the sense of identifying macro-properties with correlated micro-properties. I conclude, therefore, that the adherents of the Identity Theory can find no support in the considerations of simplicity or unity in the structure of scientific theory.

II

1. The Identity Theory asserts that pain is identical with brain state B. But what does this mean?

To say that pain is identical with brain state B is to make a general statement that each particular occurrence of pain is identical with some particular occurrence of brain state B, and also, conversely, that each particular occurrence of brain state B is identical with some particular occurrence of pain. It is clearly not intended that Plato's pain is identical with Socrates' brain state B; but rather that Plato's pain is identical with his own simultaneous brain state B. Hence, to claim that pain is identical with brain state B is to claim, among other things, that the two statements "Plato is in pain (at time t)" and "Plato is in brain state B (at time t)" *describe* or *refer to* the same event or state.

But what are we to understand by this assertion that two statements describe the same event or state? Under what conditions do two singular statements—restricting ourselves to singular statements—describe or refer to the same event or state of affairs? An answer to this question will have the general form: "Statement A describes event a and statement B describes event b, and a is identical with b." So two problems emerge: first, what particular event or state does a given singular statement describe or refer to, and second, under what conditions does the identity of events obtain?

To be told that event a and event b are the same event if and only if a and b share all properties in common gives us no real enlightenment; it gives us a definition, no doubt a valid one, but not a practically usable *criterion,* of the identity of events. I would like to see someone apply this definition to Plato's being in pain and Plato's being in brain state B and deliver an opinion as to their identity or non-identity. To say that two singular statements refer to or describe the same event if and only if they are logically equivalent is clearly inadequate for the purposes of the Identity Theory.[7] For the identity of the mental and the physical is assumed to be a factual one and not a matter of logic or meaning.

I suggest the following procedure. First, what is an event or state? An event or state can be explained as a particular (substance) having a certain property, or more generally a certain number of particulars standing in a certain relation to one another. Suppressing reference to time, we may take the expressions of the following kind as designating-expressions for events and states: "a's being F," "b's being G," "a standing in relation R to b," etc., where 'a' and 'b' refer to particulars and 'F', 'G' and 'R' to properties and relations. Thus, Socrates' being in pain, Socrates' being in brain state B, and Socrates speaking to Theaetetus are all events or states. Although we normally distinguish between

---

[7] K. Popper appears to have this concept of event in *The Logic of Scientific Discovery* (New York, Basic Books, 1959), pp. 88–90. However, a precise interpretation of Popper is uncertain.

events and states, or between events, states, and processes, I shall not attempt such a distinction here; in discussing the mind-body problem, philosophers speak indifferently in terms of events, states, and processes, and the fate of the Identity Theory does not hinge on whether mental events or states are identified with physical events, states, or processes. It suffices if the Identity Theorist concedes, as I think he would, that among the things that he wants to identify are Socrates' being in pain and Socrates' being in brain state B. With this understanding let us hereafter speak in terms of events for the sake of brevity.

Under this conception of event, the following criterion of the identity of events naturally comes to mind: The event *a's being F* and the event *b's being G* are the same event if and only if either the statements "*a* is F" and "*b* is G" are logically equivalent, or else the particular *a* is identical with the particular *b* and the property of being F (F-ness) is identical with the property of being G (G-ness). The criterion can be generalized in obvious directions so as to cover "relational events" and "compound events"; but the simple special case is all we need for the purposes at hand. Thus, on this criterion, Cicero's being a bachelor is the same event (state) as Tully's being an unmarried adult male; the Morning Star emitting yellow light is the same event as Venus emitting light of the color of the sunflower.

A singular atomic statement involving a one-place predicate—again we need not consider more general cases—has the form "*a* is F," and we may say that the statement, if true, describes or refers to the event *a's being F*. It follows that two singular statements "*a* is F" and "*b* is G" describe or refer to the same event if the event *a's being F* and the event *b's being G* are the same. Or we may say: Two singular statements describe the same event if they assert truly of the same particular that the same property holds for it.

In identifying a mental event with a physical event, the identity of the particulars involved in the events presumably is not at issue, unless one would want to say that the Socrates who has pain is different from the Socrates who is in brain state B. A radical Cartesian Dualist would claim that mental events necessarily occur to mental substance and physical events necessarily occur to material substance. Let us disregard this problem for the moment, however, and assume that both pain and brain state B can be attributed to the biological organism, Socrates. Then the problem of the identity of Socrates' being in pain and Socrates' being in brain state B reduces to the problem whether or not the property of being in pain and the property of being in brain state B are the same property.[8]

---

[8] The foregoing, which is a fragment of what is hoped to be a full systematic analysis, not here presented, of the concept of event, admittedly does not precisely

2. The problem of the identity of properties is a difficult one. Most writers[9] take logical equivalence or cointensivity as the criterion of property identity. Under such a criterion, all property-identity statements would be either logically or necessarily true, if true, and logically or necessarily false, if false. This shows that logical equivalence or cointensivity is obviously too strong as a criterion of property identity for the Identity Theory.

On the other hand, if cointensivity is too strong, mere coextensivity is too weak. In asserting that pain is identical with brain state B, the Identity Theorist intends to assert more than that there is a concomitance between occurrences of pain and occurrences of brain state B. These considerations put the Identity Theorist in a quandary: In order to state his theory in an intelligible and nontrivial way, he must produce a criterion of property identity that is weaker than cointensivity but stronger than coextensivity. Can such a criterion be found?

The task seems difficult but perhaps not impossible. The Identity Theorist may take heart in the fact that there are prima facie cases of nonanalytic and contingent property identity. The following are some of the representative examples:[10]

(1) Blue is the color of the sky.
(2) Black is the color of ravens.

---

coincide with the ordinary presystematic notion. (But then it is not clear that there is *one*, ordinary notion of event.) Some of the points at which my analysis deviates from it may be noted here. For example, Brutus' killing Caesar and Brutus' stabbing Caesar turn out, on the proposed criterion of event identity, to be different events, and similarly, "Brutus killed Caesar" and "Brutus stabbed Caesar" describe different events. Notice, however, that it is not at all absurd to say that Brutus' killing Caesar is *not the same as* Brutus' stabbing Caesar. Further, to explain Brutus' killing Caesar (why Brutus killed Caesar) is not the same as to explain Brutus' stabbing Caesar (why Brutus stabbed Caesar); also, to postdict one is not to postdict the other.

Such common notions as one description of an event being more detailed than another description of the *same* event, one description being more informative than another, and so on, have no immediate meaning under the proposed analysis. If these notions are to be clarified, a more comprehensive notion of event (say, "happening"), namely one in terms of which "Brutus killed Caesar" and "Brutus stabbed Caesar" can be said to be *about the same happening*, would have to be constructed, hopefully on the basis of the more atomistic concept of event used in this paper. Anyhow, the critical portions of the present paper do not depend on a full acceptance of the proposed analysis (see the end of the following section).

[9] For example, Rudolf Carnap in *Meaning and Necessity* (Chicago, University of Chicago Press, 1947), pp. 16ff.

[10] Some of the examples are adapted from N. L. Wilson, "The Trouble with Meanings," *Dialogue*, vol. 3 (1964), pp. 52–64.

(3) The property designated by the English word "redness" is the same as the property designated by the German word "Rot."
(4) Goodness is Plato's favorite property (i.e., the property Plato liked best).

I have tried to enumerate as many different kinds of factual property identity as I can think of. If we inspect these cases, one common characteristic is seen to emerge: in each case, at least one of the terms of the identity refers to a property via some particular(s) that stands in a certain definite relation to it. In the first two examples, properties are referred to on the basis of the particulars that *exemplify* them, as in "the color of the sky" and "the color of ravens." In the third, a property is referred to on the basis of a word that *designates* it. In the last example, reference is made to a property by way of an "intentional relation" in which a particular, Plato, stands to that property. Hence, a reasonable conjecture is that all contingent statements of property identity contain, essentially, some expression that refers to a particular or individual. This seems true, but I have no general argument to prove it. The converse of the conjecture seems more intuitively plausible: If a statement of property identity includes an essential reference to a particular, then it is nonanalytic and contingent.

These considerations are admittedly inconclusive; but perhaps it is not unwarranted to suppose that the identity of pain and brain state B, if there is such identity, is unlikely to turn out to be a contingent and nonanalytic identity of properties. Here, there is no mention of particulars in referring to the properties; nor any mention or use, implicit or explicit, of such relations as exemplification and designation, or of any intentional relation. At any rate, it seems evident that if the pain-brain state B identity is a case of factual property identity, it is unlike the usual examples of such identity and would require an explanation and justification of a special nature. And if the Identity Theorist objects to our entire procedure leading to this problem of the factual identity of properties, he is invited to propose a more reasonable alternative analysis of the concepts of event and of event identity.

The analysis of event proposed above explains why some Identity Theorists[11] are anxious to eliminate mental properties or "features" as well as mental events and states. For to allow irreducible mental properties that are exemplified is to allow irreducible mental events and states. Indeed, the problem of the identity of properties seems to be one of the central problems that confront the adherents of the Identity Theory. Whether or not my analysis of event is generally ac-

---

[11] For example, see Smart, "Sensations and Brain Processes," *op. cit.*, pp. 59–61.

ceptable, we can argue as follows: Suppose that the property of being in pain is not the same as the property of being in brain state B. Then, surely, Socrates' being in pain and Socrates' being in brain state B would have to count as distinct events. Presumably, the former is a mental event and the latter its correlated physical event, and the two are distinct. This contradicts the Identity Theory.[12]

3. The so-called location problem for mental events and states has perhaps been the strongest obstacle to the Identity Theory; the alleged difficulties raised by it seem to have persuaded more philosophers against the theory than any other single difficulty.[13] As formulated by the critics of the theory, the objection runs as follows. If a mental state is to be identical with a physical state, the two must share all properties in common. But there is one property, spatial localizability, that is not so shared; that is, physical states and events are located in space, whereas mental events and states are not. Hence, mental events and states are different from physical ones. When it is retorted that some mental events like itches and some cases of pain have fairly determinate spatial locations, it is answered that a pain or an itch may be locatable but not *having a pain* or *being itchy*. An obvious rejoinder to this move is to point out that having a hand, weighing 145 pounds, having a temperature of 97 degrees, and other so-called physical states and events have no clear spatial locations either. A hand can be located in space, but having a hand cannot; a brain can be located in space, but not a brain state; my body can be located in space, but not my body's weighing 145 pounds.

Thus, the inconclusiveness and weakness of this objection to the Identity Theory stems not so much from the possible locatability of mental states and events as from the vagueness of the general concept of spatial location for events and states. Of course, it must be admitted that we do locate explosions, fires, and deaths; but it takes only a moment's reflection to notice that we do not locate events as such. Rather, we locate events by locating the particulars or things that "undergo" them. Something explodes in an explosion, and the explosion is located where the thing that explodes is located; when there

---

[12] J. A. Shaffer writes: ". . . we cannot avoid admitting at the least the existence of *nonphysical properties* or *features*, even if we give up nonphysical events as a different class from physical events" (Shaffer's italics); "Mental Events and the Brain," *The Journal of Philosophy*, vol. 60 (1963), p. 162. [Reprinted in this volume, p. 69.] My claim is that we cannot admit nonphysical properties without admitting nonphysical events.

[13] See Norman Malcolm, "Scientific Materialism and the Identity Theory," *Dialogue*, vol. 3 (1964), pp. 115–125; J. A. Shaffer, "Recent Work on the Mind-Body Problem," *op. cit.*, pp. 96–98.

is a fire, something burns, and the fire is where the burning thing is; and, similarly, a death takes place where the dying man is located. Particulars are located first; events and states are located relatively to particulars. Or, we may say, particulars are the primary localizable entities; events and states are localizable only derivatively.[14]

In terms of our analysis of the concept of event and state, we may say that an event *a's being F* can be located derivatively at the place where the particular *a* is located. Then, what the critic of the Identity Theory who takes the location problem seriously must show is that a mental event *a's being M*, where *M* is some mental property, is nonspatial in that the particular *a* to which *M* is attributed is not a spatially localizable entity. Namely, in order to show that Socrates' being in pain is not spatially localizable, it must be shown, on this construal of the location of an event, that Socrates to whom the property of being in pain is attributed is not a spatially localizable entity. But in order to show this one must show or assume that the subjects of mental properties—or the subjects of mental events and states—are immaterial souls or mental substances in the full-fledged Cartesian sense.

The situation, therefore, seems to be this. Insofar as the notion of the location of an event is unclear and vague, it is not clear that all physical events and states have locations; and insofar as it is made clear—in terms of the location of particulars—the assertion that mental events and states lack spatial locations implies the Cartesian thesis of the immaterial soul and unextended mental substance. Hence, the objection based on the location problem is unclear and therefore inconclusive, or it begs the question at issue.

4. Can the Identity Theory claim to involve a simpler, more parsimonious ontology than the Dualist Theories? Under that theory, there would be only one system of events, namely physical ones some of which are also mental events, rather than two distinct interacting, correlating, or paralleling systems of events. And there would be fewer events, too, pain and the corresponding brain state being counted as one. It must be granted, I think, that the scheme of entities countenanced by the Identity Theory is clearly simpler than, and at least as simple as, that to be assumed by any alternative theory. But exactly what sort of ontological economy is effected by the Identity Theory? Or, equivalently, what does "fewer events" mean? The analysis of event given earlier suggests an answer to this question.

We assume an ontological scheme that includes particulars (sub-

---

[14] This point is anticipated by P. F. Strawson. See his *Individuals* (London, Methuen, 1959), p. 57.

stances) and properties as basic entities or one that includes events in addition to particulars and properties. In either case, an event can be understood in the manner explained in earlier sections on the basis of particulars and properties; and the identity of events can be explained on the basis of the identity of particulars and of properties. Let M be some mental property and P some physical property, and let a and b be particular substances. Then, factual identification of the mental event *a's being M* and the physical event *b's being P* involves (1) the identification of the properties M and P, and (2) the identification of the particulars a and b. Accordingly, the identification of the two events results in the reduction of both particulars and properties.

However, the net amount of economy thus achieved will vary depending on the alternative theory of mind that is taken as the point of comparison. An opponent of the Identity Theory may be one of the following two kinds: (a) one who rejects both (1) and (2) above, and (b) one who rejects (1) but is willing to accept (2). Philosophers of the first kind can be called "Cartesians"; they deny not only that mental properties and physical properties are identical but also that the "subjects" of physical properties or events can be the "subjects" of mental properties or events. On this view, nothing that has some mental property can have a physical one, nor vice versa; unextended mental substances are the subjects of mental happenings and the extended, unthinking matter is the substratum of physical properties. Thus, the Cartesians represent the opposite extreme of the Identity Theory: their theory involves a bifurcated system of particulars and a bifurcated system of properties, and either bifurcation is sufficient to generate a bifurcated system of events.

But a radical Dualism of this form is not the only alternative to the Identity Theory. A sort of Dualistic Materialism results if one accepts the identity of the particulars involved in the two events but not the identity of the properties. A theory of this form is materialistic in that it allows only spatio-temporally localizable particulars; and it is dualistic in that mental events are countenanced as a distinct system of events from the system of physical events. Over such a theory, the net simplicity of entities effected by the Identity Theory lies merely in the reduction of properties. Whether such an economy of entities is of much philosophical significance is a difficult question that cannot be settled here; perhaps, it cannot be settled at all. But we will do well to remind ourselves that the economy in question would have to be attained in the face of the extreme implausibility besetting the factual identification of mental properties with physical ones, and also, as I tried to show in Part I, that the economy has no scientific import and hence cannot be supported by scientific considerations. The slogan of ontological economy does not by itself sanction the identification of any two factually correlated properties. We clearly do not think that ontological economy of this kind would justify the identification of, say, thermal conductivity and electrical conductivity as one property on the basis of the Wiedemann-Franz law.

THOMAS NAGEL

Physicalism

I

It is the purpose of this paper to examine the reasons for believing that physicalism cannot possibly be true.[1] I mean by physicalism the thesis that a person, with all his psychological attributes, is nothing over and above his body, with all its physical attributes. The various theories which make this claim may be classified according to the identities which they allege between the mental and the physical.[2] These identities may be illustrated by the standard example of a quart of water which is identical with a collection of molecules, each containing two atoms of hydrogen and one of oxygen.

All states of the water are states of that collection of molecules: for the water to be in a particular bottle is for those molecules to be in that bottle; for the water to be frozen is for the molecules to be arranged in a space lattice, with strong intermolecular attractive force and relatively weak individual vibratory motion; for the water to be boiling is for the molecules to have a kinetic energy sufficient to produce a vapor pressure equal to the atmospheric pressure; and so forth. In addition to general identities like these, there will be particular ones.[3] One such is the identity between an individual splash of the

---

Reprinted from *The Philosophical Review*, LXXIV, 3 (July 1965), 339–356, by permission of the editor and Thomas Nagel.

[1] An earlier version of this paper was read at the Pacific Division A.P.A. meetings in Seattle, September 5, 1964.

[2] I shall not consider behaviorism or reductionism of any kind.

[3] Any identity both of whose terms are universal in form will be called general, even if their specification involves reference to particulars. Thus, "Water is H_2O," "For water to be frozen is for its molecules to be in condition F," and "For *this*

water and a particular sudden displacement of certain of the molecules—an identity which does not imply that a splash is always identical with that particular type of displacement. In all of these cases we can say something like the following: that the water's splashing is not anything over and above the displacement of those molecules; they are the same occurrence.

It is not clear whether every physicalist theory must assert the identity of each person with his body, nor is the connection between this identity and that of psychological with physical states easy to describe. Still, we can specify a range of possible views in terms of the latter relation alone. (1) An implausibly strong physicalism might assert the existence of a general identity between each psychological condition and a physical counterpart. (2) A weaker view would assert some general identities, particularly on the level of sensation, and particular identities for everything that remains. (3) A still weaker view might not require that a physical condition be found identical even in the particular case with every psychological condition, especially if it were an intensional one. (4) The weakest conceivable view would not even assert any particular identities, but of course it is unclear what other assertion by such a theory about the relation between mental and physical conditions might amount to a contention of physicalism.

I am inclined to believe that some weak physicalist theory of the third type is true, and that any plausible physicalism will include some state and event identities, both particular and general. Even a weak view, therefore, must be defended against objections to the possibility of identifying *any* psychological condition with a physical one. It is with such general objections that we shall be occupied.

I shall contend that they fail as objections to physicalism, but I shall also contend that they fail to express properly the real source of unhappiness with that position. This conclusion is drawn largely from my own case. I have always found physicalism extremely repellent. Despite my current belief that the thesis is true, this reaction persists, having survived the refutation of those common objections to physicalism which I once thought expressed it. Its source must therefore lie elsewhere, and I shall make a suggestion about that later.[4] First, however, it will be necessary to show why the standard objec-

---

water to be frozen is for its molecules to be in condition F" are all general identities. On the other hand, "This water's (now) being frozen is its molecules' being in condition F" is a particular identity.

[4] In Sec. V; of the other sections, II attempts to rebut some standard objections, and III contains a general discussion of identity whose results are applied to physicalism in IV.

tions fail, and what kind of identity can hold between mental and physical phenomena.

II

Since Smart refuted them, it has presumably become unnecessary to discuss those objections which rest on the confusion between identity of meaning and identity in fact.[5] We may concentrate rather on two types of objection which seem still to be current.

The first is that physicalism violates Leibniz' law, which requires that if two things are identical they have all their nonintensional and nonmodal properties in common. It is objected that sensory impressions, pains, thoughts, and so forth have various properties which brain states lack, and vice versa. I shall eventually propose a modification of Leibniz' law, since I do not believe that in its strict form it governs the relation asserted by the identity thesis. At this point, however, the thesis may be defended without resorting to such methods, through a somewhat altered version of a device employed by Smart, and earlier by U. T. Place.[6]

Instead of identifying thoughts, sensations, afterimages, and so forth with brain processes, I propose to identify a person's having the sensation with his body's being in a physical state or undergoing a physical process. Notice that both terms of this identity are of the same logical type, namely (to put it in neutral terminology) a subject's possessing a certain attribute. The subjects are the person and his body (not his brain), and the attributes are psychological conditions, happenings, and so forth, and physical ones. The psychological term of the identity must be the person's having a pain in his shin rather than the pain itself, because although it is undeniable that pains exist and people have them, it is also clear that this describes a condition of one entity, the person, rather than a relation between two entities, a person and a pain. For pains to exist *is* for people to have them. This seems to me perfectly obvious, despite the innocent suggestions of our language to the contrary.

[5] J. J. C. Smart, "Sensations and Brain Processes," *Philosophical Review*, LXVIII (1959), 141–156; republished in *The Philosophy of Mind*, ed. by V. C. Chappell (Englewood Cliffs, 1962). [Reprinted in this volume, pp. 53–66. The reference below is to the occurrence in this volume.] See also Smart's book, *Philosophy and Scientific Realism* (London, 1963), and his article "Materialism," *Journal of Philosophy*, LX (1963), 651–662, for further discussion of the identity thesis.

[6] U. T. Place, "Is Consciousness a Brain Process?," *British Journal of Psychology*, 47 (1956), republished in Chappell (ed.), *op. cit.*, pp. 107–109; for Smart, see p. 62. My formulation of the physical side of the identity differs from Smart's, and I do not accept his psychological reductionism.

So we may regard the ascription of properties to a sensation simply as part of the specification of a psychological state's being ascribed to the person. When we assert that a person has a sensation of a certain description B, this is not to be taken as asserting that there exist an x and a y such that x is a person and y is a sensation and $B(y)$, and x *has* y. Rather we are to take it as asserting the existence of only one thing, x, such that x is a person, and moreover $C(x)$, where C is the attribute "has a sensation of description B." The specification of this attribute is accomplished in part by the ascription of properties to the sensation; but this is merely part of the ascription of that psychological state to the person. This position seems to me attractive independently of physicalism, and it can be extended to psychological states and events other than sensations. Any ascription of properties to them is to be taken simply as part of the ascription of other attributes to the person who has them—as *specifying* those attributes.

I deviate from Smart in making the physical side of the identity a condition of the body rather than a condition of the brain,[7] because it seems to me doubtful that anything without a body of some conventional sort could be the subject of psychological states.[8] I do not mean to imply that the presence of a particular sensation need depend on the condition of any part of one's body outside of the brain. Making the physical term of the identity a bodily rather than a brain state merely implies that the brain is *in* a body. To identify the person's having a pain with the brain's being in state X rather than with the body's containing a brain in state X would imply, on the other hand, that if the individual's brain could have been in that state while the rest of his body was destroyed, he would still have been in the corresponding psychological state.

Given that the terms of the identity are as specified, nothing obliges us to identify a sensation or a pain or a thought with anything physical, and this disposes of numerous objections. For although I may have a visual sense impression whose attributes of form and color correspond closely to those which characterize the "Mona Lisa," my *having* the sense impression does not possess those attributes, and it is therefore no cause for worry that nothing in my brain looks like the "Mona Lisa." Given our specification of the psychological side of the identity, the demands on the physical side are considerably lessened. The physical equivalents of auditory impres-

---

[7] One might alternatively make it a physical condition of the *person*, so that the two identified attributes would be guaranteed the same subject. I cannot say how such a change would affect the argument.

[8] Cf. Norman Malcolm, "Scientific Materialism and the Identity Theory," *Dialogue*, III (1964), 124–125.

sions may be silent, those of olfactory impressions odorless, and so forth.

Most important, we can be rid of the stubbornest objection of this type, that having to do with location.[9] Brain processes are located in the brain, but a pain may be located in the shin and a thought has no location at all. But if the two sides of the identity are not a sensation and a brain process, but my *having* a certain sensation or thought and my body's *being* in a certain physical state, then they will both be going on in the same place—namely, wherever I (and my body) happen to be. It is important that the physical side of the identity is not a brain process, but rather my *body's* being in that state which may be specified as "having the relevant process going on in its brain." *That* state is not located in the brain; it has been located as precisely as it can be when we have been told the precise location of that of which it is a state—namely, my body. The same is true of my having a sensation: that is going on wherever I happen to be at the time, and its location cannot be specified more precisely than mine can. (That is, even if a pain is located in my right shin, I am *having* that pain in my office at the university.) The location of bodily sensations is a very different thing from the location of warts. It is phenomenal location, and is best regarded as one feature of a psychological attribute possessed by the *whole* person rather than as the spatial location of an event going on in a part of him.

The other type of objection which I shall discuss is that physicalism fails to account for the privacy or subjectivity of mental phenomena. This complaint, while very important, is difficult to state precisely.

There is a trivial sense in which a psychological state is private to its possessor, namely, that since it is his, it cannot be anyone else's. This is just as true of haircuts or, for that matter, of physiological conditions. Its triviality becomes clear when we regard thoughts and sensations as conditions of the person rather than as things to which the person is related. When we see that what is described as though it were a relation between two things is really a condition of one thing, it is not surprising that only one person can stand in the said relation to a given sensation or feeling. In this sense, bodily states are just as private to their possessor as the mental states with which they may be equated.

The private-access objection is sometimes expressed epistemologically. The privacy of haircuts is uninteresting because there is lacking

---

[9] Malcolm, *op. cit.*, pp. 118–120. See also Jerome Shaffer, "Could Mental States Be Brain Processes?," *Journal of Philosophy*, LVIII (1961). Shaffer thinks the difficulty can be got over, but that this depends on the possibility of a *change* in our concept of mental states, which would make it meaningful to assign them locations.

in that case a special connection between possession and knowledge which is felt to be present in the case of pains. Consider the following statement of the privacy objection.[10] "When I am in a psychological state—for example, when I have a certain sensation—it is logically impossible that I should fail to know that I am in that state. This, however, is not true of any bodily state. Therefore no psychological state is identical with any bodily state." As it happens, I believe that the first clause of this objection—namely, the incorrigibility thesis—is false, but I do not have to base my attack on that contention, for even if the incorrigibility thesis were true it would not rule out physicalism.

If state x is identical with state y it does not follow by Leibniz' law that if I know I am in state x then I know I am in state y, since the context is intensional. Therefore neither does it follow from "If I am in state x then I know I am in state x" that if I am in state y I know I am in state y. All that follows is that if I am in state y I know I am in state x. Moreover, this connection will not be a necessary one, since only one of the premises—the incorrigibility thesis—is necessary. The other premise—that x is identical with y—is contingent, making the consequence contingent.[11]

There may be more to the special-access objection than this, but I have not yet encountered a version of it which succeeds. We shall later discuss a somewhat different interpretation of the claim that mental states are subjective.

III

Let us now consider the nature of the identity which physicalism asserts. Events, states of affairs, conditions, psychological and otherwise,

[10] See Kurt Baier, "Smart on Sensations," and J. J. C. Smart, "Brain Processes and Incorrigibility," *Australasian Journal of Philosophy*, 40 (1962). This is regarded as a serious difficulty by Smart and other defenders of physicalism. See D. M. Armstrong, "Is Introspective Knowledge Incorrigible?," *Philosophical Review*, LXXII (1963), 418–419. On the other hand, Hilary Putnam has argued that all the problems about privacy and special access which can be raised about persons can be raised about machines as well. See his paper, "Minds and Machines," in *Dimensions of Mind*, ed. by Sidney Hook (New York, 1960).

[11] It is worth noting that if two mental states are necessarily connected, this connection must be mirrored on the level of the physical states with which we identify them. Although the connection between the physical states need not be a logically necessary one, that would be a desirable feature in a physicalistic theory, and it seems in fact to be present in the example of water and molecules: the water's being frozen necessarily includes its being cold, and the specification of the molecular state which *is* its being frozen entails that the molecules will have a low average kinetic energy—which is in fact the same thing as the water's being cold.

may be identical in a perfectly straightforward sense which conforms to Leibniz' law as strictly as does the identity between, say, the only horse in Berkeley and the largest mammal in Berkeley. Such identities between events may be due to the identity of two things referred to in their descriptions—for example, my being kicked by the only horse in Berkeley and my being kicked by the largest mammal in Berkeley—or they may not—for example, the sinking of the Titanic and the largest marine disaster ever to occur in peacetime. Whether they hold between things, events, or conditions, I shall refer to them as *strict* identities.

We are interested, however, in identities of a different type—between psychological and physical events, or between the boiling of water and the activity of molecules. I shall call these theoretical identities[12] and shall concentrate for the moment on their application to events and attributes rather than to things, although they hold between things as well. It is a weaker relation than strict identity, and common possession of causal and conditional attributes is crucial for its establishment.[13] Strict identities are likely to be established in other ways, and we can infer the sameness of all causal and conditional attributes. Thus, if being kicked by the only horse in Berkeley gave me a broken leg, then being kicked by the largest mammal in Berkeley had the same effect, given that they are the same creature; and if it is the case that I should not have been kicked by the only horse in Berkeley if I had stayed in my office that afternoon, then it follows that if I had stayed in my office I should not have been kicked by the largest mammal in Berkeley.

But if we lack grounds such as these, we must establish sameness of conditional attributes independently, and this depends on the discovery of general laws from which the particular conditionals follow. Our grounds for believing that a particular quart of water's boiling is the same event as a collection of molecules' behaving in a certain way are whatever grounds we may have for believing that all the causes and effects of one event are also causes and effects of the

[12] Following Hilary Putnam, *op. cit.*, who says that the "is" in question is that of theoretical identification. The word "identity" by itself is actually too strong for such cases, but I shall adopt it for the sake of convenience.

[13] An attribute, for our purposes, is signified by any sentence frame containing one free variable (in however many occurrences) where this may be a variable ranging over objects, events, and so forth. (One gets a particular instance of an attribute by plugging in an appropriate particular for the variable and converting to gerundival form.) Thus all three of the following are attributes: ". . . is boiling," ". . . will stop boiling if the kettle is taken off the fire," and ". . . will stop if the kettle is taken off the fire." A particular quart of water has the second of these attributes if and only if that water's boiling has the third, where this can be described as the possession of the third attribute by a particular instance of the first.

other, and that all true statements about conditions under which the one event would not have occurred, or about what would have happened if it had not, or about what would happen if it continued, and so forth, are also true of the other.

This is clearly more than mere constant conjunction; it is a fairly strong requirement for identity. Nevertheless it is weaker than the standard version of Leibniz' law in that it does not require possession by each term of *all* the attributes of the other. It does not require that the complex molecular event which we may identify with my being kicked by the only horse in Berkeley be independently characterizable as ridiculous—for example, on the grounds that the latter event was ridiculous and if the former cannot be said to be ridiculous, it lacks an attribute which the latter possesses. There are some attributes from the common possession of which the identity follows, and others which either do not matter or which we cannot decide whether to ascribe to one of the terms without first deciding whether the identity in question holds.

To make this precise, I shall introduce the notion of independent ascribability. There are certain attributes such as being hot or cold, or boiling or offensive, which cannot significantly be ascribed to a collection of molecules per se. It may be that such attributes *can* be ascribed to a collection of molecules, but such ascription is dependent for its significance on their primary ascription to something of a different kind, like a body of water or a person, with which the molecules are identical. Such attributes, I shall say, are not independently ascribable, to the molecules, though they may be dependently ascribable. Similarly, the property of having eighty-three trillion members is not independently ascribable to a quantity of water, though it may be possessed by a collection of H_2O molecules. Nevertheless, there is in such cases a class of attributes which are independently ascribable to both terms, and the condition for theoretical identity may be stated as follows: that the two terms should possess or lack in common all those attributes which can be independently ascribed to each of them individually—with the qualification that nothing is by this criterion to be identical with two things which are by the same criterion distinct.[14] Actually this will serve as a condition for identity in general; a strict identity will simply be one between terms sufficiently similar in type to allow independent ascription to both of *all* the same attributes, and will include such cases as the sinking of the Titanic being the largest marine disaster ever to occur in

[14] The qualification takes care of such possibly problematic claims as that I am the square root of 2, for although it may be that we share all attributes which can be independently ascribed to each of us, I also share those attributes with the square root of 3, whose attributes clearly contradict those of the square root of 2.

peacetime, or the morning star being the evening star. The identities I have characterized as theoretical hold across categories of description sufficiently different to prohibit independent ascription to both terms of all the same attributes, although, as I have observed, such ascriptions may be meaningful as *consequences* of the identity.

The question naturally arises, to what extent do particular theoretical identities depend on corresponding general ones? In the examples I have given concerning the case of water, the dependence is obvious. There the particular identities have simply been instances of general ones, which are consequences of the same theory that accounts for the common possession of relevant attributes in the particular cases. Now there is a technical sense in which every particular theoretical identity must be an instance of a general identity, but not all cases need be like that of water. Although it is essential that particular identities must follow from general laws or a general theory, this does not prevent us from distinguishing between cases in which, for example, the molecular counterpart of a macroscopic phenomenon is always the same, and those in which it varies from instance to instance. The common possession of conditional attributes can follow for a particular case from general laws, without its being true that there is a general correlation between macroscopic and microscopic phenomena of that type. For example, it may at the same time follow from general laws that types of microscopic phenomena other than the one present in this case would also share the requisite conditional properties.

The technical sense in which even in such cases the particular identity must be an instance of a general one is that it must be regarded as an instance of the identity between the macroscopic phenomenon and the disjunction of all those microscopic phenomena which are associated with it in the manner described, via general laws. For suppose we have a type of macroscopic phenomenon A and two types of microscopic phenomena B and C so associated with it. Suppose on one occasion particular cases of A and B are occurring at the same place and time, and so forth, and suppose it is asserted that since it follows from general laws that they also have all their conditional attributes in common, A is in this case identical in the specified sense with B. They do not, however, have in common the conditional attribute $F(X)$, defined as follows: "If C and not B, then X." That is, $F(A)$ but not $F(B)$. Therefore, we must identify the occurrence of A even in this case with the occurrence of the disjunction B or C. This does not prevent us, however, from introducing as a subsidiary sense of identity for particular cases that in which A is B because the disjunction B or C which is properly identical with A is in fact satisfied by B. There is of course a range of cases between the two kinds described, cases in which the disjuncts in the general identity consist of conjunctions which overlap to a greater or lesser degree, and this complicates the matter considerably.[15] Nevertheless we can, despite the technicality, differentiate roughly between particular identities which are in a narrow sense instances of general identities and those which are not—that is, which are instances only of radically disjunctive general identities. Henceforth when I refer to general identities I shall be excluding the latter.

I have concentrated on identities between states, events, and attributes because it is in such terms that physicalism is usually conceived, but if it is also part of physicalism to hold that people are their bodies, it becomes appropriate to inquire into the relation between the theoretical identity of things and the theoretical identity of their attributes. Unfortunately, I do not have a general answer to this question. The case of strict identity presents no problem, for there every attribute of one term is strictly identical with the corresponding attribute of the other; and in our standard example of theoretical identity, each attribute of the water seems to be theoretically identical with some attribute of the molecules, but not vice versa. This may be one (asymmetrical) condition for the theoretical identity of things. It is not clear, however, whether the identity of things must always be so closely tied to the identity of their attributes. For example, it might be that everything we could explain in terms of the water and its attributes could be explained in terms of the batch of molecules and their attributes, but that the two systems of explanation were so different in structure that it would be impossible to find a single attribute of the molecules which explained all and only those things explained by a particular attribute of the water.

Whether or not this is true of water, the possibility has obvious relevance to physicalism. One might be able to define a weak criterion of theoretical identity which would be satisfied in such a case, and this might in turn give sense to an identification of persons with

---

[15] A fuller treatment would have to include a discussion of the nonsymmetrical relation ". . . consists of . . ." which is distinct from identity. A macroscopic event (the freezing of some water, for example) may be identical with a microscopic event A described in general terms (average kinetic energy, spatial ordering, and the like) while at the same time consisting of a very specific collection B of microscopic events with which it is not identical, since if one of them (the motion of a particular molecule) had been different, that particular complex of microscopic events would not have occurred though both A and the macroscopic event would have. (Presumably in such cases the occurrence of B entails the occurrence of A, but more than that needs to be said about the relation between the two.) The same concept applies to the relation between World War II and the immense collection of actions and events of which it consisted, or that between the Eiffel Tower and the girders and rivets which make it up.

their bodies which did not depend on the discovery of a single physical counterpart for every psychological event or condition. I shall, however, forgo an investigation of the subject; this general discussion of identity must remain somewhat programmatic.

IV

It provides us with some things to say, however, about the thesis of physicalism. First, the grounds for accepting it will come from increased knowledge of (a) the explanation of mental events and (b) the physiological explanation of happenings which those mental events in turn explain. Second, in view of the condition of independent ascribability, physicalism need not be threatened by the difficulty that although anger may be, for example, justified, it makes no sense to say this of a physical state with which we may identify it. Third, it does not require general identities at every level: that is, there need not be, either for all persons or even for each individual, a specific physical state of the body which is *in general* identical with intending to vote Republican at the next election, or having a stomach-ache, in order that physicalism be true. It seems likely that there will be general identities of a rough kind for nonintensional states, such as having particular sensations or sensory impressions, since the physical causes of these are fairly uniform. But one can be practically certain that intensional mental states, even if in each particular case they are identical with some physical state, will not have general physical counterparts, because both the causes and the effects of a given belief or desire or intention are extremely various on different occasions even for the same individual, let alone for different persons. One might as easily hope to find a general equivalent, in molecular terms, of a building's collapsing or a bridge's being unsafe —yet each instance of such an event or circumstance is identical with some microscopic phenomenon.

The relation of intensional mental states to physical states may be even more involved than this. For one thing, if it should be the case that they are dispositional in a classical sense, then physicalism requires only that the events and states to which they are the dispositions be identical with physical events and states. It does not require that they be identical with any additional independent physical state, existing even when the disposition is not being exercised. (In fact, I do not believe that dispositions operate according to the classical Rylean model, and this will affect still further the way in which the identity thesis applies to dispositional mental states;

but this is not the place for a discussion of that issue.)

There is still another point: many intensional predicates do not just ascribe a condition to the person himself but have implications about the rest of the world and his relation to it. Physicalism will of course not require that these be identical simply with states of the person's body, narrowly conceived. An obvious case is that of knowledge, which implies not only the truth of what is known but also a special relation between this and the knower. Intentions, thoughts, and desires may also imply a context, a relation with things outside the person. The thesis that all states of a person are states of his body therefore requires a liberal conception of what constitutes a state—one which will admit relational attributes. This is not peculiar to mental states: it is characteristic of intensional attributes wherever they occur. That a sign says that fishing is forbidden does not consist simply in its having a certain geometrically describable distribution of black paint on its surface; yet we are not tempted here to deny that the sign is a piece of wood with paint on it, or to postulate a noncorporeal substance which is the subject of the sign's intensional attributes.

Even with all these qualifications, however, it may be too much to expect a specific physical counterpart for each particular psychological phenomenon. Thus, although it may be the case that what explains and is explained by a particular sensation can also explain and be explained by a particular neurological condition, it may also be that this is not precisely true of an intention, but rather that the various connections which we draw between causes and effects via the intention can be accounted for in terms of many different physical conditions, some of which also account for connections which in psychological discourse we draw via states other than the intention, and no subset of which, proper or improper, accounts for all and only those connections which the intention explains. For this reason a thoroughgoing physicalism might have to fall back on a criterion for identity between things not dependent on the identity of their attributes—a criterion of the sort envisaged at the end of the previous section.

Obviously any physicalistic *theory,* as opposed to the bare philosophical thesis of physicalism, will be exceedingly complex. We are nowhere near a physical theory of how human beings work, and I do not know whether the empirical evidence currently available indicates that we may expect with the advance of neurology to uncover one. My concern here has been only to refute the philosophical position that mental-physical identity is *impossible,* and that *no* amount of further information could constitute evidence for it.

V

Even if what might be called the standard objections have been answered, however, I believe that there remains another source for the philosophical conviction that physicalism is impossible. It expresses itself crudely as the feeling that there is a fundamental distinction between the subjective and the objective which cannot be bridged. Objections having to do with privacy and special access represent attempts to express it, but they fail to do so, for it remains when they have been defeated. The feeling is that I (and hence any "I") cannot be a mere physical object, because I possess my mental states: I am their *subject*, in a way in which no physical object can possibly be the subject of its attributes. I have a type of internality which physical things lack; so in addition to the connection which all my mental states do admittedly have with my body, they are also mine—that is, they have a particular *self* as subject, rather than merely being attributes of an object. Since any mental state must have a self as subject, it cannot be identical with a mere attribute of some object like a body, and the self which is its subject cannot therefore be a body.

Why should it be thought that for *me* to have a certain sensation—to be in a certain mental state—cannot consist merely in a physical object's being in some state, having some attribute? One might put it as follows. States of my body, physical states, are, admittedly, physical states of me, but this is not simply because they are states of that body but because in addition it is my body. And its being my body consists in its having a certain relation, perhaps a causal one, to the subject of my mental states. This leads naturally to the conclusion that I, the subject of my mental states, am something else—perhaps a mental substance. My physical states are only derivatively mine, since they are states of a body which is mine in virtue of being related in the appropriate way to my psychological states. But this is possible only if those psychological states are mine in an original, and not merely derivative, sense; therefore *their* subject cannot be the body which is derivatively mine. The feeling that physicalism leaves out of account the essential subjectivity of psychological states is the feeling that nowhere in the description of the state of a human body could there be room for a physical equivalent of the fact that *I* (or any self), and not just that body, am the subject of those states.

This, so far as I can see, is the source of my uneasiness about physicalism. Unfortunately, whatever its merits, it is no more an argument against physicalism than against most other theories of mind, including dualism, and it therefore provides us with no more reason for rejecting the former in favor of the latter than do the standard objections already discussed. It can be shown that if we follow out this type of argument, it will provide us with equally strong reasons for rejecting any view which identifies the subject of psychological states with a substance and construes the states as attributes of that substance. A noncorporeal substance seems safe only because in retreating from the physical substance as a candidate for the self, we are so much occupied with finding a subject whose states are originally, and not just derivatively, mine—one to which the physical body can be related in a way which explains how *it* can be mine—that we simply postulate such a subject without asking ourselves whether the same objections will not apply to it as well: whether indeed any substance can possibly meet the requirement that its states be *underivatively* mine.

The problem can be shown to be general in the following way: consider everything that can be said about the world without employing any token-reflexive expressions.[16] This will include the description of all its physical contents and their states, activities, and attributes. It will also include a description of all the persons in the world and their histories, memories, thoughts, sensations, perceptions, intentions, and so forth. I can thus describe without token-reflexives the entire world and everything that is happening in it—and this will include a description of Thomas Nagel and what he is thinking and feeling. But there seems to remain one thing which I cannot say in this fashion—namely, which of the various persons in the world *I* am. Even when everything that can be said in the specified manner has been said, and the world has in a sense been completely described, there seems to remain one fact which has not been expressed, and that is the fact that I am Thomas Nagel. This is not, of course, the fact ordinarily conveyed by those words, when they are used to inform someone else who the *speaker* is—for that could easily be expressed otherwise. It is rather the fact that *I* am the subject of *these* experiences; this body is my body; the subject or center of my world is this person, Thomas Nagel.

Now it follows from this not only that a sensation's being mine cannot consist simply in its being an attribute of a particular body; it follows also that it cannot consist in the sensation's being an attribute of a particular soul which is joined to that body; for nothing in the specification of that soul will determine that *it* is mine, that I am *that* person. So long as we construe psychological states as attributes of a substance, no matter what substance we pick, it can be

---

[16] I.e., expressions *functioning* as token reflexives. Such words of course lose this function in quotation and in certain cases of *oratio* (or *cogitatio*) *obliqua:* e.g., "John Smith thinks that he is Napoleon."

thrown, along with the body, into the "objective" world; its states and its relation to a particular body can be described completely without touching upon the fact that I am that person.[17] It turns out therefore that, given the requirements which led us to reject physicalism, the quest for the self, for a substance which *is* me and whose possession of a psychological attribute will *be* its being mine, is a quest for something which could not exist. The only possible conclusion is that the self is not a substance, and that the special kind of possession which characterizes the relation between me and my psychological states cannot be represented as the possession of certain attributes by a subject, no matter what that subject may be. The subjectivity of the true psychological subject is of a different kind from that of the mere subject of attributes. And if I am to extend this to cases other than my own, I must conclude that for no person is it the case that his having a particular sensation consists in some occupant of the world having a particular attribute or being in a certain state.

I shall not discuss the reasons for rejecting this position. My attitude toward it is precisely the reverse of my attitude toward physicalism, which repels me although I am persuaded of its truth. The two are of course related, since what bothers me about physicalism is the thought that I cannot be a mere physical object, cannot in fact be anything *in* the world at all, and that my sensations and so forth cannot be simply the attributes of some substance.

But if we reject this view (as it seems likely that we must) and accept the alternative that a person is something in the world and that his mental states are states of that thing, then there is no a priori reason why it should not turn out to be a physical body and those states physical states. We are thus freed to investigate the possibility, and to seek the kind of understanding of psychological states which will enable us to formulate specific physicalistic theories as neurology progresses.

[17] Cf. Wittgenstein, *Tractatus,* 5.64.

Postscript (November 1968)

I now believe that theoretical identity is not distinct from strict identity, and that the device by which I formerly defined theoretical identity can be used to explain how Leibniz' law is satisfied by identities whose terms are of disparate types. Suppose boiling is independently ascribable to a quart of water but not to the molecules which compose it. Nevertheless we can say that the molecules are boiling if they bear a certain relation to the water, and the water is boiling. The relation in question, call it R, is simply that which I formerly described as theoretical identity. It holds between a and b if (i) they possess or lack in common all those attributes which can be independently ascribed to each of them individually (call this relation S), and (ii) neither a nor b bears relation S to any third term which does not bear relation S to the other.* Let F range over nonintensional and nonmodal attributes, and let us symbolize the modal statement 'F is independently ascribable (truly or falsely) to a' as $I(F,a)$. Then

(1) $S(a,b) \equiv_{df} (F)(I(F,a) \cdot I(F,b) \cdot \supset \cdot F(a) \equiv F(b))$

(2) $R(a,b) \equiv_{df}$ (i) $S(a,b)$ & (ii) a true statement results whenever a name or definite description is substituted for 'x' in the schema $S(a,x) \equiv S(b,x)$

I claim that a true statement results whenever names or definite descriptions are substituted for 'x' and 'y' in the following schema:

(3) $(F)(I(F,x) \cdot F(x) \cdot R(x,y) \cdot \supset F(y))$

If this is correct, then when a and b are related by R they will share all the attributes independently ascribed to either of them. By Leibniz' law, therefore,

(4) $R(a,b) \equiv a = b$

* Condition (ii) is added for the reason cited in footnote 14 of my 1965 paper.

KEITH GUNDERSON

Asymmetries and Mind-Body Perplexities

*"O wad some Pow'r the giftie gie us
To see oursels as others see us!"*
from "To a Louse" by ROBERT BURNS

I

Any satisfactory solution to the mind-body problem must include an account of why the so-called "I", "subjective self", or "self as subject of experiences" seems so adept at slipping through the meshes of every nomological net of physical explanation which philosophers have been able to imagine science someday bestowing upon them.[1] Until this agility on the part of the self is either curtailed or shown to be ontologically benign the mind-body problem is not going to go away. Unless the self itself, however characterized, can be shown to be comfortably at home within the domain of the physical, many of its putative attributes—thoughts, feelings, and sensations—will not seem to be at rest there either.

Nor will it do to attempt to pre-empt the playing out of these perplexities by launching a frontal attack *à la* Hume or Ryle on allegedly quixotic views as to the nature of the self. The problem I am alluding to does not arise because of quixotic views of the self. It is just the reverse: philosophers find themselves forced to endorse

---

Reprinted, in considerably shortened and slightly rewritten form, from "Asymmetries and Mind-Body Perplexities," in *Minnesota Studies in the Philosophy of Science,* IV, edited by Michael Radner and Stephen Winokur, Minneapolis: University of Minnesota Press, 1970, 273–309, by permission of the publishers and Keith Gunderson. [The present version corresponds to pages 273–279, 284–285, 289–294 and 300–305 of the original.]

[1] I wish to thank Professor Feigl and Mrs. Judith Economos for encouraging me to write up the central ideas contained in this paper. I have also had the benefit of a number of discussions with Mr. Mischa Penn on these matters. I have no idea as to how happy they will be with the final result. Cf. the final chapter of Mrs. Economos' *The Identity Thesis* (doctoral dissertation—Department of Philosophy, UCLA). As usual, I am greatly indebted to my former colleague, Charles Chastain, with whom I have discussed this paper in detail.

quixotic views of the self primarily because they systematically fail to show how a human being might conceive of himself as being completely *in* the world.

Some kind of thoroughgoing physicalism seems intuitively plausible mainly because of a dramatic absence of reasons for supposing that were we to dissect, dismantle, and exhaustively inspect any other person we would discover anything more than a complicated organization of physical things, properties, processes, and events. Furthermore, as has been emphasized recently, we have a strong sense of many of our mental features as being embodied.[2] On the other hand there's a final persuasiveness physicalism lacks which can be traced to the conceptual hardship each person faces when trying to imagine himself being completely accounted for by any such dissection, dismantling, or inspection. It is not so much that one boggles at conceiving of *any* aspect of his self, person, or consciousness being described in physicalistic terms; it is rather that one boggles at conceiving of *every* aspect of being simultaneously so describable. For convenience of exposition I shall sometimes use the word "self" to refer to whatever there is (or isn't!) which seems to resist such description. Such reference to a self or aspect thereof will not commit me to any positive characterization of it. Neither to the view that one's self remains unchanged from moment to moment, nor to the view that it doesn't, nor to the view that it is a thing, process, or bundle of events. What I am committed to is phrasing and unpicking the following problem: If a thoroughgoing physicalism (or any kind of monism) is true, why should it even *seem* so difficult for me to view my mind or self as an item wholly in the world? And this independently of how I may construe that mind or self: whether as a substance or as a cluster of properties, processes, or events. The paradox becomes: A physicalistic (or otherwise monistic) account of the mind at the outset seems quite convincing so long as I consider anyone except myself. If, however, physicalism provides an adequate account of the minds or selves of others, why should it not, then, provide an adequate account of the nature of my mind or self so long as I lack any reason to suppose that I am utterly unique? [3] But if I am unable to see how physicalism could account for the nature of my mind or self, why then should it not seem equally implausible as a theory about the mind or self of anyone else, again assuming that I lack reasons for supposing that I am unique? In this way we teeter-totter between the problem of viewing our self as wholly in the world, or physical, and the problem of viewing

---

[2] Vesey, G. A., *The Embodied Mind*, London: Allen & Unwin, 1965.
[3] Cf. Paul Ziff's "The Simplicity of Other Minds," *The Journal of Philosophy*, Vol. LXII, No. 20: October 21, 1965, pp. 575–584.

other people who seem wholly in the world as being somewhat mental. But if the mental is after all physical, why should this be so? Although I may not initially believe that in my or anyone else's investigation of the world I or they will find need to riddle our explanations with references to immaterial selves or spirits, it still remains easy to believe that I will never turn up the whole of my self as something co-habiting with items in the natural world. Hence the presumptuousness of assuming I really do find other selves *in* the world.

II

In his *Principles of Human Knowledge* Bishop Berkeley was to write:

> But besides all that endless variety of ideas or objects of knowledge, there is likewise something which knows or perceives them; and exercises divers operations, as willing, imagining, remembering, about them. This perceiving active being is what I call MIND, SPIRIT, SOUL, or MYSELF. By which words I do not denote any one of my ideas, but a thing entirely distinct from them, wherein they exist....[4]

This is tantamount to Berkeley having asserted that he does not come upon his mind, spirit, soul, or self as an item of the world in the way in which he is able to come upon cogs or pulleys, dendrites or axons. His claim that we only have notions of the mind, spirit, soul, or self and not ideas (perceptions) of it is another way he has of expressing his belief that there is a basic difference between how it is we can have knowledge of our own mind(s) and how it is we can have knowledge of nature.

And Kant, in spite of his general disaffection with Berkeley, echoes his sentiment concerning the self when he claims that he "cannot have any representation whatsoever of a thinking being, through any outer experience, but only through self-consciousness."[5]

Furthermore, I believe it can be shown in writings from Fichte to Sartre that a well-advertised view of the self as a free or autonomous subject occurs as a simple corollary to the just discussed claim that whatever its nature the self will not be found to reside as do objects at any spatio-temporal address. As occupant of a more ethereal dwelling the self can hardly be expected to feel constrained by the zoning laws of determinism. (Compare the quotation from Schopenhauer in Section V.)

---

[4] Berkeley, George, *The Principles of Human Knowledge,* in the Meridian Books edition, pp. 65–66; 1963.

[5] *Critique of Pure Reason,* Kemp Smith translation (unabridged) p. 332.

Thomas Nagel in his recent article "Physicalism" (see this volume) writes:

> The feeling that physicalism leaves out of account the essential subjectivity of psychological states is the feeling that nowhere in the description of the state of a human body could there be room for a physical equivalent of the fact that I (or any self), and not just that body, am the subject of those states.[6]

No doubt (as Nagel himself intimates) such puzzlements are to some extent reflected in (perhaps in some sense caused by?) the peculiar linguistic role played by indexical expressions such as "I" ("now", "this", and so on) or what have been called egocentric particulars (by Russell).[7] Even so, what then needs to be shown is that the pragmatic conditions underlying the difference in use between the indexical "I" and nonindexicals do not add up to a metaphysical difference between whatever the indexical "I" denotes when it is used and the sorts of things which the nonindexicals might refer to or characterize. Only after this is done will it be easy to concur with Russell's claim concerning egocentric particulars ". . . that they are not needed in any part of the description of the world, whether physical or psychological."[8]

In brief, I believe that a major temptation to reject a physicalistic theory of mentality, *or any monistic doctrine,* and by default flirt with some variety of Cartesianism or mind/body dualism derives from the as yet inadequately assessed asymmetry between (a) how I am able to view myself as a potential object of investigation (within a spatiotemporal setting) and (b) how at first sight it seems one would be able to investigate virtually anything else including (supposedly) other people within such a setting. Given this asymmetry it is cold comfort to be told that my sensations and feelings may be identical with certain brain processes *in the way that* a lightning flash is identical with an electrical discharge or a cloud is identical with a mass of tiny particles in suspension.[9] Such comparisons may serve to assuage whatever logical qualms had been felt concerning the compatibility of an identity statement ("Sensations are identical with brain processes") with the sup-

---

[6] In *Philosophical Review*, Vol. LXXIV, No. 3, July 1965, p. 354. [Reprinted in this volume, p. 108.]

[7] Bertrand Russell, Chapter VII, "Egocentric Particulars," in *An Inquiry into Meaning and Truth*, Norton, 1940.

[8] *Ibid.*, p. 115.

[9] Cf. J. J. C. Smart's "Sensations and Brain Processes," in *The Philosophy of Mind*, edited by V. C. Chappell, Prentice-Hall, 1962. [Reprinted in this volume, pp. 53–66.] Such analogies are, of course, scattered throughout the writings of proponents of the identity thesis.

posedly synthetic empirical character of the mind-body identity thesis. (For we have learned that although a lightning flash is identical with an electrical discharge we had to make empirical discoveries to disclose it.) But as long as we seem systematically unable to view our own mind or self as something which can be wholly investigated in the way in which lightning flashes or electrical discharges or, as it seems, other people can be wholly investigated, illustrations involving lightning flashes, electrical discharges (and the like) will seem less than illustrative. It is for this reason that the seeming duality of the phenomenal and the physical does not comprise an analogue to the "complementarity" involved in the Cophenhagen interpretation of Quantum Mechanics. For both particles and waves are, *in some sense,* equally at home *in* or "out of" the world.

An invisible bull in the china shop of the physicalist's analogies is the ominous absence of whatever those arguments might be which would show one that his own self is as wholly amenable to physical investigation as are *either* clouds *or* molecules *or* lightning flashes *or* electrical discharges. The identity-analogies usually engaged in the service of physicalism involve only identities between entities rather obviously susceptible to eventual specification and characterization by expressions which conveniently locate them within a spatio-temporal framework and describe them in physicalistic ways. The question of whether my mind or self is wholly amenable to even roughly this sort of description is one of the major points at issue. It is not sufficient to argue that if other minds seem to consist of nothing other than that which can be physically located and characterized then my mind must be too, unless I suppose it is unique; for the failure to suppose it's unique can be utilized to show that other minds cannot be accounted for in a purely physicalistic way.

Should the above diagnosis be correct, any solution to the mind-body problem must proceed through (at least) two stages: At the first stage what must be overcome is a natural resistance to viewing one's own mind or self as *the sort of thing* which can be wholly investigated in a way in which other things, events, objects, (people?) can be imagined as being wholly investigated by one's own mind or self. I shall refer to the difficulties encountered at this first stage as *The Investigational Asymmetries Problem*.[10] Once such difficulties have been dissolved one may go on to attempt to answer the question of whether one's mind (and hence other minds) which *is* amenable to

[10] These asymmetries can be phrased either in terms of (1) how we find out about the minds of others as distinct from the way in which we find out about our own mind, or (2) the problem we have in finding ourselves in the world as distinct from the way we can at least imagine finding anything else in the world. Here I restrict myself to (2).

such investigation can best be characterized after such an investigation as "a certain kind of information processing system," "a coalition of computer-like routines and subroutines," or instead as "a certain type of entelechy" or as "a certain sort of vital force" and so on. I shall refer to the difficulties encountered at this second stage as *The Characterization Problem*.

I mention entelechies and vital forces in passing because I wish to emphasize that a solution to the *Investigational Asymmetries Problem* does not settle in favor of physicalism the question of whether physicalism is true. The extent to which this latter question remains unanswered is the extent to which a theory such as vitalism could blossom from our investigation of nature in general. For example, it might seem reasonable to conclude on the basis of current physical theory that there are entities (say entelechies) inexplicable within the framework of that theory. (Compare: Hans Driesch's vitalistic conclusions insofar as they were based on his investigation of the development of sea urchins and not based on his investigation of Hans Driesch.)[11]

So the problem I wish to focus on is *not simply that my self seems so private to me and hence could not be a physical object of scientific investigations carried out by others, but rather that it seems in some part so unpublic to me, and hence cannot be viewed by me at any given time as an item wholly susceptible even in principle to scientific investigations by me.* (We might call this the problem of empirically "underprivileged access" to ourselves.) But if my self could never be wholly public to me in the way that cogs or pulleys, dendrites or axons seem to be, it is easy to be persuaded that it is not really wholly public to anyone else either. Hence a thesis such as physicalism which certainly ought to be committed to the view that my mental states are public in virtue of their being physical states or processes which incontestably public still seems implausible.

What I hope to show is that the asymmetry between how I am able to investigate my self (and thereby the subjects of my thoughts, feelings, and sensations) and how it is I can investigate what I regard as other selves and other things within some spatio-temporal scheme is structurally similar to other ontologically benign asymmetries. By

[11] Driesch, Hans, *The History and Theory of Vitalism*, Macmillan & Co., 1914. Vitalistic metaphysics did not generally depend on puzzles about the self for its anti-materialistic conclusions. These conclusions were usually based upon seemingly inexplicable but publicly observable features of animals or people such as self-adaptive behavior, etc. This is one reason why the counter-examples which cybernetic machines provided to the claim that non-mechanistic explanations (involving entelechies, *et al.*) were needed to account for self-adaptive behavior did not settle certain basic mind-body problems. That is to say, puzzles about the self could be utilized on behalf of a mind-body dualism whether or not cybernetic models made reference to entelechies unnecessary in explaining behavior.

seeing why it is that these analogous asymmetries fail to thrust upon us any dualistic ontology of things, processes, or features, I think it will be shown that there is no need to suppose that the *Investigational Asymmetries* underlying the mind-body problem forces upon us a dualistic ontology of things, processes, or features.

III

Case I: The My Eyes Problem

How can I tell what both my eyes look like (at one time)? Not in the same way I can tell what someone else's eyes look like, not simply by observing them. Only by looking in mirrors, or at photographs, or at movies of me, or by asking others to tell me what my eyes look like.

There are two ways of finding out what a person's two eyes look like at one time: (1) a way of finding out about the eyes of others, and (2) a way of finding out about my own.

A familiar division. Here we have a kind of other minds problem in reverse. I can know by directly looking at them what other people's eyes look like, but I can never know what my own eyes look like by looking at them—except with the aid of mirrors, photographs, and so on. (I shall hereafter rule out the latter.)

I can imagine what it would be like to be in a position to see what anybody else's eyes look like, but I cannot imagine what it would be like to be in a position to see with my present eyes what my present eyes look like. At least I cannot imagine being in a position to see what my eyes look like, without, say, imagining something like the case where I have my current eyes removed and replaced by a different pair of eyes. But this changes the case. By "my eyes", I mean to mean "the eyes which I now possess in my body and which I now see through."

But is there any reason to suppose that the general characteristics which my eyes have differ in kind from the sorts of features which other people's eyes have and which I can see that they have by looking at them? That is to say, are we in the least bit tempted here to propagate a double ontology concerning eyes: (1) the sorts of features my eyes have and which from my point of view seem non-visible and (2) the sorts of features (or looks) everybody else's eyes have and which I am aware of whenever I look at them? Are we to imagine that there is more (or, better still, less) to other people's eyes than meets my eye since I have no reason to suppose I am unique, and, seemingly every reason to suppose there is something in eyes which cannot be investigated since I cannot investigate my own?

Consider the complications which arise if we tried to refute the testimony of mirrors, photographs, and other people as wholly adequate for our own case. We would have to assume that though we know what everyone else's eyes looked like, and know that they looked just as they looked in the mirror, ours do not look as they look in the mirror to everyone else. Ours, we might insist, have non-visible features. If we were to do this we would also have to assume that the looks of our eyes differ from any other part of the body with respect to their reflections in a mirror. We know our hands look like our hands look in the mirror; we know our stomachs look like our stomachs look in the mirror; and so on. But eyes, well, no, or maybe, or we can't tell whether they do look like they look in the mirror or that they are even the sorts of things of which it makes sense to say "they look a certain way," and so on. We would have to believe that everybody else lies with respect to our eyes, and that mirrors "lie" with respect to our eyes, though they "tell the truth" with respect to every other reflectable feature of us.

I do not conclude that my eyes look as they look in the mirror, because I adopt a simple "reverse" argument from analogy: "Since other people's eyes look like what they look like in the mirror, therefore my eyes must look like what they look like in the mirror." Rather, it is because it would take an immensely complicated and implausible theory to try to explain my eyes not looking like they look in the mirror, given that my hands do, given that my feet do, given that other people's eyes do, given that I have no reason for thinking other people are lying when they tell me what my eyes look like, and so on. Lacking a special theory for my own case, I not only accept what other people say about the looks of my eyes, and what is shown in the mirror, I have excellent reasons for accepting this. And certainly I do not conclude that my eyes are, say, "featureless." This latter absurdity, however, is one we could be needled into accepting were we to decide to "start from our own case" and reason by analogy to the nature of the eyes of others. We would be forced to submit to the conclusion, even in the face of other faces, that the eyes of others have no visible features, for our own eyes seem to us to have none. But we never seemed pressed to such calamitous conclusions, and this is because we have a perfectly good explanation of why we could never be in a position to see the features of our own eyes in the way we are in a good position (potentially) for seeing the features of anyone else's eyes. And the explanation is that in order for me to see my eyes with my eyes, my own eyes would have to be in two (actually four) places at once: in front of themselves to be looked at as well as at the point from which they are being looked at. Note too the conceptual absurdity involved in supposing we know how eyes (in general) look by "starting from our own case" and then reasoning by analogy that other eyes are as ours seem to us, i.e., featureless. What possible sense could be given to the claim that our eyes seem to us to have *or* lack features of any sort whatsoever if we suppose there are no mirrors about and so on?

Wittgenstein remarked in the *Tractatus:*

> For the form of the visual field is surely not like this [12]

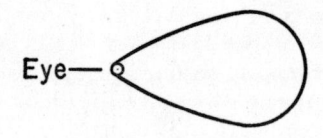

Eye—

which connects up with his earlier remarks at 5.631:[13]

> There is no such thing as the subject that thinks or entertains ideas.
> If I wrote a book called *The World as I found it*, I should have to include a report on my body, and should have to say which parts were subordinate to my will, and which were not, etc., this being a method of isolating the subject, or rather of showing that in an important sense there is no subject; for it alone could *not* be mentioned in that book.

Surely Wittgenstein here has his eye on what I have called *The Investigational Asymmetries Problem*. In other words, just as the eye does not, cannot, see itself in its own visual field, so too, the self will never, in its inventory-taking of the world, find itself in the world in the manner in which it finds other people and things. But Wittgenstein wrongly concludes from this that the self ("the subject") in "an important sense" does not exist. What I am arguing is that there's no more reason to suppose the self does not exist because it is unable to observe itself, than there is reason to suppose eyes have no visible features since one is unable to observe them in his own case. (Compare: "There is no meaning to my own utterance tokens because only items which require some degree of interpretation or disambiguation can have meaning, and I don't (generally can't) disambiguate my own remarks!") Note: Wittgenstein anticipates this move, but seems willing to accept the consequences: "You will say that this is exactly like the case of the eye and the visual field. But really you do *not* see the eye." [14] Of course. But we really *do* see eyes, and (1) have an ex-

---

[12] *Tractatus Logico-Philosophicus*, trans. by D. F. Pears and B. F. McGuiness, Routledge and Kegan Paul, 1961, p. 117.

[13] *Tractatus, loc. cit.*

[14] *Tractatus, loc. cit.*

planation of why it is we cannot observe our own, and (2) have no reason to assume our case is unlike the case of other eyes which we do observe. But if our having eyes does not guarantee that we ourselves be able to inspect their looks, their visible natures, why should we suppose that our being or having selves should guarantee that we will be in a position fully to inspect their natures, and so on? The way back into the world for the self which seems to itself not to be there, is simply its coming to realize that it is to other people what other people are to it.

The case of "my eyes," though it is a kind of other minds problem in reverse, is exactly parallel to that problem of the self which has concerned me here. For the problem of convincing myself that the looks of my eyes are (more or less) exactly like the looks of other eyes, is parallel to the problem of becoming convinced that the nature of my self is (more or less) exactly like the selves of others which, it seems, can be exhaustively described by reference to their behavior and physiology.

But another case will help to consolidate and further clarify the conceptual theses advanced in the first case. It might be noted that nowhere in this second case is any mention of a living organism involved. This should serve to erase any suggestion that the form which the *Investigational Asymmetries Problem* takes is peculiar to sentient agents.

Case II: The Self-Scanning Scanner Problem

Suppose, we have a non-conscious scanning mechanism, call it SM_1, which is able to scan what we shall call its communication cell, CC_1, somewhat after the manner in which current computing machines are able to scan symbols in their communication cells. We shall imagine CC_1 to be a cell of rather flexible size. It shall be able to expand and contract. We shall suppose that SM_1 could scan CC_1 for the appearance of symbols, or the presence of objects, say a bug or a watch or a feather. Let us also imagine that SM_1 could scan other scanners, $SM_2, SM_3, \ldots, SM_n$, all of which would differ only from SM_1 in that they'd be smaller than SM_1 during the time at which they were being scanned. Whenever a scanner such as SM_1 scans another scanner, the scanner being scanned will have to shrink suitably in order for it to appear in CC_1. (Note: It is possible to make the same points without assuming that any object being scanned by SM_1 must appear *in* SM_1's CC_1. Cf. the longer version of this paper, *op. cit.*, pp. 294–300, especially pp. 299–300.) We shall also suppose that SM_1 could scan other scanners while they were in the state of scanning things. Scanners $SM_1, SM_2, \ldots, SM_n$ will be similar in all interesting respects: in design and structure, and in the sorts of inputs, outputs, and so on which are possible for them. So now let us suppose that SM_1 is able to perform what we shall call a "complete scan" of the workings of SM_2, while SM_2 is scanning its communication cell CC_2 in which there appears some symbol or thing. Thus the nature of SM_2, its program, its actual operation while scanning CC_2, will be made available to SM_1 in the form of descriptions. Each scanner we shall suppose to be endowed with certain pattern recognition or generalization capacities. For example, each scanner will be able to recognize various instances of triangles as triangles, apples of different sizes and color, all as being apples, and so on. Thus a scanner will be equipped to answer simple questions as to how a certain item is classified. Let us imagine that such information could be stored as an entry to a list contained in some storage system which is an appendage of SM_1. Let us call this list SM_1's "World List." And let us call the list of all possible World Lists (of scanners SM_1, SM_2, . . . , SM_n) "The World List." So now let us imagine that SM_1 goes on to scan SM_3, SM_4, . . . , SM_n while each is in a state of scanning a symbol or a bug or a watch or a feather. Thus a description of each scanner scanning would be potentially available to SM_1 and could be stored in SM_1's storage system on its "World List." And if we imagine the universe in which SM_1 exists as being a universe in which there are only other scanners SM_2, SM_3, . . . , SM_n and a few objects and events—feathers, bugs, watches, scanners scanning—then we can imagine SM_1 being able to describe virtually everything in its universe. That is, it could in principle scan most everything in its universe and store a description of each item on its World List. But obviously there is going to be one description which SM_1 will never be able to insert on its own World List: namely, any complete description of SM_1 while it is in a state of scanning. SM_1 is, of course, not able to obtain information about itself while scanning in the same way that it is able to gain information about SM_2, SM_3, . . . , SM_n. In order for SM_1 to obtain information about itself scanning an X, say, in the way that it obtains information about SM_2 scanning an X, SM_1 would have to be in two places at once: where it is, and inside its own communication cell.

Nevertheless, a description of SM_1 in a state of scanning will be available to the World List of some other scanner—say SM_{27}. Hence, such a description could appear on *The* World List. All descriptions of scanners in a state of scanning could appear on *The* World List. So if we think of scanners SM_1, SM_2, . . . , SM_n as all being of a comparable nature, and the descriptions of them in a state of scanning as depicting that nature, then we can see that SM_1 in a state of scanning is the same in nature as the other scanning scanners it scans, though it will never be able to locate a description which depicts its nature of other scanners scanning which are descriptions on its (SM_1's) World List. In other words it would be utterly wrong to conclude from SM_1's failure to find a description of its own state of scanning on its World List (or for SM_1 somehow to report on the basis of this) that SM_1 possessed features different in nature from the features which other scanners scanning had and which could be revealed to SM_1. For this would be to suggest that a comparison between SM_1's features and the features of other scanners made available to SM_1 while scanning had been made and that radical differences had been found. Although scanner SM_1 is in principle unable to construe itself on the model of other scanners in a state of scanning in the restricted sense that it cannot construct a list of information about itself comparable to the lists of information it can compile about other scanners, there is no reason for it to report or for us to suppose that some kind of scanning dualism is in order. In other words, there is no reason to assert that SM_1 while in the state of scanning differs in nature from the sorts of features it finds other scanners to possess while in a state of scanning X. Hence, there is also no reason to suppose that there is more to other scanners in a state of scanning than that which could be revealed to SM_1.

The scanning mechanism may be compared to a periscope which is able to sight other ships, even parts of the ship to which it belongs, but which is unable to place itself in its own crosshairs (compare R. Ruyer's *Neo-Finalisme*).

The import of such examples for the mind-body problem should by now be transparent: the difficulty in construing our self at any given moment as an item wholly susceptible to third-person physicalistic and behavioristic descriptions is comparable to the difficulty a periscope would face in attempting to place itself between its own crosshairs.

IV

On the basis of the foregoing cases, I think it is correct to conclude that the following statements are true: (1) Even though I can never be in a position to look at them, the visual appearances which my eyes possess are identical in kind with members of the class of visual features to which the visual features of the eyes of others belong, which features are revealed to me simply by looking at other eyes (*sans* mirrors, photographs, *et al.*). (2) Whenever scanner SM_1 is in a state of scanning its communication cell, it is in a state identical in kind with the sorts of states other scanners in a state of scanning are in, and which are revealed to SM_1 whenever other scanners scanning are placed in SM_1's communication cell. (A periscope$_1$ is identical in kind with members of the class of periscopes$_2$ . . .$_n$ any one of which periscope$_1$ can place between its crosshairs.)

The two foregoing statements might all be called "metaphysically neutral." For even though it can be shown that X, say, is identical in kind with Y's, it leaves open the question as to what kind of things Y's are. Yet such a "metaphysically neutral" identity statement is, I believe, exactly what must first be shown to be true of a theory such as physicalism is to seem justified. The statement which the above analogies are designed to support is: "I am identical in kind with what I find other people to be" where by "what I find other people to be" is meant as they are (or might be) revealed to be on the basis of empirical investigation, etc. (which could in principle be found out by me). This latter qualification must be made in order to distinguish our case from the case where a mind/body dualist accepts the claim that he is identical in kind with other people but asserts that other people all have private selves not amenable to empirical investigation and derives this conclusion from his belief that his self is not amenable to being treated by himself as an object for investigation lying within the world.[15] That is I am assuming that what we find other people to be will no longer be colored by the assumption that since I cannot wholly investigate myself, then since there is no reason to assume I am unique, there is something for all people which does not yield to empirical investigation either. In other words, "what I find other people to be" will be construed as "what I find them to be *sans* use of the just mentioned assumption." This again, as argued earlier, does not load the dice in favor of physicalism. It simply seems that way, since it is obvious at the moment that unless we resort to such an assumption there is no reason to suppose other people are not wholly physical beings.

It is easy to unwittingly saddle oneself with the view that if I am an object wholly amenable to scientific investigation, I had better be able to imagine myself as being an object which I myself could wholly investigate. This I have argued is an absurd demand. And for the same reason that it's absurd to demand that I be able to see my own eyes if I am to credit them with the same sorts of features I ascribe to the eyes of others. Yet, the self-centered insistence that if I am an item susceptible to empirical investigation I ought to be able, at least in principle, to carry out the complete investigation is quite understandable. For what this really adds up to is the insistence that anyone,

---

[15] This latter belief may itself be derived from the more radical notion that the self cannot treat itself as an object for investigation *period*.

myself or others, be able to demonstrate *to my satisfaction* that I am such an item. And the insistence that it be possible to demonstrate to my satisfaction that I am such an item slips into seeming comparable to the demand that I be in a position to appreciate the demonstrations. (Compare: I must be the sort of creature which can never die, since I cannot imagine being in a position to observe my own death. And since I'm not unique, perhaps we are all immortal.)

V

Non-physicalism according to my story has an initially plausible ring which echoes from the fact that I cannot be in two places at the same time, and the tendency to wish to be in as good a position to investigate myself (empirically) as I am in (at least potentially) with respect to others. Curiously enough the failure to be able to be in two places at once in this case forces us to feel that we, as minds, or consciousnesses, are not in any place at all. As Schopenhauer was to write:

> . . . the body is an object among objects, and is conditioned by the laws of objects, although it is an immediate object. Like all objects of perception, it lies within the universal forms of knowledge, time and space, which are the conditions of multiplicity. The subject, on the contrary, which is always the knower, never the known, does not come under these forms, but is presupposed by them; it has therefore neither multiplicity nor its opposite unity. We never know it, but it is always the knower wherever there is knowledge.
>
> So then the world as idea, the only aspect in which we consider it at present, has two fundamental, necessary, and inseparable halves. The one half is the object, the forms of which are space and time, and through these multiplicity. The other half is the subject, which is not in space and time, for it is present, entire and undivided, in every percipient being.[16]

And it is this sense of non-location which tends to reinforce the view that the mind is only contingently connected with the physical. But the foregoing arguments, if correct, should rid us of any temptation to adopt either view.

So too, if I am really never in a position to exhaustively inspect the self which I am, to include it in my inventory of physical facts garnered

---

[16] Schopenhauer, Arthur, in *The World as Idea*, I, 2, pp. 5–6, in *The Philosophy of Schopenhauer*, edited by Irwin Edman, The Modern Library, 1928. Cf. George Pitcher's discussion of this passage in his *The Philosophy of Wittgenstein*, p. 147. Prentice-Hall, Inc., 1964.

through physical investigations, since I would have to be investigator and object of investigation simultaneously, we might expect this fact to reflect itself in our language. And this, I believe, is precisely what underlies the odd referential status of the indexical "I". (Recall Professor Ryle's discussion of the "systematic elusiveness of 'I' "[17] where part of his strategy was to show that the evasive reference of the indexical did not foist Cartesianism upon us.) What I have, in effect, tried to show is that the puzzle surrounding "I" is a manifestation of a deep going dissatisfaction with either physicalism or any monism, a dissatisfaction which is rooted in the seeming unpublicness of our self. That "I" when used in an utterance refers only to the user and not to any one else and is in this sense for each token-occurrence private, or non-public, is parallel to the fact that I cannot make myself an object for public inspection by me and still remain myself. That I cannot refer wholly "outward" by using "I", reflects the fact that I cannot investigate myself as a wholly public object. By saying that the use of "I" in an utterance is restricted in that it can never be used to refer wholly "outward," I wish to call attention to the fact that even in cases where I use "I" in an utterance to specify a certain person (obviously myself) who was or will be, "I" will necessarily specify as well the person I am at the moment of utterance. Consider: I say (while looking at an old photograph) "Here I was in 1950". In such cases the "I" still serves to specify the speaker (whatever else it might do). (Note: it is precisely this fact that "I" is in any utterance-token speaker-specifying, which leads to the oddity Hintikka[18] points out in the case where a person attempts to convince someone he doesn't exist by saying "I don't exist.")

This feature of the first-person pronoun indexicals, is the linguistic frosting on the factual cake: the ingredients of the latter being my (or anyone's) inability to treat myself (himself) wholly as an other person or thing. Were I able on occasion to treat myself wholly as an other person or thing, then "I" would not be, could not be, restricted in the above manner. The reflection of this fact underlying this restriction on "I" would, of course, be ploughed under were we to imagine our language *sans* egocentric particulars (following Russell). Yet in agreement with Russell we can see why in one sense "I" is not needed in our descriptions of the world. For once we are aware that the unpublic nature of my self *vis-à-vis* me does not show my self to be unpublic *simpliciter,* each of us is then in a position to see and describe ourselves

---

[17] In *Concept of Mind*, pp. 195–198, Hutchinson's University Library, 1955.
[18] Hintikka, Jaakko, "Cogito, Ergo Sum: Inference or Performance?", *The Philosophical Review*, Vol. LXXI, No. 1, Whole No. 397, January, 1962, pp. 3–32.

via an acceptance of how others see and describe us—and others do not (cannot), of course, utilize "I" in their descriptions of us.

The solution to stage one of the mind-body question, on the above analysis, turns out to be nothing more than coming to an acceptance of the fact that although we will never be in as good a position to investigate ourselves as we are to investigate others, objects, things, events, etc. this makes no more difference (ontologically) than the fact that a submarine's periscope cannot locate itself in its own crosshairs makes an ontological difference between the nature of the periscope doing the sighting and the things it can sight.

A Schopenhauerian self which cannot locate itself as just another member in the sprawly family of physical objects is comparable to a periscope which is safe from the torpedoes of its own submarine because it can never locate itself in its own crosshairs. But just as such a periscope is only safe from its own torpedoes and not the torpedoes of others, so too, such a self is only safe from spotting itself in the physical world. It is not safe from being spotted there by others.

part four
FUNCTIONALISTIC MATERIALISM

JERRY A. FODOR

Materialism

It is frequently suggested in philosophical discussions of the mind-body problem that it might be reasonable to regard mind states and brain states as contingently identical. How plausible one considers this suggestion to be depends on one's view of an extremely complicated tangle of philosophical problems to which the materialist doctrine is closely connected. Among these are problems that must clearly be faced during the course of providing an account of explanation in psychology.

For example, determining whether or not materialism can be true is part of understanding the relation between theories in psychology and theories in neurology—a relation that many philosophers believe poses a stumbling block for the doctrine of the unity of science. In particular, it is sometimes maintained that the unity of science requires that it prove possible to "reduce" psychological theories to neurological theories, the model of reduction being provided by the relation between constructs in chemistry and those in physics. This is usually taken to mean that, for each theoretical term that appears in psychology, there must be a true statement that articulates a psychophysical identity and that such statements are to be understood on the analogy of statements that identify hydrogen atoms with certain configurations of subatomic particles. On this view, neurological entities are the denotata of psychological terms, just as physical entities are the denotata of chemical terms.[1]

From *Psychological Explanation*, by Jerry A. Fodor, 90–120. © Copyright 1968 by Random House, Inc. Reprinted by permission of the publisher.

[1] Cf. Paul Oppenheim and Hilary Putnam, "Unity of Science as a Working Hypothesis," in *Minnesota Studies in the Philosophy of Science, Volume II: Concepts, Theories, and the Mind-Body Problem*, ed. Herbert Feigl, Michael Scriven and Grover Maxwell (Minneapolis: University of Minnesota Press, 1958), 3–36.

This sort of issue suggests that rather more is at stake when the question of materialism is raised than may initially meet the eye. In this chapter, I shall therefore attempt to bring out some of the logical links between the controversy about materialism and some other problems in philosophical psychology, as well as to survey a number of arguments in which the truth of materialism is directly involved.

CONCEPTUAL BACKGROUND OF CONTEMPORARY MATERIALISM

Classical empiricism sought to provide a psychological account of the ontogenesis of ideas from which it would follow that the mind could entertain no concept that was not in some sense exemplified in experience. This demonstration has seemed unsatisfactory to contemporary empiricists, who have sought to provide something stronger than psychological necessity for the existence of an experiential component in all coherent concepts.

At its crudest, contemporary empiricism has sought to guarantee an experiential basis of concepts by identifying concept attainment with learning a disposition to provide appropriate verbal and nonverbal responses to specified stimuli. Thus, learning to talk a language is said to involve forming such habits as that of saying "red" when there are red patches, or "pain" upon encountering criterial pain behaviors; paradigmatic of learning to understand a language is learning to bring the slab when someone says "slab."

In its more sophisticated manifestations, contemporary empiricism has argued that a concept is specified, in part, by reference to the kinds of evidence that are typically employed in justifying claims that something falls under that concept. Thus, the connection between the concept *pain* and pain behavior is mediated by a theory according to which giving the meaning of "pain" is, in part, specifying those behaviors that would warrant its application.

Although such versions of empiricism undoubtedly escape the charge of psychologizing, it is less clear that they avoid other traditional objections that have been raised against empiricism in its classic form. In particular, it may plausibly be objected that they fail to provide convincing analyses either of theoretical concepts or of the justification of existential claims about theoretical entities.

Very often, in the natural sciences, an investigator is confronted with a syndrome of observable phenomena, the occurrence of any large proper subset of which provides a reliable basis for the prediction of the remainder, even though it is implausible to argue that any of the phenomena cause any of the others. In such cases, the relevant form of explanation often consists in postulating some unobserved processes, events, or states to whose agency the occurrence of the syndrome is directly or indirectly attributable.

A number of factors may be relevant to determining whether such a postulation is warranted. Among these are the extent to which the data permit the elaboration of an account of theoretically interesting relations among the unobservables (as, e.g., dominance or connectedness in genetic theory, or valence in chemistry); the extent to which the postulations license inferences about those observables that are not included in the initial syndrome (as, e.g., the prediction of the phenomena of perceptual defense on the basis of the Freudian postulation of a censorship mechanism), and so on.

MATERIALISM AND INFERRED ENTITIES

The relevance of these remarks is that it is sometimes suggested that certain uses of psychological language in ordinary and technical discourse may be understood on the model of theoretical postulations in science. On the suggested analogy, behavior takes on the role of the observed syndrome and some mental event or state corresponds to the inferred entity.[2] According to this account then, learning to use everyday psychological language involves being introduced to the culturally accepted views concerning *which* mental states are involved in the etiology of which behaviors. Applying psychological predicates in the second person is then a case of making the inferences that are licensed by those views. The use of mental terms in scientific theories is thus held to be continuous with certain of their ordinary language uses, except that, in psychology, mental terms are explicitly taken to designate theoretical entities, and the explanations in which such terms figure are explicitly subject to conditions of simplicity and rigor.

Advocates of this position argue that it makes sense of the relations between, for example, talk about pain behavior and talk about pain in a way in which neither behaviorism nor dualism manages to. On the one hand, the inferred-entity account, when held in conjunction with a realistic interpretation of theoretical terms, makes it clear why behaviorists have failed to demonstrate the logical sufficiency of statements about behavior for psychological statements: existential statements about theoretical entities are *always* logically independent of

---

[2] Cf. Hilary Putnam, "Minds and Machines," in *Dimensions of Mind*, ed. Sidney Hook (New York: Collier Books, and London: Collier-Macmillan Ltd., 1960), 138–164, and C. S. Chihara and J. A. Fodor, "Operationalism and Ordinary Language: A Critique of Wittgenstein," *American Philosophical Quarterly*, II, 4 (October 1965), 281–295.

statements about the observable data. On the other hand, the present suggestion accounts for the peculiar intimacy of the relation between statements about behavior and statements about mental states, in a way in which dualistic theories do not. For if ϕs are, in the first instance, entities that are postulated in order to explain the ϕ-behavior syndrome, it is evident that the occurrence of the ϕ-behavior syndrome must provide the best possible prima facie evidence for ascriptions of ϕ.

The suggestion that the justification of second-person mental ascriptions is analogous to the justification of existential claims about theoretical entities must be sharply distinguished from the traditional claim that second-person mental ascriptions are somehow based upon analogies. The latter view is, perhaps, best interpreted as an ontogenetic hypothesis about how we might in fact come to entertain the suspicion that the behavior of other people is contingent upon antecedent or concurrent mental states, processes, and events: having noted that our own behavior has such antecedents, and having taken note of the similarity between the behavior we produce and the behavior of other people, we hypothesize correspondingly similar mental operations.

It is unclear that this speculation is either logically coherent or psychologically plausible. But even if it is a fact that no one who had never himself had pains or intentions would think of ascribing them to others, that fact would be largely irrelevant to the *justification* of such ascriptions. Traditional objections to the "argument" from analogy have correctly maintained that it is a poor inductive extrapolation that must base itself upon one case. This consideration does not, however, impugn the inferred-entity account of second-person psychological ascriptions. For if we distinguish between discovery and justification, we may correspondingly distinguish between the occasion that suggests the attribution of pains to others (conceivably having a pain oneself) and the character of the justification for such attributions (viz., that they provide the simplest systematic account of what one observes about other people's behavior).

I do not wish here to discuss the question of whether or not mental entities are plausibly treated as inferred entities. But it is important to understand the consequences of assuming that they are, since these consequences bear upon the truth of materialism in a way that has not previously been noted. I shall argue that it is not an historical accident but a simple consideration of coherence that accounts for the fact that the inferred-entity view of how one justifies the application of mental predicates is invariably held in conjunction with a materialist view of their denotata.

ONTOLOGICAL STATUS OF INFERRED ENTITIES

A reasonable reaction to the suggestion that mental states are profitably compared to theoretical entities is to remark upon its prima facie unnaturalness. Among the paradigms of theoretical entities are, for example, the microparticles of physics. But what, after all, do pains and photons have in common?

However, this line of thought badly misses the point. For to say that the referent of a term is a theoretical entity is not to provide an ontological classification—that is, is not to say what *kind* of entity it is. Rather, it is to emphasize the way in which existence claims about that entity are justified. If there are trees on Mars, then such trees are theoretical entities. Not because the putative Martian flora are in some way more mysterious or less substantial than our own, but only because our information about them is (currently) arrived at by inferences from spectroscopic analyses, seasonal color changes, and so on. At the moment when observational investigation of the Martian landscape does become possible, then existential claims about Martian trees will ipso facto become verifiable by observation, and Martian trees will ipso facto cease to be theoretical entities.[3]

Since whether or not we say of an entity that it is inferred is a question solely of the sort of justificatory arguments we use to substantiate claims about its existence, the line between observed and inferred entities is just as hard to draw as the line between observation and inference. It is, indeed, the same line. I think that there is a strong temptation to say that the larger viruses are not inferred entities *any more* —specifically because of the electron microscope. Yet it is possible to maintain that the argument from shadows on the plate to viruses on the slide is fully as complex as the argument from spectroscopic results to vegetation on Mars. What we decide to call an observation is in part determined by what we feel comfortable about calling an instrument of observation. Places in which telescopes are employed are called observatories for reasons that are not unrelated to the fact that

---

[3] R. Abelson has suggested to me a way out of the apparent paradox—namely, that we call an entity "theoretical" only when existence claims about *all* entities of that kind are based upon inferential evidence, that is, that no member of a class of entities is theoretical if any member of that class has been observed. This allows us to say either that Martian trees are theoretical entities (i.e., because they are *Martian* trees and no tree growing on Mars has yet been observed) or that Martian trees are *not* theoretical entities because they are Martian *trees* and observations of trees (albeit of trees growing on Earth) are not rare. In short, there are two concepts that are in need of simultaneous adjustment: the concept of a theoretical entity and the concept of two entities being of the same kind. If slack develops in one place, it can be taken up in the other.

no one would want to hold the craters on the moon to be theoretical entities.

I have said that the line between observation and inference is hard to *draw*, not that it is hard to stipulate. One can always decide that certain predicates, and only those, constitute one's "observation vocabulary." The difficulty lies, notoriously, in justifying such decisions. If the present view of the distinction between theoretical and observed entities is deflationary, that is because the previous attempts to draw the line between observation and inference at some epistemologically interesting point—for example, by holding that only terms for "qualia" are to count as observation terms—have uniformly proved too weak to provide an acceptable account of the justification of claims about theoretical entities, even in well-entrenched scientific theories.[4]

It appears that there is no a priori answer to the question "Where does a theory confront the data?" In principle, any nonlogical term in the vocabulary of a theory is a possible observation term. So long as no law of nature prohibits the observation of what a term denotes, whether or not observations of its denotata do in fact play a role in the confirmation of some theory depends solely upon our ingenuity in inventing instruments of observation and in devising experiments in which such instruments may be deployed. So far no philosopher has provided very convincing reasons for dismissing as a *façon de parler* scientists' occasional claims to have observed chromosomes, microparticles, distant nebulae, and so on, or for supposing that there is need for a strict sense of "strictly," in terms of which what was strictly observed in such cases were only patches and traces.

REALISM AND MATERIALISM

If, as we have supposed, the claim that T is an inferred entity is a de facto claim about the way in which existential statements about Ts are in fact justified, certain conclusions follow that are directly relevant to the inferred-entity view of psychological terms. In particular, if the assertion that T is an inferred entity is logically equivalent to the assertion that the sorts of arguments that are used to establish its existence do not in fact include reference to alleged observations of Ts, then the claim that T is an inferred entity can be true *only where it is logically possible to observe* (makes sense to speak of observing) *that something is a T*. Another way of making the same point is that on a realistic analysis of theoretical entities it makes no sense to say

---

[4] Cf. Carl G. Hempel, "The Empiricist Criterion of Meaning," in *Logical Positivism*, ed. A. J. Ayer (New York: The Free Press, 1959), 108–129.

that something is *necessarily* a theoretical entity, since statements of the form "*T* has not been observed" are never analytic in cases in which *T* ranges over physical entities, states, events, and so on.

On this analysis, claims about *inferences* to *T* can be true only where talk about *observations* of *T* makes sense. It is this consequence of the realistic view of theoretical entities that has serious implications for the inferred-entity account of second-person psychological ascriptions. For, so far, the inferred-entity account has not provided for the possibility, in principle, of the observational verification of such ascriptions. On the contrary, it looks as though the claim is that the existence of other people's psychological states is *necessarily* inferred since, prima facie, there is no sense in talking of directly observing other people's mental states. If, however, "*X* observationally verified the truth of *P*" is logically false wherever *P* is a second-person psychological ascription, then it follows that the claim that psychological entities are inferred entities is simply the denial of a necessarily false statement and hence itself necessarily true. But this in turn entails that the notion of a theoretical term is somehow being misused when second-person psychological predicates are likened to such terms since, as we have just seen, it is characteristic of bona fide theoretical entities that statements asserting that they *are* theoretical entities must invariably be contingent.

It should be emphasized that the present argument is not impugned by the fact that there is a perfectly good ordinary-language use of such remarks as "*X* observed that *Y* was in pain." For the whole point about the inferred-entity view is that it offers an analysis of such remarks according to which they too announce inferential judgments. That is, according to the inferred-entity view, the cases in which we (properly, but colloquially) claim to have directly observed that some psychological predicate applies are simply those cases in which our (presumably unconscious) inferences from behavior to psychological state are based on unusually good evidence—for example, in which a very substantial or very reliable part of the behavior syndrome that is characteristically associated with the psychological state is on view. Now the present argument claims that for there to be any sense to the assertion that the justification of a certain existential statement in a theory is inferential there must be something that that theory would, in principle, count as a corresponding observational justification of that statement. But the inferred-entity theory does not count as observations those verifications of second-person mental ascriptions that would be described as observational in ordinary language.

The argument that we have been considering does not by any means show that the inferred-entity account of second-person mental ascriptions is false. But it does show that that account is incoherent unless some sense can be given to the notion of direct observational verification of such ascriptions. And, as far as I can see, saying that the inferred-entity view must assign some sense to the notion of an observational confirmation of second-person psychological ascriptions is tantamount to saying that whoever holds the inferred-entity view is committed to some form of materialism. For if some statements of psychophysical identities are true, it could be claimed that some neurological observations would count as noninferential verifications of second-person mental ascriptions. If X has observed the neurological event N, and N is identical with the mental event E, it follows that X has observed E. (I assume—what is by no means obvious—that there is some sense of "observe" in which it is not intensional.) On the other hand, if one assumes that *no* psychophysical identity statements are true, it is extremely unclear what other candidates for observational verifications of second-person mental ascriptions the inferred-entity view could possibly offer.

ARGUMENTS AGAINST MATERIALISM

Problems about materialism are thus linked with other problems currently central in the philosophy of mind. We shall presently see that they also involve some rather general issues in the theory of language. In the remainder of this chapter, we shall examine a number of questions about the status of the psychophysical identity statements in terms of which materialism is articulated. We turn first to a discussion of what is perhaps the most important argument for the view that no statement of the form "x is y" could be significant where x is a mental term, y is a physiological term, "is" means identity, and all terms bear their current senses.

This argument bases itself upon an appeal to an extended form of a principle of logic known as Leibniz' Law. Leibniz' Law states that no proposition of the form "x is identical with y" can be true unless, for each nonintensional predicate F, $Fx \equiv Fy$. That is, the law states that if x is identical with y, then every nonintensional predicate true of x is also true of y and vice versa.

Now it has frequently been suggested that Leibniz' Law can be extended to provide a further condition upon the truth of identity statements. In particular what has been called the Law of Transferable Epithets states that if x is identical with y, and if Fx makes sense (is linguistically possible), then Fy must also make sense (be linguistically possible).

If the Law of Transferable Epithets is true, it would appear to have some serious implications for materialistic accounts of mental predicates. For example, it clearly makes sense to say that the firing of neuron N took place three inches from the base of Smith's skull. Therefore, according to the Law of Transferable Epithets, the firing of neuron N could not be identical with, say, one of Smith's wishes unless it also made sense to say that the wish took place three inches from the base of his skull. But since this latter remark is alleged to be nonsensical, it follows that the program of identifying wishes with neural events must be abandoned.

Three kinds of moves can be made against this argument; I am not at this point certain whether any of them is successful.

In the first place, it may simply be denied that such statements as "The wish happened three inches from the base of his skull" are properly described as absurd, nonsensical, and so on. For, it may be said, even though such statements certainly *sound* odd, no violation of a linguistic rule is involved in making them. Analogously, it might be said that the oddity of claiming that one craves a cool refreshing drink of H_2O is not an argument against the chemical theory of water. For, though that would be an odd-sounding thing to claim to crave, the oddity presumably cannot be traced to the violation of any rule of language.

The argument hinges on the fact that it is in general not clear which of the indefinitely many regularities that are true of our use of a word ought to be attributed to the operation of the rules that determine the meaning of the word.[5] Thus, it is perhaps a statistically certifiable regularity about "H_2O" that it is more often used by persons who possess a high-school degree than by persons who do not. But, clearly, no one would suppose that that regularity is in any sense a consequence of a linguistic rule governing the use of "H_2O," or that the fact that that regularity obtains contributes in any sense to the meaning "H_2O." Similarly, it is a regularity about "H_2O" that it is characteristically used in technical contexts. But it is by no means obvious that departing from that regularity ought to be counted as inventing a new sense of "H_2O." Nor is it a good argument against the identification of H_2O with water that references to the latter occur in contexts in which references to the former would be odd.

By parity of argument, according to the materialist, oddities may result when one departs from the regularity that predicates of spatial location are not to be applied to such terms as "wish." But unless it is demonstrated that such departures constitute violations of the meaning rules of English, the oddities they engender provide no case against those psychophysical identity statements in which "wish" appears. Still

[5] For discussion of this, cf. Jerry A. Fodor, "On Knowing What We Would Say," *The Philosophical Review*, LXXIII, 2 (April 1964), 198–212.

less do they indicate that allowing the application of spatial predicates to wishes ipso facto constitutes an equivocation on "wish."

This is one of the points, it seems to me, at which the philosopher must find his lack of a general theory of the semantics of natural languages most vexing. In the absence of a well-motivated account of the differences between those regularities that are the consequence of a speaker's adherence to meaning rules and those that are not, it is hard to see what ought to be deduced from the truth of the allegation that a given way of talking is odd. Correspondingly, in the absence of a well-motivated account of change of meaning, it is hard to know how to decide when departing from a regularity that some word obeys amounts to an implicit equivocation on the word. It should be emphasized that appeals to the naïve intuitions of speakers can be of relatively little use in deciding these issues—first, because the cases about which philosophers disagree are, not surprisingly, precisely those cases about which intuition tends to be unclear; second, because we have no way of distinguishing those intuitions that can properly be attributed to the informant's linguistic mastery from those that stem from his philosophical commitments. No doubt we ought to believe an informant who tells us that it sounds odd to attribute places to wishes; but must we also believe him when he intuits that the source of the oddity is linguistic?[6] (Needless to say, this question is also pertinent when one serves as one's own informant.)

In short, the materialist can correctly argue that the fact that a way of talking is odd is not a conclusive reason for abandoning the premises that lead one to talk that way. His antagonist can reply, equally plausibly, that it is at best not clear that the materialist is talking sense when he states a psychophysical identity and that one ought, in general, to avoid ways of talking that may be nonsensical. Barring an account of meaning on which both sides can agree, the argument would appear to rest there.

A more interesting line of defense for the materialist would perhaps be to deny that the putative Law of Transferable Epithets is valid. That is, he might both maintain that there are circumstances in which it would be rational to accept an identification that violated that law and deny that such circumstances invariably involve fallacies of equivocation.

The point to be noted rests on an asymmetry between Leibniz' Law and the Law of Transferable Epithets. In particular, the denial of Leibniz's Law trivially implies contradictions if we permit substitutivity of identity to operate as usual. That is, from Fx and not Fy and "x is identical with y," it is possible to derive both Fx and *not Fx*. Our

---

[6] For further discussion, cf. Fodor, *op. cit.*

grounds for refusing to accept any identification that violates Leibniz' Law are thus as good as our grounds for requiring arguments to be consistent.

However, no corresponding consideration holds in the case of the Law of Transferable Epithets. In particular, from the premises that "The form of words 'Fx' makes sense," "x is identical with y," and "The form of words 'Fy' makes no sense, no contradiction follows. Substitutivity of identity does not hold across quotation marks, roughly because what makes sense depends upon what linguistic conventions have in fact been adopted, and it is surely logically possible that conventions should have been adopted for "Fx," and that x should in fact be identical with y, yet that no conventions should have been adopted for "Fy."

One might put it that "We say ———" and "We do not say ———" are themselves intensional contexts. It is therefore hardly surprising that Leibniz' Law should fail to hold for terms that occur in those contexts.

Given the possibility in principle of violating the Law of Transferable Epithets, it is not too hard to find cases in the history of science where it is tempting to say that that law was in fact violated. It appears that scientific discoveries do sometimes provide for ways of talking to which no sense could previously have been assigned. Nor is it invariably evident in such cases that the intuitively correct analysis is that the meanings of key terms have been altered.

It seems clear, for example, that prior to the adoption of atomic theories of matter, no definite sense could have been attached to the claim that the smallest sample of water is larger than the smallest sample of hydrogen, or to any similar assertion. I suppose it would now be universally admitted, on the one hand, that some such claims are meaningful and true, and, on the other, that it is implausible to say that words like "water" underwent a change of meaning when the atomic theory was adopted. Similarly, it is often noted that it requires the assumption that the Earth is round in order to render coherent speculations about the distance around the Earth. Here again, it is hard to see how a case could be made for an interpretation on which the sentence "The Earth is round" is equivocal. For that would presumably entail that there is or was one sense of "Earth" in which "The Earth is round" is logically false and one sense of "Earth" in which "The Earth is round" is logically true so that, in either sense, to make the empirical discovery that the Earth is round is logically impossible.

There remains to be discussed one further counter to the use of the Law of Transferable Epithets in order to demonstrate the incoherence of statements that articulate psychophysical identities. It may plausibly be suggested that the materialist's apparent violation of the Law of Transferable Epithets derives not from supposing that there are true psychophysical identity statements, but rather from supposing that the variables in such statements range over *entities*. In particular, on the present view, the materialist thesis should be so formulated as to involve mental and physiological *states*. Thus, a typical psychophysical identity statement would be "Having a wish is being in such and such a physiological condition" rather than "A wish is such and such a physiological condition." Since, for example, spatial predicates do not apply to states but to the entities that are in them ("John is three feet from the door," but not "Having an inflamed tonsil is three feet from the door"), such predicates will apply to *neither* the neurological *nor* the mental terms that are involved in psychophysical identity statements; hence the strictures upon the transferability of epithets will be trivially satisfied by such statements.

If there is a difficulty with this sort of suggestion, it is that it places a restriction upon the grammar of statements that relate neurological and psychological terms that is not satisfied by paradigm cases of statements that clearly do articulate theoretical identifications. Consider, for example, colds. It is true to say that having a cold is just having a certain set of symptoms with a certain etiology. That is, there is a state-to-state identification between colds and physiological conditions that is analogous to the state-to-state identifications that we are supposing may obtain for wishes and neurological conditions. But in the case of colds it is proper to say that *since* having a cold is just being in a certain condition, it follows that a cold is just that condition. That is, we are committed both to "Having a cold is having a certain set of symptoms with a certain etiology," *and* to "A cold is a certain set of symptoms with a certain etiology," *and* to the principle that the former of these statements entails the latter. If, however, we allow the same inference in the case of psychological states and physiological states—for example, if we are allowed to infer that since having a pain is just being in such and such a physiological state, it follows that the pain is just that state—we find ourselves once again committed to locutions that are in apparent violation of the Law of Transferable Epithets.

In short, the suggestion that psychophysical identities be construed as state-to-state identities does manage to provide a way of holding a materialist view without violating the strictures on transferability. But it does so at the price of an apparently arbitrary restriction against employing a form of inference that otherwise appears to be valid: the inference from "Having an X is just being in state Y" to "an X is a Y."

It seems to me that, on balance, the case against the possibility that some psychophysical identity statements are significant has not been proved. Nor does it seem that the dispute is likely to be settled until more insight has been gained into the criteria for meaning change in natural languages on the one hand, and, on the other, into the relation between meaning change and theoretical revision in the empirical sciences. That both problems are likely to be difficult is indicated by the consideration that the first directly involves the distinction between analytic and synthetic propositions, while the second involves questions about the conventional status of scientific theories and laws.

MATERIALISM AND THE RELATION BETWEEN PSYCHOLOGY AND NEUROLOGY

For purposes of the present investigation, we are primarily interested in materialism as it bears upon problems about psychological explanation. We need, therefore, to clarify the implications of the materialist view for an account of the relations between psychological and neurological theories. I shall argue that while it is by no means evident that materialism must be regarded as conceptually incoherent, it is equally unclear that the truth of materialism would entail the views of the relation between psychology and neurology that have often been held in conjunction with it. In particular, to claim that mind states and brain states are contingently identical need not be to hold that psychological theories are reducible to neurological theories. Nor would the truth of materialism entail that the relevant relation between psychological and neurological constructs is that the latter provide "microanalyses" of the former. It is to these issues that we now proceed.

Let us commence by trying to form some picture of how the problem of the relation between psychology and neurology emerges during the course of attempts to provide systematic scientific explanations of behavior.

Such attempts have characteristically exhibited two phases that, although they may be simultaneous in point of history, are nevertheless distinguishable in point of logic. In the first phase, the psychologist attempts to arrive at theories that provide what are often referred to as "functional" characterizations of the mechanisms responsible for the production of behavior. To say that the psychologist is seeking functional characterizations of psychological constructs is at least to say that, in this phase of explanation, the criteria employed for individuating such constructs are based primarily upon hypotheses about the role they play in the etiology of behavior. Such hypotheses are constrained by two general considerations. On the one hand, by the principle that the psychological states, processes, and so on hypothesized to be responsible for the production of behavior must be supposed to be sufficiently complex to account for whatever behavioral capacities the organism can be demonstrated to possess; on the other, by the principle that specific aspects of the character of the organism's behavior must be explicable by reference to specific features of the hypothesized underlying states and processes or of their interactions.

Thus, for example, a psychologist might seek to explain failures of memory by reference to the decay of a hypothetical memory "trace," an attempt being made to attribute to the trace properties that will account for such observed features of memory as selectivity, stereotyping, and so forth. As more is discovered about memory—for example, about the effects of pathology upon memory, or about differences between "short-" and "long-term" memory—the properties attributed to the trace, and to whatever other psychological systems are supposed to interact with it, must be correspondingly elaborated. It is, of course, the theorist's expectation that, at some point, speculations about the character of the trace will lead to confirmable experimental predictions about previously unnoticed aspects of memory, thus providing independent evidence for the claim that the trace does in fact have the properties it is alleged to have.

To say that, in the first phase of psychological explanation, the primary concern is with determining the functional character of the states and processes involved in the etiology of behavior is thus to say that, at that stage, the hypothesized psychological constructs are individuated primarily or solely by reference to their alleged causal consequences. What one knows (or claims to know) about such constructs is the effects their activity has upon behavior. It follows that phase-one psychological theories postulate functionally equivalent mechanisms when and only when they postulate constructs of which the behavioral consequences are, in theoretically relevant respects, identical.

This sort of point has sometimes been made by comparing first-phase psychological theories with descriptions of a "machine table"—that is, of the sets of directions for performing computations—of a digital computer. Neurological theories, correspondingly, are likened to descriptions of the "hardware"; that is, of the physical machinery into which such tables are programmed.[7] Since two physical realizations of the same table—that is, two computers capable of performing the mathematically identical set of computations in mathematically identical ways—may differ arbitrarily in their physical structure, mathematical equivalence is independent of physical similarity: two machines may, in this sense, share functionally equivalent "psychological"

[7] Cf. Putnam, *op. cit.*

mechanisms even though they have neither parts nor configurations of parts in common.

The second phase of psychological explanation has to do with the specification of those biochemical systems that do, in fact, exhibit the functional characteristics enumerated by phase-one theories. The image that suggests itself to many psychologists is that of opening a "black box": having arrived at a phase-one theory of the kinds of operations performed by the mechanisms that are causally responsible for behavior, one then "looks inside" to see whether or not the nervous system does in fact contain parts capable of performing the alleged functions. The situation is more complicated, however, than this image suggests since the notion of a "part," when applied to the nervous systems of organisms, is less than clear. The physiological psychologist's task of determining what, if any, organization into subsystems the nervous system of an organism exhibits is precisely the problem of determining whether the nervous system has subsystems whose functional characteristics correspond with those required by antecedently plausible psychological theories.

The two phases of psychological explanation thus condition one another. On the one hand, it is clear that a psychological theory that attributes to an organism a state or process that the organism has no physiological mechanisms capable of realizing is ipso facto incorrect. If memory is a matter of forming traces, then there must be subsystems of the nervous system that are capable of going from one steady state to another and that are capable of remaining in the relevant states for periods that are at least comparable to known retention periods. If no such mechanisms exist, then the trace is the wrong model for the functional organization of memory.

On the other hand, the relevant notion of a neurological subsystem is that of a biochemical mechanism whose operation can correspond to some state or process that is postulated by a satisfactory psychological theory. To say that the goals of physiological psychology are set by the attempt to find mechanisms that correspond to certain functions is to say that it is the psychological theory that articulates these functions that determines the principle of individuation for neurological mechanisms. Once again, analogies to the analysis of less complicated systems may be helpful. What makes a carburetor part of an engine is not the spatial contiguity of its own parts (the parts of fuel injectors exhibit no such contiguity) nor is it the homogeneity of the materials of which it is composed. It is rather the fact that its operation corresponds to a function that is detailed in the theory of internal-combustion engines and that there is no sub- or superpart of the carburetor whose operation corresponds to that function.

The problem, then, is one of fit and mutual adjustment: on the one hand, there is a presumed psychological theory, which requires possibly quite specific, complex, and detailed operations on the part of the neurological mechanisms that underlie behavior; on the other hand, there is a putative articulation of the nervous system into subsystems that must be matched to these functional characteristics and that must also attempt to maximize anatomical, morphological, and biochemical plausibility. This extremely complex situation is sometimes abbreviated by materialist philosophers into the claim that identification between psychological and neurological states is established on the basis of constant correlation and simplicity. We have seen that it is an open question whether the relevant relation is identification. Our present point is that the evidence required to justify postulating the relation is something considerably more complex than mere correlation. It is rather a nice adjustment of the psychological characterization of function to considerations of neurological plausibility, and vice versa.

MICROANALYSIS AND FUNCTIONAL ANALYSIS

This discussion of the way in which psychological and neurological theories integrate during the course of the development of scientific explanations of behavior is, to be sure, no more than the barest sketch. But, insofar as the sketch is at all plausible, it suggests that the reductivist view of the relation between psychological and neurological theories is seriously misleading, even if one accepts a materialistic account of the relation between psychological and neurological constructs. The suggestion is that if materialism is true, a completed account of behavior would contain statements that identify certain neural mechanisms as having functions detailed during the course of phase-one theory construction and that some such statements would hold for each psychological construct. But such statements, clearly, are quite different in kind from those that articulate paradigmatic cases of reductive analysis.

This distinction seems to have been pretty widely missed by materialists, particularly in the literature that relates discussions of materialism to problems about the unity of science. Oppenheim and Putnam, for example, are explicit in referring to neurological theories, such as those of Hebb, as constituting "micro-reductions" of the corresponding psychological theories of memory, learning, motivation, and so on. On the Oppenheim-Putnam account, "the essential feature of micro-reduction is that the branch [of science] B_1 [which provides the micro-reduction of B_2] deals with the parts of the objects dealt with by B_2." [8]

Our present point is that it is difficult to understand how this could be the correct model for the relation between psychological and neurological theories. Psychological entities (sensations, for example) are not readily thought of as capable of being microanalyzed into *anything*, least of all neurons or states of neurons. Pains do not have parts, so brain cells are not parts of pains.

It is, in short, conceivable that there may be true psychophysical identity statements, but it seems inconceivable that such statements are properly analyzed as expressing what Place (1956) has called identities of composition, that is, as expressing relations between wholes and their parts. It should be emphasized that not all statements of identities *are* identities of composition. Compare "Her hat is a bundle of straw" with "He is the boy I knew in Chicago."

It is worth pursuing at some length the difference between the present view of the relation between psychological and neurological constructs and the view typical of reductivist materialism. In reductive analysis (microanalysis), one asks: "What does X consist of?" and the answer has the form of a specification of the microstructure of Xs. Thus: "What does water consist of?" "Two atoms of hydrogen linked with one atom of oxygen." "What does lightning consist of?" "A stream of electrons." And so on. In typical cases of functional analysis, by contrast, one asks about a part of a mechanism *what role it plays* in the activities that are characteristic of the mechanism as a whole: "What does the camshaft do?" "It opens the valves, permitting the entry into the cylinder of fuel, which will then be detonated to drive the piston." Successful microanalysis is thus often contingent upon the development of powerful instruments of observation or precise methods of dissection. Successful functional analysis, on the other hand, requires an appreciation of the sorts of activity that are characteristic of a mechanism and of the contribution made by the functioning of each part of the mechanism to the economy of the whole.

Since microanalysis and functional analysis are very different ways of establishing relations between scientific theories, or between ordinary-language descriptions, conceptual difficulties may result when the vocabulary of one kind of analysis is confounded with the vocabulary of the other.

If I speak of a device as a "camshaft," I am implicitly identifying it by reference to its physical structure, and so I am committed to the view that it exhibits a characteristic and specifiable decomposition into physical parts. But if I speak of the device as a "valve lifter," I

---

[8] Cf. Oppenheim and Putnam, *op. cit.*, p. 6.

am identifying it by reference to its function and I therefore undertake no such commitment. There is, in particular, no sense to the question "What does a valve lifter consist of?" If this is understood as a request for microanalysis—that is, as analogous to such questions as "What does water consist of?" (There *is*, of course, sense to the question "What does *this* valve lifter consist of?" but the generic valve lifter must be *functionally* defined, and functions do not have parts.) One might put it that being a valve lifter is not reducible to (is not a matter of) being a collection of rods, springs, and atoms, in the sense in which being a camshaft is. The kinds of questions that it makes sense to ask about camshafts need not make sense, and are often impertinent, when asked about valve lifters.

It is, then, conceivable that serious confusions could be avoided if we interpreted statements that relate psychological and neurological constructs not as articulating microanalyses but as attributing certain psychological functions to corresponding neurological systems. For example, philosophers and psychologists who have complained that it is possible to trace an input from afferent to central to efferent neurological systems without once encountering motives, strategies, drives, needs, hopes, along with the rest of the paraphernalia of psychological theories, have been right in one sense but wrong in another, just as one would be if one argued that a complete mechanical account of the operation of an internal-combustion engine never encounters such a thing as a valve lifter. In both cases, the confusion occurs when a term that properly figures in functional accounts of mechanisms is confounded with terms that properly appear in mechanistic accounts, so that one is tempted to think of the function of a part as though it were itself one part among others.

From a functional point of view, a camshaft is a valve lifter and *this* valve lifter (i.e., this particular mechanism for lifting valves) may be "nothing but" a camshaft. But a mechanistic account of the operations of internal-combustion engines does not seek to replace the concept of a valve lifter with the concept of a camshaft, nor does it seek to "reduce" the former to the latter. What it does do is to explain *how* the valves get lifted: that is, what mechanical transactions are involved when the camshaft lifts the valves. In the same way, presumably, neurological theories seek to explain what biochemical transactions are involved when drives are reduced, motives entertained, objects perceived, and so on.

In short, drives, motives, strategies, and such are, on the present view, internal states postulated in attempts to account for behavior, perception, memory, and other phenomena in the domain of psychological theories. In completed accounts, they could presumably serve to characterize the functional aspects of neurological mechanisms;

that is, they would figure in explanations of how such mechanisms operate to determine the molar behavior of an organism, its perceptual capacities, and so on. But this does not entail that drives, motives, and strategies have microanalyses in terms of neurological systems any more than valve lifters can be microanalyzed into camshafts.

There are still further philosophically pertinent differences between the suggestion that psychophysical identity statements should be understood as articulating functional analyses and the suggestion that they should be analyzed as micro-reductions.

When, in paradigmatic cases, entities in one theory are reduced to entities in another, it is presupposed that both theories have available conceptual mechanisms for saying what the entities have in common. For example, given that water can be "reduced" to H_2O, it is possible to say what all samples of water have in common either in the language of viscosity, specific gravity, and so on at the macrolevel, or in chemical language at the microlevel. It is patent that functional analysis need not share this property of reductive analysis. When we identify a certain mousetrap with a certain mechanism, we do not thereby commit ourselves to the possibility of saying in mechanistic terms what all members of the set of mousetraps have in common. Because it is (roughly) a sufficient condition for being a mousetrap that a mechanism be customarily *used* in a certain way, there is nothing in principle that requires that a pair of mousetraps *have* any shared mechanical properties. It is, indeed, because "mousetrap" is functionally rather than mechanically defined that "building a better mousetrap"—that is, building a mechanically novel mousetrap, which functions better than conventional mousetraps do—is a reasonable goal to set oneself.

It is a consequence of this consideration that the present interpretation of the relation between neurological and psychological constructs is compatible with very strong claims about the ineliminability of mental language from behavioral theories. Let us suppose that there are true psychophysical statements that identify certain neurological mechanisms as the ones that possess certain psychologically relevant functional properties. It still remains quite conceivable that identical psychological functions could sometimes be ascribed to anatomically heterogeneous neural mechanisms. In that case, mental language will be required to state the conditions upon such ascriptions of functional equivalence. It is, in short, quite conceivable that a parsing of the nervous system by reference to anatomical or morphological similarities may often fail to correspond in any uniform way to its parsing in terms of psychological function. Whenever this occurs, explicit reference to the character of such functions will be required if we are to be able to say what we take the brain states that we classify together to have in common.

Every mousetrap can be identified with some mechanism, and being a mousetrap can therefore be identified with being a member of some (indefinite) set of possible mechanisms. But enumerating the set is not a way of dispensing with the notion of a mousetrap; that notion is required to say what all the members of the set have in common and, in particular, what credentials would be required to certify a putative new member as belonging to the set.

Such considerations may be extended to suggest not only that a *plausible* version of materialism will need to view psychological theories as articulating the functional characteristics of neural mechanisms, but also that that is the *only* version of materialism that is likely to prove coherent. Consider the following argument, which Sellars has offered as a refutation of materialism:

> Suppose I am experiencing a circular red raw feel . . . (in certain cases) the most careful and sophisticated introspection will fail to refute the following statement: "There is a finite subregion ΔR of the raw feel patch ψr, and a finite time interval Δt, such that during Δt no property of ΔR changes."

The refutation may now proceed by appeal to Leibniz' Law. Suppose there is a brain state ϕ_r which is held to be identical with the psychological state ψ_r that one is in when one senses something red (i.e., with the "red raw feel"). Then substitution of ϕ_r for ψ_r permits the inference: there is a finite region ΔR of the brain state ϕ_r and a finite time interval Δt, such that during Δt no property of ΔR changes.

> But this, as even pre-Utopian neurophysiology shows us, is factually false. . . . Thus, during, say, 500 milliseconds, the 5° region at the center of my phenomenal circle does not change in any property, whereas no region of the physical brain-event can be taken small enough such that *none* of its properties change during a 500-millisecond period.[9]

The point of this argument is, I think, entirely independent of its appeal to such dubious psychological entities as "red raw feels." For it seems pretty clear that the principles we employ for individuating neurological states are in general different from, and logically inde-

---

[9] Paul E. Meehl, "The Compleat Autocerebroscopist: A Thought-Experiment on Professor Feigl's Mind-Body Identity Thesis," in *Mind, Matter, and Method: Essays in Philosophy and Science in Honor of Herbert Feigl*, ed. Paul K. Feyerabend and Grover Maxwell (Minneapolis: University of Minnesota Press, 1966), 103–180, where the argument is attributed to Sellars. [See pages 167ff. in that volume.]

pendent of, those that we employ for individuating psychological states. Since what counts as one sensation, one wish, one desire, one drive, and so on is not specified by reference to the organism's neurophysiology, it seems hardly surprising that an organism may persist in a given psychological condition while undergoing neurological change. If a materialist theory is so construed as to deny this, then materialism is certain to prove *contingently* false.

Nor does Sellars' argument depend solely upon the possibility of there being differences in "grain" between neurological and psychological variation. The problem is not just that slight changes in neurophysiology may be compatible with continuity of psychological state. It is rather that we have no right to assume a priori that the nervous system may not sometimes produce indistinguishable psychological effects by *radically* different physiological means. How much redundancy there may be in the nervous system is surely an open empirical question. It would be extraordinarily unwise if the claims for materialism or for the unity of science were to be formulated in such fashion as to require that for each distinguishable psychological state there must be one and only one corresponding brain state.

I see no way to accommodate such considerations that does not involve a wholesale employment of the notion of functional equivalence. For the point on which Sellars' argument turns is precisely that there may very well be sets of neurologically distinct brain states, whose members are nevertheless psychologically indistinguishable. In such cases, identification of the psychological state with any member of such a set produces problems with the substitutivity of identity.

It seems clear that a materialist can avoid these difficulties only at the price of assuming that the objects appropriate for identification with psychological states are sets of *functionally equivalent* neurological states. In particular, it must be true of any two members of such a set that an organism may alternate between them without thereby undergoing psychological change.

This is tantamount to saying that a materialist must recognize as scientifically relevant a taxonomy of neurological states according to their psychological functions. Such a taxonomy defines a "natural kind" (although very likely not the same natural kind as emerges from purely anatomical and biochemical considerations). Thus, a reasonable version of materialism might hold that psychological theories and neurological theories both involve taxonomies defined over the same objects (brain states), but according to different principles. What we require of the members of a set of anatomically similar brain states is *not* what we require of the members of a set of functionally equivalent brain states. Yet in neither case need the classification be arbitrary. The psychological consequences of being in one or another brain state are either distinguishable or they are not. If they are distinguishable, it is a question of fact whether or not the distinction is of the kind that psychological theories recognize as systematic and significant.

It is tempting to suppose that there must be only one principle of sorting (taxonomy by physical similarity), on pain of there otherwise being chaos, that either there is *one* kind of scientifically relevant similarity or there is *every* kind. It is, however, unnecessary to succumb to any such temptation. What justifies a taxonomy, what makes a kind "natural," is the power and generality of the theories that we are enabled to formulate when we taxonomize in that way. Classifying together all the entities that are made up of the same kinds of parts is one way of taxonomizing fruitfully, but if we can find other principles for sorting brain states, principles that permit simple and powerful accounts of the etiology of behavior, then that is itself an adequate justification for sorting according to those principles.

It would seem, then, that both the traditional approach to materialism and the traditional approach to the unity of science are in need of liberalization. In the first case, if he is to accommodate the sort of problem that Sellars has raised, the materialist will have to settle for identifications of psychological states with sets of functionally equivalent brain states, and this means that the materialist thesis is at best no clearer than the notoriously unclear notion of functional equivalence. In the second case, it appears that if the doctrine of the unity of science is to be preserved, it will have to require something less (or other) than reducibility as the relation between constructs in neurology and those in psychology. It seems, then, that scientific theories can fit together in more than one way, perhaps in many ways. If this is correct, then reduction is only one kind of example of a relation between scientific theories that satisfies reasonable constraints on the unity of science. It would be interesting to know what other kinds of examples there are.

HILARY PUTNAM

The Nature of Mental States

The typical concerns of the Philosopher of Mind might be represented by three questions: (1) How do we know that other people have pains? (2) Are pains brain states? (3) What is the analysis of the concept *pain*? I do not wish to discuss questions (1) and (3) in this paper. I shall say something about question (2).[1]

I. IDENTITY QUESTIONS

"Is pain a brain state?" (Or, "Is the property of having a pain at time *t* a brain state?")[2] It is impossible to discuss this question sensibly without saying something about the peculiar rules which have grown up in the course of the development of "analytical philosophy"—rules which, far from leading to an end to all conceptual confusions, themselves represent considerable conceptual confusion. These rules —which are, of course, implicit rather than explicit in the practice of most analytical philosophers—are (1) that a statement of the form

---

Reprinted from *Art, Mind, and Religion*, edited by W. H. Capitan and D. D. Merrill, Pittsburgh: University of Pittsburgh Press, 1967, 37–48. by permission of the publishers and Hilary Putnam; originally published under the title "Psychological Predicates," this has been changed at the request of the author.

[1] I have discussed these and related topics in the following papers: "Minds and Machines," in *Dimensions of Mind*, ed. Sidney Hook, New York, 1960, pp. 148–179; "Brains and Behavior," in *Analytical Philosophy, second series*, ed. Ronald Butler, Oxford, 1965, pp. 1–20; and "The Mental Life of Some Machines," in *Intentionality, Minds, and Perception*, ed. Hector-Neri Castañeda, Detroit, 1967, pp. 177–200.

[2] In this paper I wish to avoid the vexed question of the relation between *pains* and *pain states*. I only remark in passing that one common argument *against* identification of these two—viz., that a pain can be in one's arm but a state (of the organism) cannot be in one's arm—is easily seen to be fallacious.

"being A is being B" (e.g., "being in pain is being in a certain brain state") can be *correct* only if it follows, in some sense, from the meaning of the terms A and B; and (2) that a statement of the form "being A is being B" can be philosophically *informative* only if it is in some sense reductive (e.g. "being in pain is having a certain unpleasant sensation" is not philosophically informative; "being in pain is having a certain behavior disposition" is, if true, philosophically informative). These rules are excellent rules if we still believe that the program of reductive analysis (in the style of the 1930's) can be carried out; if we don't, then they turn analytical philosophy into a mug's game, at least so far as "is" questions are concerned.

In this paper I shall use the term 'property' as a blanket term for such things as being in pain, being in a particular brain state, having a particular behavior disposition, and also for magnitudes such as temperature, etc.—i.e., for things which can naturally be represented by one-or-more-place predicates or functors. I shall use the term 'concept' for things which can be identified with synonymy-classes of expressions. Thus the concept *temperature* can be identified (I maintain) with the synonymy-class of the word 'temperature.'[3] (This is like saying that the number 2 can be identified with the class of all pairs. This is quite a different statement from the peculiar statement that 2 *is* the class of all pairs. I do not maintain that concepts *are* synonymy-classes, whatever that might mean, but that they can be identified with synonymy-classes, for the purpose of formalization of the relevant discourse.)

The question "What is the concept *temperature?*" is a very "funny" one. One might take it to mean "What is temperature? Please take my question as a conceptual one." In that case an answer might be (pretend for a moment 'heat' and 'temperature' are synonyms) "temperature is heat," or even "the concept of temperature is the same concept as the concept of heat." Or one might take it to mean "What are *concepts*, really? For example, what is 'the concept of tempera-

[3] There are some well-known remarks by Alonzo Church on this topic. Those remarks do not bear (as might at first be supposed) on the identification of concepts with synonymy-classes as such, but rather support the view that (in formal semantics) it is necessary to retain Frege's distinction between the normal and the "oblique" use of expressions. That is, even if we say that the concept of temperature *is* the synonymy-class of the word 'temperature,' we must not thereby be led into the error of supposing that 'the concept of temperature' is synonymous with 'the synonymy-class of the word "temperature"'—for then 'the concept of temperature' and 'der Begriff der Temperatur' would not be synonymous, which they are. Rather, we must say that 'the concept of temperature' *refers to* the synonymy-class of the word 'temperature' (on this particular reconstruction); but that class is *identified* not as "the synonymy class to which such-and-such a word belongs," but in another way (e.g., as the synonymy-class whose members have such-and-such a characteristic use).

ture'?" In that case heaven knows what an "answer" would be. (Perhaps it would be the statement that concepts *can be identified with* synonymy-classes.)

Of course, the question "What is the property temperature?" is also "funny." And one way of interpreting it is to take it as a question about the concept of temperature. But this is not the way a physicist would take it.

The effect of saying that the property P_1 can be identical with the property P_2 only if the terms P_1, P_2 are in some suitable sense "synonyms" is, to all intents and purposes, to collapse the two notions of "property" and "concept" into a single notion. The view that concepts (intensions) *are* the same as properties has been explicitly advocated by Carnap (e.g., in *Meaning and Necessity*). This seems an unfortunate view, since "temperature is mean molecular kinetic energy" appears to be a perfectly good example of a true statement of identity of properties, whereas "the concept of temperature is the same concept as the concept of mean molecular kinetic energy" is simply false.

Many philosophers believe that the statement "pain is a brain state" violates some rules or norms of English. But the arguments offered are hardly convincing. For example, if the fact that I can know that I am in pain without knowing that I am in brain state S shows that pain cannot be brain state S, then, by exactly the same argument, the fact that I can know that the stove is hot without knowing that the mean molecular kinetic energy is high (or even that molecules exist) shows that it is *false* that temperature is mean molecular kinetic energy, physics to the contrary. In fact, all that immediately follows from the fact that I can know that I am in pain without knowing that I am in brain state S is that the concept of pain is not the same concept as the concept of being in brain state S. But either pain, or the state of being in pain, or some pain, or some pain state, might still be brain state S. After all, the concept of temperature is not the same concept as the concept of mean molecular kinetic energy. But temperature is mean molecular kinetic energy.

Some philosophers maintain that both 'pain is a brain state' and 'pain states are brain states' are unintelligible. The answer is to explain to these philosophers, as well as we can, given the vagueness of all scientific methodology, what sorts of considerations lead one to make an empirical reduction (i.e., to say such things as "water is H_2O," "light is electro-magnetic radiation," "temperature is mean molecular kinetic energy"). If, without giving reasons, he still maintains in the face of such examples that one cannot imagine parallel circumstances for the use of 'pains are brain states' (or, perhaps, 'pain states are brain states') one has grounds to regard him as perverse.

Some philosophers maintain that "P_1 is P_2" is something that can be true, when the 'is' involved is the 'is' of empirical reduction, only when the properties P_1 and P_2 are (a) associated with a spatio-temporal region; and (b) the region is one and the same in both cases. Thus "temperature is mean molecular kinetic energy" is an admissible empirical reduction, since the temperature and the molecular energy are associated with the same space-time region, but "having a pain in my arm is being in a brain state" is not, since the spatial regions involved are different.

This argument does not appear very strong. Surely no one is going to be deterred from saying that mirror images are light reflected from an object and then from the surface of a mirror by the fact that an image can be "located" three feet *behind* the mirror! (Moreover, one can always find *some* common property of the reductions one is willing to allow—e.g., temperature is mean molecular kinetic energy—which is not a property of some one identification one wishes to disallow. This is not very impressive unless one has an argument to show that the very purposes of such identification depend upon the common property in question.)

Again, other philosophers have contended that all the predictions that can be derived from the conjunction of neurophysiological laws with such statements as "pain states are such-and-such brain states" can equally well be derived from the conjunction of the same neurophysiological laws with "being in pain is correlated with such-and-such brain states," and hence (sic!) there can be no methodological grounds for saying that pains (or pain states) *are* brain states, as opposed to saying that they are *correlated* (invariantly) with brain states. This argument, too, would show that light is only correlated with electromagnetic radiation. The mistake is in ignoring the fact that, although the theories in question may indeed lead to the same predictions, they open and exclude different *questions*. "Light is invariantly correlated with electromagnetic radiation" would leave open the questions "What is the light then, if it isn't the same as the electromagnetic radiation?" and "What makes the light accompany the electromagnetic radiation?"—questions which are excluded by saying that the light *is* the electromagnetic radiation. Similarly, the purpose of saying that pains are brain states is precisely to exclude from empirical meaningfulness the questions "What is the pain, then, if it isn't the same as the brain state?" and "What makes the pain accompany the brain state?" If there are grounds to suggest that these questions represent, so to speak, the wrong way to look at the matter, then those grounds are grounds for a theoretical identification of pains with brain states.

If all arguments to the contrary are unconvincing, shall we then conclude that it is meaningful (and perhaps true) to say either that pains are brain states or that pain states are brain states?

(1) It is perfectly meaningful (violates no "rule of English," involves no "extension of usage") to say "pains are brain states."

(2) It is not meaningful (involves a "changing of meaning" or "an extension of usage," etc.) to say "pains are brain states."

My own position is not expressed by either (1) or (2). It seems to me that the notions "change of meaning" and "extension of usage" are simply so ill-defined that one cannot in fact say *either* (1) or (2). I see no reason to believe that either the linguist, or the man-on-the-street, or the philosopher possesses today a notion of "change of meaning" applicable to such cases as the one we have been discussing. The *job* for which the notion of change of meaning was developed in the history of the language was just a *much* cruder job than this one.

But, if we don't assert either (1) or (2)—in other words, if we regard the "change of meaning" issue as a pseudo-issue in this case—then how are we to discuss the question with which we started? "Is pain a brain state?"

The answer is to allow statements of the form "pain is *A*," where 'pain' and '*A*' are in no sense synonyms, and to see whether any such statement can be found which might be acceptable on empirical and methodological grounds. This is what we shall now proceed to do.

II. IS PAIN A BRAIN STATE?

We shall discuss "Is pain a brain state?," then. And we have agreed to waive the "change of meaning" issue.

Since I am discussing not what the concept of pain comes to, but what pain is, in a sense of 'is' which requires empirical theory-construction (or, at least, empirical speculation), I shall not apologize for advancing an empirical hypothesis. Indeed, my strategy will be to argue that pain is *not* a brain state, not on *a priori* grounds, but on the grounds that another hypothesis is more plausible. The detailed development and verification of my hypothesis would be just as Utopian a task as the detailed development and verification of the brain-state hypothesis. But the putting-forward, not of detailed and scientifically "finished" hypotheses, but of schemata for hypotheses, has long been a function of philosophy. I shall, in short, argue that pain is not a brain state, in the sense of a physical-chemical state of the brain (or even the whole nervous system), but another *kind* of state entirely. I propose the hypothesis that pain, or the state of being in pain, is a functional state of a whole organism.

To explain this it is necessary to introduce some technical notions. In previous papers I have explained the notion of a Turing Machine and discussed the use of this notion as a model for an organism. The notion of a Probabilistic Automaton is defined similarly to a Turing Machine, except that the transitions between "states" are allowed to be with various probabilities rather than being "deterministic." (Of course, a Turing Machine is simply a special kind of Probabilistic Automaton, one with transition probabilities 0, 1.) I shall assume the notion of a Probabilistic Automaton has been generalized to allow for "sensory inputs" and "motor outputs"—that is, the Machine Table specifies, for every possible combination of a "state" and a complete set of "sensory inputs," an "instruction" which determines the probability of the next "state," and also the probabilities of the "motor outputs." (This replaces the idea of the Machine as printing on a tape.) I shall also assume that the physical realization of the sense organs responsible for the various inputs, and of the motor organs, is specified, but that the "states" and the "inputs" themselves are, as usual, specified only "implicitly"—i.e., by the set of transition probabilities given by the Machine Table.

Since an empirically given system can simultaneously be a "physical realization" of many different Probabilistic Automata, I introduce the notion of a *Description* of a system. A Description of S where S is a system, is any true statement to the effect that S possesses distinct states $S_1, S_2, \ldots, S_n$ which are related to one another and to the motor outputs and sensory inputs by the transition probabilities given in such-and-such a Machine Table. The Machine Table mentioned in the Description will then be called the Functional Organization of S relative to that Description, and the S_i such that S is in state S_i at a given time will be called the Total State of S (at that time) relative to that Description. It should be noted that knowing the Total State of a system relative to a Description involves knowing a good deal about how the system is likely to "behave," given various combinations of sensory inputs, but does *not* involve knowing the physical realization of the S_i as, e.g., physical-chemical states of the brain. The S_i, to repeat, are specified only *implicitly* by the Description—i.e., specified *only* by the set of transition probabilities given in the Machine Table.

The hypothesis that "being in pain is a functional state of the organism" may now be spelled out more exactly as follows:

(1) All organisms capable of feeling pain are Probabilistic Automata.

(2) Every organism capable of feeling pain possesses at least one Description of a certain kind (i.e., being capable of feeling pain *is* possessing an appropriate kind of Functional Organization).

(3) No organism capable of feeling pain possesses a decomposition

into parts which separately possess Descriptions of the kind referred to in (2).

(4) For every Description of the kind referred to in (2), there exists a subset of the sensory inputs such that an organism with that Description is in pain when and only when some of its sensory inputs are in that subset.

This hypothesis is admittedly vague, though surely no vaguer than the brain-state hypothesis in its present form. For example, one would like to know more about the kind of Functional Organization that an organism must have to be capable of feeling pain, and more about the marks that distinguish the subset of the sensory inputs referred to in (4). With respect to the first question, one can probably say that the Functional Organization must include something that resembles a "preference function," or at least a preference partial ordering, and something that resembles an "inductive logic" (i.e., the Machine must be able to "learn from experience"). (The meaning of these conditions, for Automata models, is discussed in my paper "The Mental Life of Some Machines.") In addition, it seems natural to require that the Machine possess "pain sensors," i.e., sensory organs which normally signal damage to the Machine's body, or dangerous temperatures, pressures, etc., which transmit a special subset of the inputs, the subset referred to in (4). Finally, and with respect to the second question, we would want to require at least that the inputs in the distinguished subset have a high disvalue on the Machine's preference function or ordering (further conditions are discussed in "The Mental Life of Some Machines"). The purpose of condition (3) is to rule out such "organisms" (if they can count as such) as swarms of bees as single pain-feelers. The condition (1) is, obviously, redundant, and is only introduced for expository reasons. (It is, in fact, empty, since everything is a Probabilistic Automaton under *some* Description.)

I contend, in passing, that this hypothesis, in spite of its admitted vagueness, is far *less* vague than the "physical-chemical state" hypothesis is today, and far more susceptible to investigation of both a mathematical and an empirical kind. Indeed, to investigate this hypothesis is just to attempt to produce "mechanical" models of organisms—and isn't this, in a sense, just what psychology is about? The difficult step, of course, will be to pass from models of *specific* organisms to a *normal form* for the psychological description of organisms—for this is what is required to make (2) and (4) precise. But this too seems to be an inevitable part of the program of psychology.

I shall now compare the hypothesis just advanced with (a) the hypothesis that pain is a brain state, and (b) the hypothesis that pain is a behavior disposition.

III. FUNCTIONAL STATE VERSUS BRAIN STATE

It may, perhaps, be asked if I am not somewhat unfair in taking the brain-state theorist to be talking about *physical-chemical* states of the brain. But (a) these are the only sorts of states ever mentioned by brain-state theorists. (b) The brain-state theorist usually mentions (with a certain pride, slightly reminiscent of the Village Atheist) the incompatibility of his hypothesis with all forms of dualism and mentalism. This is natural if physical-chemical states of the brain are what is at issue. However, functional states of whole systems are something quite different. In particular, the functional-state hypothesis is *not* incompatible with dualism! Although it goes without saying that the hypothesis is "mechanistic" in its inspiration, it is a slightly remarkable fact that a system consisting of a body and a "soul," if such things there be, can perfectly well be a Probabilistic Automaton. (c) One argument advanced by Smart is that the brain-state theory assumes only "physical" properties, and Smart finds "non-physical" properties unintelligible. The Total States and the "inputs" defined above are, of course, neither mental nor physical *per se,* and I cannot imagine a functionalist advancing this argument. (d) If the brain-state theorist does mean (or at least allow) states other than physical-chemical states, then his hypothesis is completely empty, at least until he specifies *what* sort of "states" he *does* mean.

Taking the brain-state hypothesis in this way, then, what reasons are there to prefer the functional-state hypothesis over the brain-state hypothesis? Consider what the brain-state theorist has to do to make good his claims. He has to specify a physical-chemical state such that *any* organism (not just a mammal) is in pain if and only if (a) it possesses a brain of a suitable physical-chemical structure; and (b) its brain is in that physical-chemical state. This means that the physical-chemical state in question must be a possible state of a mammalian brain, a reptilian brain, a mollusc's brain (octopuses are mollusca, and certainly feel pain), etc. At the same time, it must *not* be a possible (physically possible) state of the brain of any physically possible creature that cannot feel pain. Even if such a state can be found, it must be nomologically certain that it will also be a state of the brain of any extra-terrestrial life that may be found that will be capable of feeling pain before we can even entertain the supposition that it may *be* pain.

It is not altogether impossible that such a state will be found. Even though octopus and mammal are examples of parallel (rather than sequential) evolution, for example, virtually identical structures (physically speaking) have evolved in the eye of the octopus and in the eye of the mammal, notwithstanding the fact that this organ has evolved from different kinds of cells in the two cases. Thus it is at least possible that parallel evolution, all over the universe, might *always* lead to *one and the same* physical "correlate" of pain. But this is certainly an ambitious hypothesis.

Finally, the hypothesis becomes still more ambitious when we realize that the brain state theorist is not just saying that *pain* is a brain state; he is, of course, concerned to maintain that *every* psychological state is a brain state. Thus if we can find even one psychological predicate which can clearly be applied to both a mammal and an octopus (say "hungry"), but whose physical-chemical "correlate" is different in the two cases, the brain-state theory has collapsed. It seems to me overwhelmingly probable that we can do this. Granted, in such a case the brain-state theorist can save himself by *ad hoc* assumptions (e.g., defining the disjunction of two states to be a single "physical-chemical state"), but this does not have to be taken seriously.

Turning now to the considerations *for* the functional-state theory, let us begin with the fact that we identify organisms as in pain, or hungry, or angry, or in heat, etc., on the basis of their *behavior*. But it is a truism that similarities in the behavior of two systems are at least a reason to suspect similarities in the functional organization of the two systems, and a much *weaker* reason to suspect similarities in the actual physical details. Moreover, we expect the various psychological states—at least the basic ones, such as hunger, thirst, aggression, etc.—to have more or less similar "transition probabilities" (within wide and ill-defined limits, to be sure) with each other and with behavior in the case of different species, because this is an artifact of the way in which we identify these states. Thus, we would not count an animal as *thirsty* if its "unsatiated" behavior did not seem to be directed toward drinking and was not followed by "satiation for liquid." Thus any animal that we count as capable of these various states will at least *seem* to have a certain rough kind of functional organization. And, as already remarked, if the program of finding psychological laws that are not species-specific—i.e., of finding a normal form for psychological theories of different species—ever succeeds, then it will bring in its wake a delineation of the kind of functional organization that is necessary and sufficient for a given psychological state, as well as a precise definition of the notion "psychological state." In contrast, the brain-state theorist has to hope for the eventual development of neurophysiological laws that are species-independent, which seems much less reasonable than the hope that psychological laws (of a sufficiently general kind) may be species-independent, or, still weaker, that a species-independent *form* can be found in which psychological laws can be written.

IV. FUNCTIONAL STATE VERSUS BEHAVIOR-DISPOSITION

The theory that being in pain is neither a brain state nor a functional state but a behavior disposition has one apparent advantage: it appears to agree with the way in which we verify that organisms are in pain. We do not in practice know anything about the brain state of an animal when we say that it is in pain; and we possess little if any knowledge of its functional organization, except in a crude intuitive way. In fact, however, this "advantage" is no advantage at all: for, although statements about how we verify that x is A may have a good deal to do with what the concept of being A comes to, they have precious little to do with what the property A *is*. To argue on the ground just mentioned that pain is neither a brain state nor a functional state is like arguing that heat is not mean molecular kinetic energy from the fact that ordinary people do not (they think) ascertain the mean molecular kinetic energy of something when they verify that it is hot or cold. It is not necessary that they should; what is necessary is that the marks that they take as indications of heat should in fact be explained by the mean molecular kinetic energy. And, similarly, it is necessary to our hypothesis that the marks that are taken as behavioral indications of pain should be explained by the fact that the organism is in a functional state of the appropriate kind, but not that speakers should *know* that this is so.

The difficulties with "behavior disposition" accounts are so well known that I shall do little more than recall them here. The difficulty —it appears to be more than "difficulty," in fact—of specifying the required behavior disposition except as "the disposition of X to behave as if X were in *pain*," is the chief one, of course. In contrast, we *can* specify the functional state with which we propose to identify pain, at least roughly, without using the notion of pain. Namely, the functional state we have in mind is the state of receiving sensory inputs which play a certain role in the Functional Organization of the organism. This role is characterized, at least partially, by the fact that the sense organs responsible for the inputs in question are organs whose function is to detect damage to the body, or dangerous extremes of temperature, pressure, etc., and by the fact that the "inputs" themselves, whatever their physical realization, represent a condition that the organism assigns a high disvalue to. As I stressed in "The Mental Life of Some Machines," this does *not* mean that the Machine will always *avoid* being in the condition in question ("pain"); it only means that the condition will be avoided unless not avoiding it is necessary to the attainment of some more highly valued goal. Since the behavior of the Machine (in this case, an organism) will depend not merely on the sensory inputs, but also on the Total State (i.e., on other values, beliefs, etc.), it seems hopeless to make any general statement about how an organism in such a condition *must* behave; but this does not mean that we must abandon hope of characterizing the condition. Indeed, we have just characterized it.[4]

Not only does the behavior-disposition theory seem hopelessly vague; if the "behavior" referred to is peripheral behavior, and the relevant stimuli are peripheral stimuli (e.g., we do not say anything about what the organism will do if its brain is operated upon), then the theory seems clearly false. For example, two animals with all motor nerves cut will have the same actual and potential "behavior" (viz., none to speak of); but if one has cut pain fibers and the other has uncut pain fibers, then one will feel pain and the other won't. Again, if one person has cut pain fibers, and another suppresses all pain responses deliberately due to some strong compulsion, then the actual and potential peripheral behavior may be the same, but one will feel pain and the other won't. (Some philosophers maintain that this last case is conceptually impossible, but the only evidence for this appears to be that *they* can't, or don't want to, conceive of it.)[5] If, instead of pain, we take some sensation the "bodily expression" of which is easier to suppress—say, a slight coolness in one's left little finger—the case becomes even clearer.

Finally, even if there *were* some behavior disposition invariantly correlated with pain (species-independently!), and specifiable without using the term 'pain,' it would still be more plausible to identify being in pain with some state whose presence *explains* this behavior disposition—the brain state or functional state—than with the behavior disposition itself. Such considerations of plausibility may be somewhat subjective; but if other things *were* equal (of course, they aren't) why shouldn't we allow considerations of plausibility to play the deciding role?

V. METHODOLOGICAL CONSIDERATIONS

So far we have considered only what might be called the "empirical" reasons for saying that being in pain is a functional state, rather than

---

[4] In "The Mental Life of Some Machines" a further, and somewhat independent, characteristic of the pain inputs is discussed in terms of Automata models—namely the spontaneity of the inclination to withdraw the injured part, etc. This raises the question, which is discussed in that paper, of giving a functional analysis of the notion of a spontaneous inclination. Of course, still further characteristics come readily to mind—for example, that feelings of pain are (or seem to be) *located* in the parts of the body.

[5] Cf. the discussion of "super-spartans" in "Brains and Behavior."

a brain state or a behavior disposition; viz., that it seems more likely that the functional state we described is invariantly "correlated" with pain, species-independently, than that there is either a physical-chemical state of the brain (must an organism have a *brain* to feel pain? perhaps some ganglia will do) or a behavior disposition so correlated. If this is correct, then it follows that the identification we proposed is at least a candidate for consideration. What of methodological considerations?

The methodological considerations are roughly similar in all cases of reduction, so no surprises need be expected here. First, identification of psychological states with functional states means that the laws of psychology can be derived from statements of the form "such-and-such organisms have such-and-such Descriptions" together with the identification statements ("being in pain is such-and-such a functional state," etc.). Secondly, the presence of the functional state (i.e., of inputs which play the role we have described in the Functional Organization of the organism) is not merely "correlated with" but actually explains the pain behavior on the part of the organism. Thirdly, the identification serves to exclude questions which (if a naturalistic view is correct) represent an altogether wrong way of looking at the matter, e.g., "What *is* pain if it isn't either the brain state or the functional state?" and "What causes the pain to be always accompanied by this sort of functional state?" In short, the identification is to be tentatively accepted as a theory which leads to both fruitful predictions and to fruitful *questions,* and which serves to discourage fruitless and empirically senseless questions, where by 'empirically senseless' I mean "senseless" not merely from the standpoint of verification, but from the standpoint of what there in fact *is.*

DAVID K. LEWIS

An Argument for the Identity Theory

I. INTRODUCTION

The (Psychophysical) Identity Theory is the hypothesis that—not necessarily but as a matter of fact—every experience[1] is identical with some physical state.[2] Specifically, with some neurochemical state. I contend that we who accept the materialistic working hypothesis that physical phenomena have none but purely physical explanations must accept the identity theory. This is to say more than do most friends of the theory, who say only that we are free to accept it, and should for the sake of some sort of economy or elegance. I do not need to make a

---

Reprinted from *The Journal of Philosophy*, LXIII, 1 (January 6, 1966), 17–25, by permission of the editor and David K. Lewis.

[1] Experiences herein are to be taken in general as universals, not as abstract particulars. I am concerned, for instance, with pain, an experience that befalls many people at many times; or with pain of some definite sort, an experience which at least *might* be common to different people at different times. Both are universals, capable of repeated instantiation. The latter is a narrower universal than the former, as crimson of some definite shade is narrower than red, but still a universal. I am not concerned with the particular pain of a given person at a given time, an abstract entity which cannot itself recur but can only be similar—at best, exactly similar—to other particular pains of other people or at other times. We might identify such abstract particulars with pairs of a universal and a single concrete particular instance thereof; or we might leave them as unanalyzed, elementary beings, as in Donald C. Williams, "On the Elements of Being," *Review of Metaphysics*, 7 (1953): 3–18 and 171–192. [All but the first sentence of this note was added in October 1969.]

[2] States also are to be taken in general as universals. I shall not distinguish between processes, events, phenomena, and states in a strict sense.

case for the identity theory on grounds of economy,[3] since I believe it can and should rest on a stronger foundation.

My argument is this: The definitive characteristic of any (sort of) experience as such is its causal role, its syndrome of most typical causes and effects. But we materialists believe that these causal roles which belong by analytic necessity to experiences belong in fact to certain physical states. Since those physical states possess the definitive characteristics of experience, they must be the experiences.

My argument parallels an argument which we will find uncontroversial. Consider cylindrical combination locks for bicycle chains. The definitive characteristic of their state of being unlocked is the causal role of that state, the syndrome of its most typical causes and effects: namely, that setting the combination typically causes the lock to be unlocked and that being unlocked typically causes the lock to open when gently pulled. That is all we need know in order to ascribe to the lock the state of being or of not being unlocked. But we may learn that, as a matter of fact, the lock contains a row of slotted discs; setting the combination typically causes the slots to be aligned; and alignment of the slots typically causes the lock to open when gently pulled. So alignment of slots occupies precisely the causal role that we ascribed to being unlocked by analytic necessity, as the definitive characteristic of being unlocked (for these locks). Therefore alignment of slots is identical with being unlocked (for these locks). They are one and the same state.

II. THE NATURE OF THE IDENTITY THEORY

We must understand that the identity theory asserts that certain physical states are experiences, introspectible processes or activities, not that they are the supposed intentional objects that experiences are experiences *of*. If these objects of experience really exist separate from experiences of them, or even as abstract parts thereof, they may well also be something physical. Perhaps they are also neural, or perhaps they are abstract constituents of veridically perceived surroundings, or perhaps they are something else, or nothing at all; but that is another story. So I am not claiming that an experience of seeing red, say, is itself somehow a red neural state.

---

[3] I am therefore invulnerable to Brandt's objection that the identity theory is not clearly more economical than a certain kind of dualism. "Doubts about the Identity Theory," in *Dimensions of Mind*, Sidney Hook, ed. (New York: NYU Press, 1960), pp. 57–67.

Shaffer has argued that the identity theory is impossible because (abstract particular) experiences are, by analytic necessity, unlocated, whereas the (abstract particular) neural events that they supposedly are have a location in part of the subject's nervous system.[4] But I see no reason to believe that the principle that experiences are unlocated enjoys any analytic, or other, necessity. Rather it is a metaphysical prejudice which has no claim to be respected. Or if there is, after all, a way in which it is analytic that experiences are unlocated, that way is irrelevant: perhaps in our presystematic thought we regard only concreta as located in a primary sense, and abstracta as located in a merely derivative sense by their inherence in located concreta. But this possible source of analytic unlocatedness for experiences does not meet the needs of Shaffer's argument. For neural events are abstracta too. Whatever unlocatedness accrues to experiences not because they are mental but because they are abstract must accrue as much to neural events. So it does not discriminate between the two.

The identity theory says that experience-ascriptions have the same reference as certain neural-state-ascriptions: both alike refer to the neural states which are experiences. It does not say that these ascriptions have the same sense. They do not; experience-ascriptions refer to a state by specifying the causal role that belongs to it accidentally, in virtue of causal laws, whereas neural-state-ascriptions refer to a state by describing it in detail. Therefore the identity theory does not imply that whatever is true of experiences as such is likewise true of neural states as such, nor conversely. For a truth about things of any kind *as such* is about things of that kind not by themselves, but together with the sense of expressions by which they are referred to as things of that kind.[5] So it is pointless to exhibit various discrepancies between what is true of experiences as such and what is true of neural states as such. We can explain those discrepancies without denying psychophysical identity and without admitting that it is somehow identity of a defective sort.

We must not identify an experience itself with the attribute that is predicated of somebody by saying that he is having that experience.[*]

---

[4] "Could Mental States Be Brain Processes?", *The Journal of Philosophy*, 58, 26 (Dec. 21, 1961): 813–822.

[5] Here I have of course merely applied to states Frege's doctrine of sense and reference. See "On Sense and Reference," in *Translations from the Philosophical Writings of Gottlob Frege*, Peter Geach and Max Black, eds. (New York: Oxford, 1960), pp. 56–78.

[*] Here I mean to deny all identities of the form ⌜α is identical with the attribute of having α⌝ where α is an experience-name definable as naming the occupant of a specified causal role. I deny, for instance, that pain is identical with the attribute of having pain. On my theory, 'pain' is a *contingent* name—that is, a name with different denotations in different possible worlds—since in any world, 'pain' names

The former *is* whatever state it is that occupies a certain definitive causal role; the latter is the attribute of *being in* whatever state it is that occupies that causal role. By this distinction we can answer the objection that, since experience-ascriptions and neural-state-descriptions are admittedly never synonymous and since attributes are identical just in case they are predicated by synonymous expressions, therefore experiences and neural states cannot be identical attributes. The objection does establish a nonidentity, but not between experiences and neural states. (It is unfair to blame the identity theory for needing the protection of so suspiciously subtle a distinction, for a parallel distinction is needed elsewhere. Blue is, for instance, the color of my socks, but blue is not the attribute predicated of things by saying they are the color of my socks, since '. . . is blue' and '. . . is the color of my socks' are not synonymous.)

III. THE FIRST PREMISE: EXPERIENCES DEFINED BY CAUSAL ROLES

The first of my two premises for establishing the identity theory is the principle that the definitive characteristic of any experience as such is its causal role. The definitive causal role of an experience is expressible by a finite[6] set of conditions that specify its typical causes and its typical effects under various circumstances. By analytic necessity these conditions are true of the experience and jointly distinctive of it.

My first premise is an elaboration and generalization of Smart's theory that avowals of experience are, in effect, of the form 'What is going on in me is like what is going on in me when . . .' followed

---

whatever state happens in that world to occupy the causal role definitive of pain. If state X occupies that role in world V while another state Y (incompatible with X) occupies that role in world W, then 'pain' names X in V and Y in W. I take 'the attribute of having pain', on the other hand, as a *non-contingent* name of that state or attribute Z that belongs, in any world, to whatever things have pain in that world—that is, to whatever things have in that world the state named in that world by 'pain'. (I take states to be attributes of things of a special kind: attributes of things at times.) Thus Z belongs in V to whatever things have X in V, and in W to whatever things have Y in W; hence Z is identical neither with X nor with Y.

Richard Montague, in "On the Nature of Certain Philosophical Entities," *Monist* 53 (1969): 172–173, objects that I seem to be denying a logical truth having as its instances all identities of the form ⌜α is identical with the attribute of having α⌝ where α is a *non-contingent* name of a state which is (either contingently or necessarily) an experience. I would agree that such identities are logically true; but those are not the identities I mean to deny, since I claim that our ordinary experience-names—'pain' and the like—are *contingent* names of states. [This note was added in October 1969.]

[6] It would do no harm to allow the set of conditions to be infinite, so long as it is recursive. But I doubt the need for this relaxation.

by specification of typical stimuli for, or responses to, the experience.[7] I wish to add explicitly that . . . may be an elaborate logical compound of clauses if necessary; that . . . must specify typical causes or effects of the experience, not mere accompaniments; that these typical causes and effects may include other experiences; and that the formula does not apply only to first-person reports of experience.

This is not a materialist principle, nor does it ascribe materialism to whoever speaks of experiences. Rather it is an account of the parlance common to all who believe that experiences are something or other real and that experiences are efficacious outside their own realm. It is neutral between theories—or a lack of any theory—about what sort of real and efficacious things experiences are: neural states or the like, pulsations of ectoplasm or the like, or just experiences and nothing else. It is not neutral, however, between all current theories of mind and body. Epiphenomenalist and parallelist dualism are ruled out as contradictory because they deny the efficacy of experience. Behaviorism as a thoroughgoing dispositional analysis of all mental states, including experiences,[8] is likewise ruled out as denying the reality and *a fortiori* the efficacy of experiences. For a pure disposition is a fictitious entity. The expressions that ostensibly denote dispositions are best construed as syncategorematic parts of statements of the lawlike regularities in which (as we say) the dispositions are manifest.

Yet the principle that experiences are defined by their causal roles is itself behaviorist in origin, in that it inherits the behaviorist discovery that the (ostensibly) causal connections between an experience and its typical occasions and manifestations somehow contain a component of analytic necessity. But my principle improves on the original behavioristic embodiment of that discovery in several ways:

First, it allows experiences to be something real and so to be the effects of their occasions and the causes of their manifestations, as common opinion supposes them to be.

---

[7] *Philosophy and Scientific Realism* (New York: Humanities Press, 1963), ch. v. Smart's concession that his formula does not really translate avowals is unnecessary. It results from a bad example: 'I have a pain' is not translatable as 'What is going on in me is like what goes on when a pin is stuck into me', because the concept of pain might be introduced without mention of pins. Indeed; but the objection is no good against the translation 'What is going on in me is like what goes on when (i.e. when and because) my skin is damaged'. [See J. J. C. Smart, "Sensations and Brain Processes," pp. 53–66 in this volume; and James W. Cornman, "The Identity of Mind and Body," pp. 73–79 in this volume.]

[8] Any theory of mind and body is compatible with a dispositional analysis of mental states other than experiences or with so-called "methodological behaviorism."

Second, it allows us to include other experiences among the typical causes and effects by which an experience is defined. It is crucial that we should be able to do so in order that we may do justice, in defining experiences by their causal roles, to the introspective accessibility which is such an important feature of any experience. For the introspective accessibility of an experience is its propensity reliably to cause other (future or simultaneous) experiences directed intentionally upon it, wherein we are aware of it. The requisite freedom to interdefine experiences is not available in general under behaviorism; interdefinition of experiences is permissible only if it can in principle be eliminated, which is so only if it happens to be possible to arrange experiences in a hierarchy of definitional priority. We, on the other hand, may allow interdefinition with no such constraint. We may expect to get mutually interdefined families of experiences, but they will do us no harm. There will be no reason to identify anything with one experience in such a family without regard to the others—but why should there be? Whatever occupies the definitive causal role of an experience in such a family does so by virtue of its own membership in a causal isomorph of the family of experiences, that is, in a system of states having the same pattern of causal connections with one another and the same causal connections with states outside the family, viz., stimuli and behavior. The isomorphism guarantees that if the family is identified *throughout* with its isomorph then the experiences in the family will have their definitive causal roles. So, *ipso facto,* the isomorphism requires us to accept the identity of all the experiences of the family with their counterparts in the causal isomorph of the family.[9]

Third, we are not obliged to define an experience by the causes and effects of exactly all and only its occurrences. We can be content rather merely to identify the experience as that state which is *typically* caused in thus-and-such ways and *typically* causes thus-and-such effects, saying nothing about its causes and effects in a (small) residue of exceptional cases. A definition by causes and effects in typical cases suffices to determine what the experience is, and the fact that the experience has some characteristics or other besides its definitive causal role confers a sense upon ascriptions of it in some exceptional cases for which its definitive typical causes and effects are absent (and likewise upon

---

[9] Putnam discusses an analogous case for machines: a family of ("logical" or "functional") states defined by their causal roles and mutually interdefined, and a causally isomorphic system of ("structural") states otherwise defined. He does not equate the correlated logical and structural states. "Minds and Machines," in *Dimensions of Mind,* pp. 148–179. [See also Hilary Putnam, "The Nature of Mental States," reprinted in this volume, pp. 150–161, especially section III.]

denials of it in some cases for which they are present). Behaviorism does not acknowledge the fact that the experience is something apart from its definitive occasions and manifestations, and so must require that the experience be defined by a strictly necessary and sufficient condition in terms of them. Otherwise the behaviorist has merely a partial explication of the experience by criteria, which can never give more than a presumption that the experience is present or absent, no matter how much we know about the subject's behavior and any lawlike regularities that may govern it. Relaxation of the requirement for a strictly necessary and sufficient condition is welcome. As anybody who has tried to implement behaviorism knows, it is usually easy to find conditions which are *almost* necessary and sufficient for an experience. All the work—and all the complexity which renders it incredible that the conditions found should be known implicitly by every speaker—comes in trying to cover a few exceptional cases. In fact, it is just impossible to cover some atypical cases of experiences behavioristically: the case of a perfect actor pretending to have an experience he does not really have; and the case of a total paralytic who cannot manifest any experience he does have (both cases under the stipulation that the pretense or paralysis will last for the rest of the subject's life no matter what happens, in virtue of regularities just as lawlike as those by which the behaviorist seeks to define experiences).

It is possible, and probably good analytic strategy, to reconstrue any supposed pure dispositional state rather as a state defined by its causal role. The advantages in general are those we have seen in this case: the state becomes recognized as real and efficacious; unrestricted mutual interdefinition of the state and others of its sort becomes permissible; and it becomes intelligible that the state may sometimes occur despite prevention of its definitive manifestations.[10]

I do not offer to prove my principle that the definitive characteristics of experiences as such are their causal roles. It would be verified by exhibition of many suitable analytic statements saying that various experiences typically have thus-and-such causes and effects. Many of these statements have been collected by behaviorists; I inherit these although I explain their status somewhat differently. Behaviorism is widely accepted. I am content to rest my case on the argument that my principle can accommodate what is true in behaviorism and can escape attendant difficulties.

[10] Quine advocates this treatment of such dispositional states as are worth saving in *Word and Object* (Cambridge, Mass.: MIT Press, and New York: Wiley, 1960), pp. 222–225. "They are conceived as built-in, enduring structural traits."

IV. THE SECOND PREMISE: EXPLANATORY ADEQUACY OF PHYSICS

My second premise is the plausible hypothesis that there is some unified body of scientific theories, of the sort we now accept, which together provide a true and exhaustive account of all physical phenomena (i.e. all phenomena describable in physical terms). They are unified in that they are cumulative: the theory governing any physical phenomenon is explained by theories governing phenomena out of which that phenomenon is composed and by the way it is composed out of them. The same is true of the latter phenomena, and so on down to fundamental particles or fields governed by a few simple laws, more or less as conceived of in present-day theoretical physics. I rely on Oppenheim and Putnam for a detailed exposition of the hypothesis that we may hope to find such a unified physicalistic body of scientific theory and for a presentation of evidence that the hypothesis is credible.[11]

A confidence in the explanatory adequacy of physics is a vital part, but not the whole, of any full-blooded materialism. It is the empirical foundation on which materialism builds its superstructure of ontological and cosmological doctrines, among them the identity theory. It is also a traditional and definitive working hypothesis of natural science —what scientists say nowadays to the contrary is defeatism or philosophy. I argue that whoever shares this confidence must accept the identity theory.

My second premise does not rule out the existence of nonphysical phenomena; it is not an ontological thesis in its own right. It only denies that we need ever explain physical phenomena by nonphysical ones. Physical phenomena are physically explicable, or they are utterly inexplicable insofar as they depend upon chance in a physically explicable way, or they are methodologically acceptable primitives. All manner of nonphysical phenomena may coexist with them, even to the extent of sharing the same space-time, provided only that the nonphysical phenomena are entirely inefficacious with respect to the physical phenomena. These coexistent nonphysical phenomena may be quite unrelated to physical phenomena; they may be causally independent but for some reason perfectly correlated with some physical phenomena (as experiences are, according to parallelism); they may be epiphenomena, caused by some physical phenomena but not them-

---

[11] "Unity of Science as a Working Hypothesis," in *Minnesota Studies in the Philosophy of Science*, II, Herbert Feigl, Michael Scriven, and Grover Maxwell, eds. (Minneapolis: Univ. of Minnesota Press, 1958), pp. 3–36.

selves causing any (as experiences are, according to epiphenomenalism). If they are epiphenomena they may even be correlated with some physical phenomena, perfectly and by virtue of a causal law.

V. CONCLUSION OF THE ARGUMENT

But none of these permissible nonphysical phenomena can be experiences. For they must be entirely inefficacious with respect to all physical phenomena. But all the behavioral manifestations of experiences are (or involve) physical phenomena and so cannot be effects of anything that is inefficacious with respect to physical phenomena. These behavioral manifestations are among the typical effects definitive of any experience, according to the first premise. So nothing can be an experience that is inefficacious with respect to physical phenomena. So nothing can be an experience that is a nonphysical phenomenon of the sort permissible under the second premise. From the two premises it follows that experiences are some physical phenomena or other.

And there is little doubt which physical phenomena they must be. We are far from establishing positively that neural states occupy the definitive causal roles of experiences, but we have no notion of any other physical phenomena that could possibly occupy them, consistent with what we do know. So if nonphysical phenomena are ruled out by our confidence in physical explanation, only neural states are left. If it could be shown that neural states do not occupy the proper causal roles, we would be hard put to save materialism itself.

A version of epiphenomenalism might seem to evade my argument: let experiences be nonphysical epiphenomena, precisely correlated according to a causal law with some simultaneous physical states which are themselves physically (if at all) explicable. The correlation law (it is claimed) renders the experiences and their physical correlates causally equivalent. So the nonphysical experiences have their definitive physical effects after all—although they are not needed to explain those effects, so there is no violation of my second premise (since the nonphysical experiences redundantly redetermine the effects of their physical correlates). I answer thus: at best, this position yields nonphysical experiences alongside the physical experiences, duplicating them, which is not what its advocates intend. Moreover, it is false that such a physical state and its epiphenomenal correlate are causally equivalent. The position exploits a flaw in the standard regularity theory of cause. We know on other grounds that the theory must be corrected to discriminate between genuine causes and the spurious causes which are their epiphenomenal correlates. (The "power on" light does not cause the motor to go, even if it is a lawfully perfect correlate of the electric current that really causes the motor to go.) Given a satisfactory correction, the nonphysical correlate will be evicted from its spurious causal role and thereby lose its status as the experience. So this epiphenomenalism is not a counterexample.

The dualism of the common man holds that experiences are nonphysical phenomena which are the causes of a familiar syndrome of physical as well as nonphysical effects. This dualism is a worthy opponent, daring to face empirical refutation, and in due time it will be rendered incredible by the continuing advance of physicalistic explanation. I have been concerned to prevent dualism from finding a safe fall-back position in the doctrine that experiences are nonphysical and physically inefficacious. It is true that such phenomena can never be refuted by any amount of scientific theory and evidence. The trouble with them is rather that they cannot be what we call experiences. They can only be the nonphysical epiphenomena or correlates of physical states which are experiences. If they are not the experiences themselves, they cannot rescue dualism when it is hard-pressed. And if they cannot do that, nobody has any motive for believing in them. Such things may be—but they are of no consequence.

part five
ELIMINATIVE MATERIALISM

PAUL K. FEYERABEND

Mental Events and the Brain

Shaffer's note (*The Journal of Philosophy*, **60**, 6: 160)† and the preceding discussion to which it refers show very clearly the dilemma of any identity hypothesis concerning mental events and brain processes. Such hypotheses are usually put forth by physiologically inclined thinkers who want also to be empiricists. Being physiologically inclined, they want to assert the *material* character of mental processes. Being empiricists, they want their assertion to be a testable statement about *mental* processes. They try to combine the two tendencies in an empirical statement of the form:

> X is a mental process of kind A ≡
> X is a central process of kind α   (H)

But this hypothesis backfires. It not only implies, as it is intended to imply, that mental events have physical features; it also seems to imply (if read from the right to the left) that some physical events, viz. central processes, have nonphysical features. It thereby replaces a dualism of events by a dualism of features. Moreover, this consequence seems to be the result of the way in which the physiologist has *formulated* his thesis. Even if he is a convinced monist he seems to be forced, by the very content of his thesis of monism, to acknowledge the correctness of a *dualistic* point of view.

For a dualist this predicament is proof of the untenability of monism. But surely he is too rash in drawing this conclusion! H implies dualism. Hence, dualism will be true *provided* H is true. However, if *monism* is correct, then H is false: there are then *no* mental processes

---

Reprinted from *The Journal of Philosophy*, LX, 11 (May 23, 1963), 295-296, by permission of the editor and Paul K. Feyerabend.

† [Reprinted in this volume, pp. 67-72.]

in the usual (nonmaterialistic) sense. This shows that the discussion of the content of H regarded as an empirical hypothesis is not at all sufficient for deciding the issue between monism and dualism. It also shows *that the monist misstates his case when defending* H.

The proper procedure for him to adopt is to develop his theory without any recourse to existent terminology. If he wants to use H at all, he ought to use it for *redefining* 'mental process' (if he intends to perpetuate ancient terminology, that is). The empirical character of his theory is not endangered thereby. After all, a physiological theory of epilepsy does not become an empty tautology on account of the fact that it does not make use of the phrase—or of the notion—'possessed by the devil', 'devil' here occurring in its *theological* sense. There are enough independent predictions available, many more predictions in fact than the mentalist could ever provide—or would even be willing to provide (think only of the tremendous field of the physiology of perception).

However, so it is usually objected, unless a connection is established with previous language, we do not know what we are talking about, and we are therefore not able to formulate our observational results. This objection assumes that the terms of a general point of view and of a corresponding language can obtain meaning only by being related to the terms of some other point of view that is familiar and known by all. Now if that is indeed the case, then how did the latter point of view and the latter language ever obtain its familiarity? And if it could obtain its familiarity without help "from outside," as it obviously did, then there is no reason to assume that a different point of view cannot do equally well. (Besides, we learn the ordinary idiom when we are small children; is it assumed that a grown-up physiologist will be incapable of doing what a small child does quite well?) Moreover, observational results always have to be formulated with respect to a certain background of theory (with respect to a certain language-game, to use more fashionable terminology). There is no reason why physiology should not by itself be capable of forming such a background. We have to conclude, then, that the reasonableness—and the success—of a purely physiological approach to human beings is not at all dependent on the outcome of an analysis of H.

"Bridge-laws" such as H play a most important role within the current theory of explanation and reduction. If our comments above are correct, then it follows that these theories are inadequate as measures of the success of theory construction.

RICHARD RORTY

Mind-Body Identity, Privacy, and Categories

I. INTRODUCTORY

Current controversies about the Mind-Body Identity Theory form a case-study for the investigation of the methods practiced by linguistic philosophers. Recent criticisms of these methods question that philosophers can discern lines of demarcation between "categories" of entities, and thereby diagnose "conceptual confusions" in "reductionist" philosophical theories. Such doubts arise once we see that it is very difficult, and perhaps impossible, to draw a firm line between the "conceptual" and the "empirical," and thus to differentiate between a statement embodying a conceptual confusion and one that expresses a surprising empirical result. The proponent of the Identity Theory (by which I mean one who thinks it sensible to assert that empirical inquiry will discover that *sensations* (not thoughts) are identical with certain brain-processes[1]) holds that his opponents' arguments to the effect that empirical inquiry *could* not identify brain-processes and sensations are admirable illustrations of this difficulty. For, he argues, the classifications of linguistic expressions that are the ground of his

---

Reprinted from *The Review of Metaphysics*, XIX, 1 (September 1965), 24–54, by permission of the editor and Richard Rorty.

[1] A proponent of the Identity Theory is usually thought of as one who predicts that empirical inquiry *will* reach this result—but few philosophers in fact stick their necks out in this way. The issue is not the truth of the prediction, but whether such a prediction makes sense. Consequently, by "Identity Theory" I shall mean the assertion that it does make sense.

I include only sensations within the scope of the theory because the inclusion of thoughts would raise a host of separate problems (about the reducibility of intentional and semantic discourse to statements about linguistic behavior), and because the form of the Identity Theory which has been most discussed in the recent literature restricts itself to a consideration of sensations.

opponents' criticism are classifications of a language which is as it is because it is the language spoken at a given stage of empirical inquiry. But the sort of empirical results that would show brain processes and sensations to be identical would also bring about changes in our ways of speaking. These changes would make these classifications out of date. To argue against the Identity Theory on the basis of the way we talk now is like arguing against an assertion that supernatural phenomena are identical with certain natural phenomena on the basis of the way in which superstitious people talk. There is simply no such thing as a method of classifying linguistic expressions that has results guaranteed to remain intact despite the results of future empirical inquiry. Thus in this area (and perhaps in all areas) there is no method which will have the sort of magisterial neutrality of which linguistic philosophers fondly dream.

In this paper I wish to support this general line of argument. I shall begin by pressing the claims of the analogy between mental events and supernatural events. Then I shall try to rebut the objection which seems generally regarded as fatal to the claims of the Identity Theory —the objection that "privacy" is of the essence of mental events, and thus that a theory which holds that mental events might *not* be "private" is *ipso facto* confused. I shall conclude with some brief remarks on the implications of my arguments for the more general metaphilosophical issues at stake.

2. THE TWO FORMS OF THE IDENTITY THEORY

The obvious objection to the identity theory is that "identical" either means a relation such that

$$(x)\,(y)\,[(x = y) \supset (F)\,(Fx \equiv Fy)]$$

(the relation of "strict identity") or it does not. If it does, then we find ourselves forced into

> saying truthfully that physical processes such as brain processes are dim or fading or nagging or false, and that mental phenomena such as after-images are publicly observable or physical or spatially located or swift,[2]

and thus using meaningless expressions, for

[2] James Cornman, "The Identity of Mind and Body," *Journal of Philosophy*, 59 (1962), p. 490. [Reprinted in this volume, p. 77. References below are to the occurrence in this volume.]

we may say that the above expressions are meaningless in the sense that they commit a category mistake; i.e., in forming these expressions we have predicated predicates, appropriate to one logical category, of expressions that belong to a different logical category. This is surely a conceptual mistake.[3]

But if by "identical" the Identity Theory does *not* mean a relation of strict identity, then what relation *is* intended? How does it differ from the mere relation of "correlation" which, it is admitted on all sides, might without confusion be said to hold between sensations and brain-processes?

Given this dilemma, two forms of the identity theory may be distinguished. The first, which I shall call the *translation* form, grasps the first horn, and attempts to show that the odd-sounding expressions mentioned above do not involve category-mistakes, and that this can be shown by suitable translations into "topic neutral" language of the sentences in which these terms are originally used.[4] The second, which I shall call the *disappearance* form, grasps the second horn, and holds that the relation in question is not strict identity, but rather the sort of relation which obtains between, to put it crudely, existent entities and non-existent entities when reference to the latter once served (some of) the purposes presently served by reference to the former—the sort of relation that holds, e.g., between "quantity of caloric fluid" and "mean kinetic energy of molecules." There is an obvious sense of "same" in which what used to be called "a quantity of caloric fluid" is *the same thing* as what is now called a certain mean kinetic energy of molecules, but there is no reason to think that all features truly predicated of the one may be sensibly predicated of the other.[5] The

---

[3] Cornman, p. 77.

[4] Cf. J. J. C. Smart, "Sensations and Brain Processes," reprinted in *The Philosophy of Mind*, ed. by V. C. Chappell (Englewood Cliffs, 1962), pp. 160–172 [reprinted in this volume, pp. 53–66; references below are to the occurrence in this volume], esp. pp. 59–61, and especially the claim that "When a person says 'I see a yellowish-orange after-image' he is saying something like this: 'There is something going on which is like what is going on when I have my eyes open, am awake, and there is an orange illuminated in good light in front of me, that is, when I really see an orange'" (p. 61). For criticisms of Smart's program of translation, see Cornman, op. cit.; Jerome Shaffer, "Could Mental States Be Brain Processes?," *Journal of Philosophy* 58, (1961), pp. 812–822; Shaffer, "Mental Events and the Brain," *Journal of Philosophy*, 60 (1963), pp. 160–166 [reprinted in this volume, pp. 67–72]. See also the articles cited in the first footnote to Smart's own article.

[5] No statement of the disappearance form of the theory with which I am acquainted is as clear and explicit as Smart's statement of the translation form. See, however, Feyerabend, "Mental Events and the Brain," *Journal of Philosophy*, 60 (1963), pp. 295–296 [reprinted in this volume, pp. 172–173], and "Materialism and the

translation form of the theory holds that if we really understood what we were saying when we said things like "I am having a stabbing pain" we should see that since we are talking about "topic-neutral" matters, we might, for all we know, be talking about brain-processes. The disappearance form holds that it is unnecessary to show that suitable translations (into "topic-neutral" language) of our talk about sensations can be given—as unnecessary as to show that statements about quantities of caloric fluid, when properly understood, may be seen to be topic-neutral statements.[6]

From the point of view of this second form of the theory, it is a mistake to assume that "X's are nothing but Y's" entails "All attributes meaningfully predicable of X's are meaningfully predicated of Y's," for this assumption would forbid us ever to express the results of scientific inquiry in terms of (in Cornman's useful phrase) "cross-category identity."[7] It would seem that the verb in such statements as "Zeus's thunderbolts are discharges of static electricity" and "Demoniacal possession is a form of hallucinatory psychosis" is the "is" of identity, yet it can hardly express *strict* identity. The disappearance form of the Identity Theory suggests that we view such statements as elliptical for e.g., "What people used to call 'demoniacal possession' is a form of hallucinatory psychosis," where the relation in question *is* strict identity. Since there is no reason why "what people call 'X'" should be in the same "category" (in the Rylean sense) as "X," there is no need to claim, as the translation form of the theory must, that topic-neutral translations of statements using "X" are possible.

In what follows, I shall confine myself to a discussion and defense of the disappearance form of the theory. My first reason for this is that I believe that the analysis of "Sensations are identical with certain brain-processes" proposed by the disappearance form (viz., "What people now call 'sensations' are identical with certain brain-processes") accomplishes the same end as the translation form's program of topic-neutral translation—namely, avoiding the charge of "category-mis-

---

Mind-Body Problem," *The Review of Metaphysics*, 17 (1963), pp. 49–67. See also Wilfrid Sellars, "The Identity Approach to the Mind-Body Problem," *ibid.*, 18 (1965). My indebtedness to this and other writings of Sellars will be obvious in what follows.

[6] Both forms agree, however, on the requirements which would have to be satisfied if we are to claim that the empirical discovery in question has been made. Roughly, they are (1) that one-one or one-many correlations could be established between every type of sensation and some clearly demarcated kind(s) of brain-processes; (2) that every known law which refers to sensations would be subsumed under laws about brain-processes; (3) that new laws about sensations be discovered by deduction from laws about brain-processes.

[7] Cornman, p. 79.

take," while preserving the full force of the traditional materialist position. My second reason is that I believe that an attempt to defend the translation form will inevitably get bogged down in controversy about the adequacy of proposed topic-neutral translations of statements about sensations. There is obviously a sense of "adequate translation" in which the topic-neutrality of the purported translations *ipso facto* makes them inadequate. So the proponent of the translation form of the theory will have to fall back on a weaker sense of "adequate translation." But the weaker this sense becomes, the less impressive is the claim being made, and the less difference between the Identity Theory and the non-controversial thesis that certain brain-processes may be constantly correlated with certain sensations.

3. THE ANALOGY BETWEEN DEMONS AND SENSATIONS

At first glance, there seems to be a fatal weakness in the disappearance form of the Identity Theory. For normally when we say "What people call 'X's' are nothing but Y's" we are prepared to add that "There are no X's." Thus when, e.g., we say that "What people call 'caloric fluid' is nothing but the motion of molecules" or "What people call 'witches' are nothing but psychotic women" we are prepared to say that there are no witches, and no such thing as caloric fluid. But it seems absurd to say that there might turn out to be no such things as sensations.

To see that this disanalogy is not fatal to the Identity Theory, let us consider the following situation. A certain primitive tribe holds the view that illnesses are caused by demons—a different demon for each sort of illness. When asked what more is known about these demons than that they cause illness, they reply that certain members of the tribe—the witch-doctors—can see, after a meal of sacred mushrooms, various (intangible) humanoid forms on or near the bodies of patients. The witch-doctors have noted, for example, that a blue demon with a long nose accompanies epileptics, a fat red one accompanies sufferers from pneumonia, etc., etc. They know such further facts as that the fat red demon dislikes a certain sort of mold which the witch-doctors give people who have pneumonia. (There are various competing theories about what demons do when not causing diseases, but serious witch-doctors regard such speculations as unverifiable and profitless.)

If we encountered such a tribe, we would be inclined to tell them that there are no demons. We would tell them that diseases were caused by germs, viruses, and the like. We would add that the witch-doctors were not seeing demons, but merely having hallucinations. We would be quite right, but would we be right on *empirical* grounds? What empirical criteria, built into the demon-talk of the tribe, go unsatisfied? What predictions which the tribesmen make fail to come true? If there are none, a sophisticated witch-doctor may reply that all modern science can do is to show (1) that the presence of demons is constantly correlated with that of germs, viruses, and the like, and (2) that eating certain mushrooms sometimes makes people think they see things that aren't really there. This is hardly sufficient to show that there are no demons. At best, it shows that if we forget about demons, then (a) a simpler account of the cause and cure of disease and (b) a simpler account of why people make the perceptual reports they do, may be given.

What do we reply to such a sophisticated witch-doctor? I think that all that we would have left to say is that the simplicity of the accounts which can be offered if we forget about demons *is* an excellent reason for saying that there are no demons. Demon-discourse is one way of describing and predicting phenomena, but there are better ways. We *could* (as the witch-doctor urges) tack demon-discourse on to modern science by saying, first, that diseases are caused by the compresence of demons and germs (each being a necessary, but neither a sufficient, condition) and, second, that the witch-doctors (unlike drunkards and psychotics) really do see intangible beings (about whom, alas, nothing is known save their visual appearances). If we did so, we would retain all the predictive and explanatory advantages of modern science. We would know as much about the cause and cure of disease, and about hallucinations, as we did before. We would, however, be burdened with problems which we did not have before: the problem of why demons are visible only to witch-doctors, and the problem of why germs cannot cause diseases all by themselves. We avoid both problems by saying that demons do not exist. The witch-doctor may remark that this use of Occam's Razor has the same advantage as that of theft over honest toil. To such a remark, the only reply could be an account of the practical advantages gained by the use of the Razor in the past.

Now the Identity Theorist's claim is that sensations may be to the future progress of psycho-physiology as demons are to modern science. Just as we now want to deny that there are demons, future science may want to deny that there are sensations. The only obstacle to replacing sensation-discourse with brain-discourse seems to be that sensation-statements have a reporting as well as an explanatory function. But the demon case makes clear that the discovery of a new way of explaining the phenomena previously explained by reference to a certain sort of entity, *combined with a new account of what is being reported by observation-statements about that sort of entity,* may give good reason for saying that there are no entities of that sort. The absurdity of saying "Nobody has ever felt a pain" is no greater than that of saying "Nobody has ever seen a demon," *if* we have a suitable answer to the question "What *was* I reporting when I said I felt a pain?" To this question, the science of the future may reply "You were reporting the occurrence of a certain brain-process, and it would make life simpler for us if you would, in the future, *say* 'My C-fibers are firing' instead of saying 'I'm in pain'." In so saying, he has as good a prima facie case as the scientist who answers the witch-doctor's question "What *was* I reporting when I reported a demon?" by saying "You were reporting the content of your hallucination, and it would make life simpler if, in the future, you would describe your experiences in those terms."

Given this prima facie analogy between demons and sensations, we can now attend to some disanalogies. We may note, first, that there is no simple way of filling in the blank in "What people called 'demons' are nothing but ———." For neither "hallucinatory contents" nor "germs" will do. The observational and the explanatory roles of "demon" must be distinguished. We need to say something like "What people who reported seeing demons were reporting was simply the content of their hallucinations," and *also* something like "What people explained by reference to demons can be explained better by reference to germs, viruses, etc." Because of the need for a relatively complex account of how we are to get along without reference to demons, we cannot *identify* "What we called 'demons' " with anything. So, instead, we simply deny their existence. In the case of sensations, however, we can give a relatively simple account of how to get along in the future. Both the explanatory *and* the reporting functions of statements about sensations can be taken over by statements about brain-processes. Therefore we are prepared to identify "What we called 'sensations' " with brain-processes, and to say "What we called 'sensations' turn out to be nothing but brain-processes."

Thus this disanalogy does not have the importance which it appears to have at first. In both the demon case and the sensation case, the proposed reduction has the same pragmatic consequences: namely, that we should stop asking questions about the causal and/or spatio-temporal relationships holding between the "reduced" entities (demons, sensations) and the rest of the universe, and replace these with questions about the relationships holding between certain other entities (germs, hallucinatory experiences, brain-processes) and the rest of the universe. It happens, for the reasons just sketched, that the proposed reduction is put in the form of a denial of existence in one case, and of an identification in another case. But "There are no demons" and "What people call 'sensations' are nothing but brain processes" can both equally well be paraphrased as "Elimination of the referring use of the expression in question ('demon,' 'sensation') from our language would leave our ability to describe and predict undiminished."

Nevertheless, the claim that there might turn out to be no such thing as a "sensation" seems scandalous. The fact that a witch-doctor might be scandalized by a similar claim about demons does not, in itself, do much to diminish our sense of shock. In what follows, I wish to account for this intuitive implausibility. I shall argue that it rests *solely* upon the fact that elimination of the referring use of "sensation" from our language would be in the highest degree *impractical*. If this can be shown, then I think that the Identity Theorist will be cleared of the charge of "conceptual confusion" usually leveled against him. Rather than proceeding directly to this argument, however, I shall first consider a line of argument which has often been used to show that he *is* guilty of this charge. Examining this line of argument will permit me to sketch in greater detail what the Identity Theorist is and is not saying.

4. THE ELIMINABILITY OF OBSERVATION TERMS

The usual move made by the opponents of the Identity Theory is to compare suggested reduction of sensations to brain-processes to certain other cases in which we say that "X's turn out to be nothing but Y's." There are two significantly different classes of cases and it might seem that the Identity Theorist confuses them. First, there is the sort of case in which both "X" and "Y" are used to refer to observable entities, and the claim that "What people called 'X's' are nothing but Y's" is backed up by pointing out that the statement "This is an X" commits one to an empirically false proposition. For example, we say that "What people called 'unicorn horns' are nothing but narwhal horns," and urge that we cease to respond to a perceptual situation with "This is a unicorn horn." We do this because "This is a unicorn horn" commits one to the existence of unicorns, and there are, it turns out, no unicorns. Let us call this sort of case *identification of observables with other observables*. Second, there is the sort of case in which "X" is used to refer to an observable entity and "Y" is used to refer to an unobservable entity. Here we do not (typically) back up the claim that "What people called 'X's' are nothing but Y's" by citing an empirically false proposition presupposed by "This is an X." For example, the statement that "What people call 'tables' are nothing but clouds of molecules" does not suggest, or require as a ground, that people who say "This is a table" hold false beliefs. Rather, we are suggesting that something *more* has been found out about the sort of situation reported by "This is a table." Let us call this second sort of case *identification of observables with theoretical entities.*

It seems that we cannot assimilate the identification of sensations with brain-processes to either of these cases. For, unlike the typical case of identification of observables with other observables, we do not wish to say that people who have reported sensations in the past have (necessarily) any empirically disconfirmed beliefs. People are not wrong about sensations in the way in which they were wrong about "unicorn horns." Again, unlike the typical case of the identification of observables with theoretical entities, we do not want to say that brain-processes are "theoretical" or unobservable. Furthermore, in cases in which we identify an observable X with an unobservable Y, we are usually willing to accept the remark that "That does not show that there are no X's." The existence of tables is not (it would seem) impugned by their identification with clouds of electrons, as the existence of unicorn horns is impugned by their identification with narwhal horns. But a defender of the disappearance form of the Identity Theory *does* want to impugn the existence of sensations.

Because the claim that "What people call 'sensations' may turn out to be nothing but brain-processes" cannot be assimilated to either of these cases, it has been attacked as trivial or incoherent. The following dilemma is posed by those who attack it: either the Identity Theorist claims that talk about sensations presupposes some empirically disconfirmed belief (and what could it be?) or the "identity" which he has in mind is the uninteresting sort of identity which holds between tables and clouds of molecules (mere "theoretical replaceability").

The point at which the Identity Theorist should attack this dilemma is the premiss invoked in stating the second horn—the premiss that the identification of tables with clouds of molecules does not permit us to infer to the non-existence of tables. This premiss is true, but *why* is it true? That there is room for reflection here is apparent when we place the case of tables side-by-side with the case of demons. If there is any point to saying that tables are nothing but clouds of molecules it is presumably to say that, in principle, we could stop making a referring use of "table," and of any extensionally equivalent term, and still leave our ability to describe and predict undiminished. But this would seem just the point of (and the justification for) saying that there are no demons. Why does the realization that nothing would be lost by the dropping of "table" from our vocabulary still leave us with the conviction that there are tables, whereas the same realization about demons leaves us with the conviction that there are no demons? I suggest that the only answer to this question which will stand examination is that although we could *in principle* drop "table," it would be monstrously inconvenient to do so, whereas it is both possible in principle and convenient in practice to drop "demon." The reason "But there still are tables" sounds so plausible is that nobody would dream of suggesting that we stop reporting our experiences in table-talk and start reporting them in molecule-talk. The reason "There are no demons" sounds so plausible is that we are quite willing to suggest that the witch-doctors stop reporting their experiences in demon-talk and start reporting them in hallucination-talk.

A conclusive argument that this practical difference is the *only* relevant difference would, obviously, canvass all the other differences which might be noted. I shall not attempt this. Instead, I shall try to make my claim plausible by sketching a general theory of the conditions under which a term may cease to have a referring use without those who made such a use being convicted of having held false beliefs.

Given the same sorts of correlations between X's and Y's, we are more likely to say "X's are nothing but Y's" when reference to X's is habitually made in non-inferential reports, and more likely to say "There are no X's" when such reference is never or rarely made. (By "non-inferential report" I mean a statement in response to which questions like "How did you know?" "On what evidence do you say . . . ?" and "What leads you to think . . . ?" are normally considered misplaced and unanswerable, but which is nonetheless capable of empirical confirmation.) Thus we do not say that the identification of temperature with the kinetic energy of molecules shows that there is no such thing as temperature, since "temperature" originally (i.e., before the invention of thermometers) stood for something which was always reported non-inferentially, and still is frequently so reported. Similarly for all identifications of familiar macro-objects with unfamiliar micro-objects. But since in our culture-circle we do not *habitually* report non-inferentially the presence of caloric fluid, demons, etc., we do not feel unhappy at the bald suggestion that there are no such things.

Roughly speaking, then, the more accustomed we are to "X" serving as an observation-term (by which I mean a term habitually used in non-inferential reports) the more we prefer, when inquiry shows the possibility of accounting for the phenomena explained by reference to X's without such reference, to "identify" X's with some sort of Y's, rather than to deny existence to X's *tout court. But the more grounds we have for such identification, the more chance there is that we shall stop using "X" in non-inferential reports,* and thus the greater chance of our eventually coming to accept the claim that "there are no X's" with equanimity. This is why we find borderline cases, and gradual shifts from assimilations of X's to Y's to an assertion that X's do not exist. For example, most people do not report the presence of pink rats non-inferentially (nor inferentially, for that matter), but some do.

The recognition that they are in the minority helps those who do so to admit that there are no pink rats. But suppose that the vast majority of us had always seen (intangible and uncatchable) pink rats; would it not then be likely that we should resist the bald assertion that there are no pink rats and insist on something of the form "pink rats are nothing but . . ."? It might be a very long time before we came to drop the habit of reporting pink rats and began reporting hallucinations instead.

The typical case-history of an observation-term ceasing to have a referring use runs the following course: (1) X's are the subjects of both inferential and non-inferential reports;[8] (2) empirical discoveries are made which enable us to subsume X-laws under Y-laws and to produce new X-laws by studying Y's; (3) inferential reports of X's cease to be made; (4) non-inferential reports of X's are reinterpreted either (4a) as reports of Y's, *or* (4b) as reports of mental entities (thoughts that one is seeing an X, hallucinatory images, etc.); (5) non-inferential reports of X's cease to be made (because their place is taken by non-inferential reports either of Y's or of thoughts, hallucinatory images, etc.); (6) we conclude that there simply are no such things as X's.

This breakdown of stages lets us pick out two crucial conditions that must be satisfied if we are to move from "X's are nothing but Y's" (stage 2) to "there are no X's" (stage 6). These conditions are;

(A) The Y-laws must be *better* at explaining the kinds of phenomena explained by the X-laws (not just equally good). Indeed, they must be sufficiently better so that *the inconvenience of changing one's linguistic habits by ceasing to make inferential reports about X's is less than the inconvenience of going through the routine of translating one's X-reports into Y-reports in order to get satisfactory explanations of the phenomena in question.* If this condition is not satisfied, the move from stage (2) to stage (3) will not be made, and thus no later move will be made.

(B) Either Y-reports may themselves be made non-inferentially, or X-reports may be treated as reports of mental entities. For we must be able to have some answer to the question "What *am* I reporting when I non-inferentially report about an X?," and the only answers available are "you're reporting on a Y" or "you're reporting on some merely mental entity." If neither answer is available, we can move neither to (4a) nor to (4b), nor, therefore, on to (5) and (6).

---

[8] Note that if X's are *only* referred to in inferential reports—as in the case of "neutrons" and "epicycles," no philosophically interesting reduction takes place. For in such cases there is no hope of getting rid of an explanandum; all we get rid of is a putative explanation.

Now the reason we move from stage (2) to stage (3) in the case of demons is that (A) is obviously satisfied. The phenomena which we explained by reference to the activity of demons are so much better explained in other ways that it is simpler to stop inferring to the existence of demons altogether than to continue making such inferences, and then turning to laws about germs and the like for an explanation of the behavior of the demons. The reason why we do *not* move from (2) to (3)—much less to (6)—in the case of temperature or tables is that explanations formulated in terms of temperatures are so good, on the ground which they were originally intended to cover, that we feel no temptation to stop talking about temperatures and tables merely because we can, in some cases, get more precise predictions by going up a level to laws about molecules. The reason why we move on from (3) to (4) in the case of demons is that the alternative labeled (4b) is readily available—we can easily consign experiences of demons to that great dumping-ground of out-dated entities, the Mind. There were no experiences of demons, we say, but only experiences of mental images.

Now it seems obvious that, in the case of sensations, (A) will not be satisfied. The inconvenience of ceasing to talk about sensations would be so great that only a fanatical materialist would think it worth the trouble to cease referring to sensations. If the Identity Theorist is taken to be predicting that some day "sensation," "pain," "mental image," and the like will drop out of our vocabulary, he is almost certainly wrong. But if he is saying simply that, at no greater cost than an inconvenient linguistic reform, we *could* drop such terms, he is entirely justified. And I take this latter claim to be all that traditional materialism has ever desired.

Before leaving the analogy between demons and sensations, I wish to note one further disanalogy which an opponent of the Identity Theory might pounce upon. Even if we set aside the fact that (A) would not be satisfied in the case of sensations, such an opponent might say, we should note the difficulty in satisfying (B). It would seem that there is no satisfactory answer to the question "What *was* I non-inferentially reporting when I reported on my sensations?" For neither (4a) nor (4b) seems an available option. The first does not seem to be available because it is counter-intuitive to think of, e.g., "I am having my C-fibers stimulated," as capable of being used to make a non-inferential report. The second alternative is simply silly—there is no point in saying that when we report a sensation we are reporting some "merely mental" event. For sensations are *already* mental events. The last point is important for an understanding of the prima facie absurdity of the disappearance form of the Identity Theory. The reason why most statements of the form "there might turn out to be no X's at all" can be accepted with more or less equanimity in the context of forecasts of scientific results is that we are confident we shall always be able to "save the phenomena" by answering the question "But what about all those X's we've been accustomed to observe?" with some reference to thoughts-of-X's, images-of-X's, and the like. Reference to mental entities provides non-inferential reports of X's with something to have been about. But when we want to say "There might turn out to be no mental entities at all," we cannot use this device. This result makes clear that if the analogy between the past disappearance of supernatural beings and the possible future disappearance of sensations is to be pressed, we must claim that alternative (4a) is, appearances to the contrary, still open. That is, we must hold that the question "What *was* I non-inferentially reporting when I non-inferentially reported a stabbing pain?" can be sensibly answered "You were reporting a stimulation of your C-fibers."

Now why should this *not* be a sensible answer? Let us begin by getting a bad objection to it out of the way. One can imagine someone arguing that this answer can only be given if a stimulation of C-fibers is strictly identical with a stabbing pain, and that such strict identification involves category-mistakes. But this objection presupposes that "A report of an X is a report of a Y" entails that "X's are Y's." If we grant this presupposition we shall not be able to say that the question "What was I reporting when I reported a demon?" is properly answered by "You were reporting the content of an hallucination which you were having." However, if we ask why this objection is plausible, we can see the grain of truth which it embodies and conceals. We are usually unwilling to accept "You were reporting a Y" as an answer to the question "What *was* I non-inferentially reporting when I non-inferentially reported an X?" unless (a) Y's are themselves the kind of thing we habitually report on non-inferentially, and (b) there does not exist already an habitual practice of reporting Y's non-inferentially. Thus we accept "the content of an hallucination" as a sensible answer because we know that such contents, being "mental images," are just the sort of thing which does get non-inferentially reported (once it is recognized for what it is) and because we are not accustomed to making non-inferential reports in the form "I am having an hallucinatory image of . . . ."[9] To take an example of answers to this sort of question that are *not* sensible, we reject the claim that when we report on a table

---

[9] Note that people who *become* accustomed to making the latter sort of reports may be no longer accept explanations of their erroneous non-inferential reports by reference to hallucinations. For they know what mental images are like, and they know that *this* pink rat was not an hallucinatory content. The more frequent case, fortunately, is that they just cease to report pink rats and begin reporting hallucinations, for their hallucinations no longer deceive them.

we are reporting on a mass of whirling particles, for either we think we know under what circumstances we should make such a report, and know that these circumstances do not obtain, or we believe that the presence of such particles can only be inferred and never observed.

The oddity of saying that when I think I am reporting on a stabbing pain I am actually reporting on a stimulation of my C-fibers is similar to these last two cases. We either imagine a situation in which we can envisage ourselves non-inferentially reporting such stimulation (periscope hitched up to a microscope so as to give us a view of our trepanned skull, overlying fibers folded out of the way, stimulation evident by change in color, etc., etc.), or else we regard "stimulation of C-fibers" as not the sort of thing which *could* be the subject of a non-inferential report (but inherently a "theoretical" state of affairs whose existence can only be inferred, and not observed). In either case, the assertion that we have been non-inferentially reporting on a brain-process all our lives seems absurd. So the proponent of the disappearance form of the Identity Theory must show that reports of brain-processes are neither incapable of being non-inferential nor, if non-inferential, necessarily made in the way just imagined (with the periscope-microscope gadget) or in some other peculiar way. But now we must ask who bears the burden of proof. Why, after all, should we think that brain-processes are *not* a fit subject-matter for non-inferential reports? And why should it not be the case that the circumstances in which we make non-inferential reports about brain-processes are just those circumstances in which we make non-inferential reports about sensations? For this will in fact be the case if, when we were trained to say, e.g., "I'm in pain" we were in fact being trained to respond to the occurrence within ourselves of a stimulation of C-fibers. If this is the case, the situation will be perfectly parallel to the case of demons and hallucinations. We *will*, indeed, have been making non-inferential reports about brain-processes all our lives *sans le savoir*.

This latter suggestion can hardly be rejected a priori, unless we hold that we can only be taught to respond to the occurrence of A's with the utterance "A!" if we were able, prior to this teaching, to be aware, when an A was present, that it was present. But this latter claim is plausible only if we assume that there is an activity which can reasonably be called "awareness" prior to the learning of language. I do not wish to fight once again the battle which has been fought by Wittgenstein and many of his followers against such a notion of awareness. I wish rather to take it as having been won, and to take for granted that there is no a priori reason why a brain-process is inherently unsuited to be the subject of a non-inferential report. The distinction between observation-terms and non-observation-terms is relative to linguistic practices (practices which may change as inquiry progresses), rather than capable of being marked out once and for all by distinguishing between the "found" and the "made" elements in our experience. I think that the recognition of this relativity is the first of the steps necessary for a proper appreciation of the claims of the Identity Theory. In what follows, I want to show that this first step leads naturally to a second: the recognition that the distinction between *private* and *public* subject-matters is as relative as that between items signified by observation-terms and items not so signified.

The importance of this second step is clear. For even if we grant that reports of brain-processes may be non-inferential, we still need to get around the facts that reports of sensations have an epistemological peculiarity that leads us to call them reports of *private* entities, and that brain-processes are intrinsically *public* entities. Unless we can overcome our intuitive conviction that a report of a private matter (with its attendant infallibility) cannot be identified with a report of a public matter (with its attendant fallibility), we shall not be able to take seriously the claim of the proponents of the disappearance form of the Identity Theory that alternative (4a) is open, and hence that nothing prevents sensations from disappearing from discourse in the same manner, and for the same reasons, as supernatural beings have disappeared from discourse. So far in this paper I have deliberately avoided the problem of the "privacy" of sensations, because I wished to show that if this problem *can* be surmounted, the Identity Theorist may fairly throw the burden of proof onto his opponent by asking whether a criterion can be produced which would show that the identification of sensations and brain-processes involves a conceptual confusion, while absolving the claim that demons do not exist of such a confusion. Since I doubt that such a criterion *can* be produced, I am inclined to say that if the problem about "privacy" is overcome, then the Identity Theorist has made out his case.

5. THE "PRIVACY" OBJECTION

The problem that the privacy of first-person sensation reports presents for the Identity Theory has recently been formulated in considerable detail by Baier.[10] In this section, I shall confine myself to a discussion of his criticism of Smart's initial reply to this argument. Smart holds that the fact that "the language of introspective reports has a different logic from the logic of material processes" is no objection to the

[10] Kurt Baier, "Smart on Sensations," *Australasian Journal of Philosophy*, 40 (1962), pp. 57–68.

Identity Theory, since we may expect that empirical inquiry can and will change this logic:

> It is obvious that until the brain-process theory is much improved and widely accepted there will be no criteria for saying 'Smith has an experience of such-and-such a sort' except Smith's introspective reports. So we have adopted a rule of language that (normally) what Smith says goes.[11]

Baier thinks that this reply "is simply a confusion of the privacy of the subject-matter and the availability of external evidence." [12] Baier's intuition is that the difference between a language-stratum in which the fact that a report is sincerely made is sufficient warrant for its truth, and one in which this situation does not obtain, seems so great as to call for an explanation—and that the only explanation is that the two strata concern different subject-matters. Indeed Baier is content to let the mental-physical distinction stand or fall with the distinction between "private" subject-matters and "public" subject-matters, and he therefore assumes that to show that "introspective reports are necessarily about something private, and that being about something private is *incompatible with being* about something public" [13] is to show, once and for all, that the Identity Theory involves a conceptual confusion. Baier, in short, is undertaking to show that "once private, always private."

He argues for his view as follows:

> To say that one day our physiological knowledge will increase to such an extent that we shall be able to make absolutely reliable encephalograph-based claims about people's experiences, is only to say that, if carefully checked, our encephalograph-based claims about 'experiences' will always be *correct,* i.e. will make the *same claims* as a *truthful* introspective report. If correct encephalograph-based claims about Smith's experiences contradict Smith's introspective reports, we shall be entitled to infer that he is *lying.* In that sense, what Smith says will no longer go. But we cannot of course infer that he is making a mistake, for that is nonsense. . . . *However good the evidence may be, such a physiological theory can never be used to show to the sufferer that he was mistaken in thinking that he had a pain, for such a mistake is inconceivable.* The sufferer's epistemological authority must therefore be better than the best physiological theory can ever be. Physiology can therefore never provide a person with more than *evidence* that someone else is having an experience of one sort or another. It can never lay down *criteria* for saying that someone is having an experience of a

---

[11] Smart, "Sensations and Brain Processes," p. 63.
[12] Baier, p. 63.
[13] Baier, p. 59.

certain sort. Talk about brain-processes therefore must be about something other than talk about experiences. Hence, introspective reports and brain-process talk cannot be merely different ways of talking about the same thing.[14]

Smart's own reply to this line of argument is to admit that

No physiological evidence, say from a gadget attached to my skull, could make me withdraw the statement that I have a pain when as a matter of fact I feel a pain. For example, the gadget might show no suitable similarities of cerebral processes on the various occasions on which I felt a pain.... I must, I think, agree with Baier that if the sort of situation which we have just envisaged did in fact come about, then I should have to reject the brain process thesis, and would perhaps espouse dualism.[15]

But this is not the interesting case. The interesting case is the one in which suitable similarities are in fact found to occur—the same similarities in all subjects—until one day (long after all empirical generalizations about sensations *qua* sensations have been subsumed under physiological laws, and long after direct manipulation of the brain has become the exclusive method of relieving pain) somebody (call him Jones) thinks he has no pain, but the encephalograph says that the brain-process correlated with pain did occur. (Let us imagine that Jones himself is observing the gadget, and that the problem about whether he might have made a mistake is a problem for Jones; this eliminates the possibility of lying.) Now in most cases in which one's observation throws doubt on a correlation which is so central to current scientific explanations, one tries to eliminate the possibility of observational error. But in Baier's view it would be absurd for Jones to do this, for "a mistake is inconceivable." Actually, however, it is fairly clear what Jones' first move would be—he will begin to suspect that he does not know what pain is—i.e., that he is not using the word "pain" in the way in which his fellows use it.[16]

So now Jones looks about for independent verification of the hypothesis that he does not use "I am in pain" incorrectly. But here he runs up against the familiar difficulty about the vocabulary used in making introspective reports—the difficulty of distinguishing between "misuse of language" and "mistake in judgment," between (a) recognizing the state of affairs which obtains for what it is, but describing it wrongly because the words used in the description are not the

[14] Baier, pp. 64–65; italics added.
[15] Smart, "Brain Processes and Incorrigibility—a Reply to Professor Baier," *Australasian Journal of Philosophy*, 40 (1962), p. 68.
[16] This problem will remain, of course, even if Jones merely *thinks* about whether he is in pain, but does not say anything.

right words, and (b) being able to describe it rightly once it is recognized for what it is, but not in fact recognizing it for what it is (in the way in which one deceived by an illusion does not recognize the situation for what it is). If we do not have a way of determining which of these situations obtains, we do not have a genuine contrast between misnaming and misjudging. To see that there is no genuine contrast in this case, suppose that Jones was not burned prior to the time that he hitches on the encephalograph, but now he is. When he is, the encephalograph says that the brain-process constantly correlated with pain-reports occurs in Jones' brain. However, although he exhibits pain-behavior, Jones thinks that he does not feel pain. (But, now as in the past, he both exhibits pain-behavior and thinks that he feels pain when he is frozen, stuck, struck, racked, etc.) Now is it that he does not know that *pain* covers what you feel when you are burned as well as what you feel when you are stuck, struck, etc.? Or is it that he really does not feel pain when he is burned? Suppose we tell Jones that what he feels when he is burned is *also* called "pain." Suppose he then admits that he does feel *something*, but insists that what he feels is quite *different* from what he feels when he is stuck, struck, etc. Where does Jones go from here? Has he failed to learn the language properly, or is he correctly (indeed infallibly) reporting that he has different sensations than those normally had in the situation in question? (Compare the parallel question in the case of a man who uses "blue" in all the usual ways except that he refuses to grant that blue is a color—on the ground that it is so different from red, yellow, orange, violet, etc.)

The only device which would decide this question would be to establish a convention that anyone who sincerely denied that he felt a pain while exhibiting pain-behavior and being burned ipso facto did not understand how to use "pain." This denial would *prove* that he lacked such an understanding. But this would be a dangerous path to follow. For not to understand when to use the word "pain" in non-inferential reports is presumably to be unable to know which of one's sensations to call a "pain." And the denial that one felt pain in the circumstances mentioned would only prove such inability if one indeed *had* the sensation normally called a pain. So now we would have a public criterion, satisfaction of which would count as showing that the subject had such a sensation—i.e., that he felt a pain even though he did not think that he did. But if such a criterion exists, its application over-rides any contradictory report that he may make—for such a report will be automatically disallowed by the fact that it constitutes a demonstration that he does not know what he is talking about. The dilemma is that either a report about one's sensations which violates a certain public criterion is a sufficient condition for saying that the reporter does not know how to use "pain" in the correct way, or there is no such criterion. If there is, the fact that one cannot be mistaken about pains does not entail that sincere reports of pain cannot be over-ridden. If there is not, then there is no way to answer the question formulated at the end of the last paragraph, and hence no way to eliminate the possibility that Jones may not know what pain is. Now since the a priori probability that he does not is a good deal higher than the a priori probability that the psycho-physiological theory of Jones' era is mistaken, this theory has little to fear from Jones. (Although it would have a great deal to fear from a sizable accumulation of cases like Jones'.)

To sum up this point, we may look back at the italicized sentence in the above quotation from Baier. We now see that the claim that "such a mistake is inconceivable" is an ellipsis for the claim that a mistake, made *by one who knows what pain is,* is inconceivable, for only this expanded form will entail that when Jones and the encephalograph disagree, Jones is always right. But when formulated in this way our infallibility about our pains can be seen to be empty. Being infallible about something would be useful only if we could draw the usual distinction between misnaming and misjudging, and, having ascertained that we were not misnaming, know that we were not misjudging. But where there are no criteria for misjudging (or to put it more accurately, where in the crucial cases the criteria for misjudging turn out to be the same as the criteria for misnaming) then to say that we are infallible is to pay ourselves an empty compliment. Our neighbors will not hesitate to ride roughshod over our reports of our sensations unless they are assured that we know our way around among them, and we cannot satisfy them on this point unless, up to a certain point, we tell the same sort of story about them as they do. The limits of permissible stories are flexible enough for us to be able to convince them occasionally that we have odd sensations, but not flexible enough for us to use these surprising sensations to break down, at one blow, well-confirmed scientific theories. As in the case of other infallible pronouncements, the price of retaining one's epistemological authority is a decent respect for the opinions of mankind.

Thus the common-sense remark that first-person reports always will be a better source of information about the occurrence of pains than any other source borrows its plausibility from the fact that we normally do not raise questions about a man's ability to use the word "pain" correctly. Once we *do* raise such questions seriously (as in the case of Jones), we realize that the question (1) "Does he know which sensations are called 'pains'?" and (2) "Is he a good judge of whether he is in pain or not?" are simply two ways of asking the same question: viz.,

"Can we fit his pain-reports into our scheme for explaining and predicting pains?" or, more bluntly, "Shall we disregard his pain-reports or not?" And once we see this we realize that if "always be a better source of information" means "will never be over-ridden on the sort of grounds on which presumed observational errors are over-ridden elsewhere in science," then our common-sensical remark is probably false. If "always be a better source of information" means merely "can only be over-ridden on the basis of a charge of misnaming, and never on the basis of a charge of misjudging," then our common-sensical remark turns out to depend upon a distinction that is not there.

This Wittgensteinian point that sensation-reports must conform to public criteria or else be disallowed may also be brought out in the following way. We determine whether to take a surprising first-person report of pain or its absence seriously (that is, whether to say that the sensation reported is something that science must try to explain) by seeing whether the reporter's overall pattern of pain-reporting is, by the usual behavioral and environmental criteria, normal. Now suppose that these public criteria (for "knowing how to use 'pain'") change as physiology and technology progress. Suppose, in particular, that we find it convenient to speed up the learning of contrastive observation predicates (such as "painful," "tickling," etc.) by supplying children with portable encephalographs-cum-teaching-machines which, whenever the appropriate brain-process occurs, murmur the appropriate term in their ears. Now "appropriate brain-process" will start out by meaning "brain-process constantly correlated with sincere utterances of 'I'm in pain' by people taught the use of 'pain' in the old rough-and-ready way." But soon it will come to mean, "the brain-process which we have always programmed the machine to respond to with a murmur of 'pain.'" (A meter is [now, but was not always] what matches the Standard Meter; intelligence is [now, but was not always] what intelligence tests test; pains will be (but are not now) what the Standard "Pain"-Training Program calls "pain.") Given this situation, it would make sense to say things like "You say you are in pain, and I'm sure you are sincere, but you can see for yourself that your brain is not in the state to which you were trained to respond to with "Pain," so apparently the training did not work, and you do not yet understand what pain is." In such a situation, our "inability to be mistaken" about our pains would remain, but our "final epistemological authority" on the subject would be gone, for there would be a standard procedure for overriding our reports. Our inability to be mistaken is, after all, no more than our ability to have such hypothetical statements as "If you admit that I'm sincere and that I know the language, you have to accept what I say" accepted by our fellows. But this asset can only be converted into final epistemological authority if we can secure both admissions. Where a clear-cut public criterion *does* exist for "knowing the language," inability to be mistaken does not entail inability to be over-ridden.

Now Baier might say that if such criteria did exist, then we should no longer be talking about what we presently mean by "pains." I do not think that this needs to be conceded,[17] but suppose that it is. Would this mean that there was now a subject-matter which was not being discussed—viz., the private subject-matter the existence of which Baier's argument was intended to demonstrate? That we once had contact with such a subject-matter, but lost it? These rhetorical questions are meant to suggest that Baier's explanation of the final epistemological authority of first-person reports of pains by the fact that this "logic" is "a function of this type of subject-matter" rather than, as Smart thinks, a convention—is an explanation of the obscure by the more obscure. More precisely, it will not be an explanation of the epistemological authority in question—but only an unenlightening redescription of it—unless Baier can give a meaning to the term "private subject-matter" other than "kind of thing which is reported in reports which cannot be over-ridden." These considerations show the need for stepping back from Baier's argument and considering the criteria which he is using to demarcate distinct subject-matters.

6. "PRIVACY" AS A CRITERION OF CATEGOREAL DEMARCATION

The closest Baier comes to giving a definition of "private subject-matter" is to say that

> We must say that 'I have a pain' is about 'something private,' because in making this remark we report something which is (1) *necessarily owned* . . . (2) *necessarily exclusive and unsharable* . . . (3) *necessarily imperceptible by the senses* . . . (4) *necessarily asymmetrical*, for whereas it makes no sense to say 'I could see (or hear) that I had a pain,' it makes quite good sense to say 'I could see (or hear) that *he* had a pain'; (5) something about the possession of which the person who claims to possess it could not possibly examine, consider, or weigh any evidence, although other people could . . . and lastly (6) it is something about which the person whose private state it is has final epistemo-

---

[17] My reasons for thinking this concession unnecessary are the same as those presented in some recent articles by Hilary Putnam: cf. "Minds and Machines," *Dimensions of Mind*, ed. S. Hook (New York, 1961), pp. 138–161, esp. pp. 153–160; "The Analytic and the Synthetic," *Minnesota Studies in the Philosophy of Science*, III, pp. 358–397; "Brains and Behavior," in *Analytic Philosophy*, II, ed. by R. J. Butler (Oxford, 1965). [See also Hilary Putnam, "The Nature of Mental States," reprinted in this volume, pp. 150–161, especially section I.]

logical authority, for it does not make sense to say 'I have a pain unless I am mistaken.' [18]

Now this definition of "something private" entails that nothing could be private except a state of a person, and is constructed to delimit all and only those states of a person which we call his "mental" states. To say that mental states are private is to say simply that mental states are described in the way in which mental states are described. But it is not hard to take *any* Rylean category of terms (call it *C*), list all the types of sentence-frames which do and do not make sense when their gaps are filled with terms belonging to this category, and say that "something *C*" is distinguished by the fact that it is "necessarily X," "necessarily Y," etc. where "X" and "Y" are labels for the fact that certain sentence-frames will or will not receive these terms as gap-fillers. For example, consider the thesis that:

> We must say that 'The devil is in that corner' is about 'something supernatural' because in making this report we report something which is *necessarily intangible,* since it makes no sense to ask about the texture of his skin, not *necessarily simply-located,* since it does not follow from the fact that a supernatural being is in the corner that the same supernatural being is not simultaneously at the other side of the globe, *necessarily immortal,* since it does not make sense to say that a supernatural being has died, *necessarily perceptible to exorcists,* since it would not make sense to say that a man was an exorcist and did not perceive the devil when he was present.... .

Are devils hallucinations? No, because when one reports an hallucination one reports something which, though intangible, is simply-located, is neither mortal nor immortal, and is not always perceptible to exorcists. Are reports of devils reports of hallucinations? No, because reports of devils are reports of something supernatural and reports of hallucinations are reports of something private. Is it simply because we lack further information about devils that we take exorcists' sincere reports as the best possible source for information about them? No, for this suggestion confuses the supernatural character of the subject-matter with the availability of external evidence. Those without the supernatural powers with which the exorcist is gifted may find ways of gathering *evidence* for the presence of supernatural beings, but they can never formulate an overriding and independent *criterion* for saying that such a being is present. Their theories might become so good that we might sometimes say that a given exorcist was *lying,* but we could never say that he was *mistaken.*

---

[18] Baier, "Smart on Sensations," p. 60; the numbers in parentheses have been added.

If this pastiche of Baier's argument seems beside the point, it is presumably either (1) because the language-game I have described is not in fact played, or else (2) because "necessarily intangible, not necessarily simply-located, necessarily immortal, and necessarily perceptible to exorcists" does not delimit a subject-matter in the way in which "necessarily owned, exclusive, imperceptible by the senses, asymmetrical, etc., etc." does. In (1) one has to ask "what if it *had* been played?" After all, if the technique of detecting distinct subject-matters which Baier uses is a generally applicable technique, and not just constructed *ad hoc* to suit our Cartesian intuitions, then it ought to work on imaginary as well as real language games. But if it is, we ought to be able to formulate rules for applying it which would tell us *why* (2) is the case. For if we cannot, and if the language-game described once was played, then Baier's objection to the Identity Theory is an objection to the theory that reports of visible supernatural beings are reports of hallucinations. Baier gives no more help in seeing what these rules would be. But I think that the root of Baier's conviction that "something private" is a suitable candidate for being a "distinct subject matter" is the thesis that certain terms are *intrinsically* observation predicates, and signify, so to speak, "natural explananda." When in quest of such predicates we look to the "foundations" of empirical knowledge, we tend to rapidly identify "observation predicate" with "predicate occurring in report having final epistemological authority" with "predicate occurring in report about something private." This chain of identifications leaves us with the suspicion that if there were no longer a private subject-matter to be infallible about, the whole fabric of empirical inquiry about public matters would be left up in the air, unsupported by any absolute epistemological authority. The suggestion that the distinction between items reportable in infallible reports and items not so reportable is "ultimate," or "irreducible," or "categorical," owes its intuitive force to the difficulty of imagining a stage in the progress of inquiry in which there was not *some* situation in which absolute epistemological authority about *something* would be granted to *somebody*.

There probably could *not* be such a stage, for inquiry cannot proceed if everything is to be doubted at once, and if inquiry is even to get off the ground we need to get straight about what is to be questioned and what not. These practical dictates show the kernel of truth in the notion that inquiry cannot proceed without a foundation. Where we slide from truth into error is in assuming that certain items are *naturally* reportable in infallible reports, and thus assume that the items presently so reportable always were and always will be reportable (and conversely for items not presently so reportable). A pain looks like the paradigm of such an item, with the situation described by "seems to me as if I were seeing something red" almost as well-qualified. But in both cases, we can imagine situations in which we should feel justified in over-riding sincere reports using these predicates. More important, we see that the device which we should use to justify ourselves in such situations—viz., "The reporter may not know how to use the word . . . "—is one which can apply in *all* proposed cases. Because this escape-hatch is always available, and because the question of whether the reporter does know how to use the word or not is probably not itself a question which could ever be settled by recourse to any absolute epistemological authority, the situation envisaged by Baier—namely, the body of current scientific theory foundering upon the rock of a single over-riding report—can probably never arise. Baier sees a difference in kind between the weight of evidence produced by such a theory and the single, authoritative, *criterion* provided by such a report. But since there can be no over-riding report until the ability of the speaker to use the words used in the report is established, and since this is to be established only by the weight of the evidence and not by recourse to any single criterion, this difference in kind (even though it may indeed be "firmly embedded in the way we talk" for millennia) is always capable of being softened into a difference of degree by further empirical inquiry.

7. REDUCTIONIST PHILOSOPHICAL THEORIES AND CATEGOREAL DISTINCTIONS

In the preceding sections of this paper I have constantly invoked the fact that language changes as empirical discoveries are made, in order to argue that the thesis that "What people now call 'sensations' might be discovered to be brain-processes" is sensible and unconfused. The "deviance" of a statement of this thesis should not, I have been urging, blind us to the facts that (a) entities referred to by expressions in one Rylean category may also be referred to by expressions in another, (b) expressions in the first category may drop out of the language once this identity of reference is realized, and (c) the thesis in question is a natural way of expressing the result of this realization in the case of "sensation" and "brain-process." Now a critic might object that this strategy is subject to a *reductio ad absurdum*. For the same fact about linguistic change would seem to justify the claim that *any* statement of the form (S) "What people call 'X's' may be discovered to be Y's" is *always* sensible and unconfused. Yet this seems paradoxical, for consider the result of substituting, say "neutrino" for "X" and "mushroom" for "Y." If the resulting statement is not conceptually confused, what statement is?

In answer to this objection, I should argue that it is a mistake to attribute "conceptual confusions" to *statements*. No statement can be known to express a conceptual confusion simply by virtue of an acquaintance with the meanings of its component terms. Confusion is a property of people. Deviance is a property of utterances. Deviant utterances made by using sentences of the form (S) *may* betoken confusion on the part of the speaker about the meanings of words, but it may simply indicate a vivid (but unconfused) imagination, or perhaps (as in the neutrino-mushroom case) merely idle fancy. Although the making of such statements may be prima facie evidence of conceptual confusion—i.e., of the fact that the speaker is insufficiently familiar with the language to find a non-deviant way of making his point—this evidence is only prima facie, and questioning may bring out evidence pointing the other way. Such questioning may show that the speaker actually has some detailed suggestions about possible empirical results which would point to the discovery in question, or that he has no such suggestions, but is nevertheless not inclined to use the relevant words in any *other* deviant utterances, and to cheerfully admit the deviance of his original utterance. The possibility of such evidence, pointing to imagination or to fancy rather than to confusion, shows that from the fact that certain questions are typically asked, and certain statements typically made, by victims of conceptual confusion, it does not follow that all those who use the sentences used to ask these questions or to make these statements are thus victimized.

This confusion about confusion is due to the fact that philosophers who propound "reductionist" theories (such as "There is no insensate matter," "There are no minds," "There are no physical objects," etc.) often *have* been conceptually confused. Such theories are often advocated as solutions to pseudo-problems whose very formulation involves deviant uses of words—uses which in fact result from a confusion between the uses of two or more senses of the same term, or between two or more related terms (e.g., "name" and "word") or between the kind of questions appropriately asked of entities referred to by one set of terms and the kind appropriately asked of entities referred to by another. (That these deviant uses *are* the result of such confusion, it should be noticed, is only capable of being determined by questioning of those who use them—and we only feel *completely* safe in making this diagnosis when the original user has, in the light of the linguistic facts drawn to his attention, admitted that his putative "problem" has been dissolved.) Because reductionist theories may often be choked off at the source by an examination of uses of language, anti-reductionist philosophers have lately become prone to use "conceptual confusion" or "category-mistake" as an all-purpose diagnosis for any deviant utterance in the mouth of a philosopher. But this is a mistake. Predictions of the sort illustrated by (S) may be turned to confused purposes, and they may be made by confused people. But we could only infer with certainty from the deviance of the utterance of a sentence of the form (S) to the conceptual confusion of the speaker if we had a map of the categories which are exhibited in all possible languages, and were thus in a position to say that the cross-category identification envisaged by the statement was eternally impossible. In other words, we should only be in a position to make this inference with certainty if we knew that empirical inquiry could *never* bring about the sort of linguistic change which permits the non-deviant use of "There are no X's" in the case of the "X's" to which the statement in question refers. But philosophers are in no position to say that such change is impossible. The hunt for categoreal confusions at the source of reductionist philosophical theories is an extremely valuable enterprise. But their successes in this enterprise should not lead linguistic philosophers to think that they can do better what metaphysicians did badly—namely, prove the irreducibility of entities. Traditional materialism embodied many confusions, but at its heart was the unconfused prediction about future empirical inquiry which is the Identity Theory. The confusions may be eradicated without affecting the plausibility or interest of the prediction.[19]

[19] I have been greatly helped in preparing this paper by the comments of Richard Bernstein, Keith Gunderson, Amélie Rorty, and Richard Schmitt.

RICHARD J. BERNSTEIN

The Challenge of Scientific Materialism

What is scientific materialism? And what is the challenge that it presents to the contemporary philosopher? In order to answer these questions, let us first locate the felt difficulty that sets the context for this challenge. Consider the following two quotations. The first is by J. J. C. Smart:

> It seems to me that science is increasingly giving us a viewpoint whereby organisms are able to be seen as physicochemical mechanisms: it seems that even the behavior of man himself will one day be explicable in mechanistic terms. There does seem to be, so far as science is concerned, nothing in the world but increasingly complex arrangements of physical constituents. All except for one place: in consciousness. That is, for a full description of what is going on in a man you would have to mention not only physical processes in his tissues, glands, nervous system, and so forth, but also his states of consciousness: his visual, auditory and tactual sensations, his aches and pains. . . . So sensations, states of consciousness, do seem to be the one sort of thing left outside the physicalist picture, and for various reasons I just cannot believe that this can be so. That everything should be explicable in terms of physics . . . except the occurrence of sensations seems to me to be frankly unbelievable.[1]

In radical opposition to this, consider what Merleau-Ponty has to say:

> The whole universe of science is built upon the world as directly experienced, and if we want to subject science itself to rigorous

Reprinted from the *International Philosophical Quarterly*, VIII, 2 (June 1968), 252–275, by permission of the editor and Richard J. Bernstein.

[1] "Sensations and Brain Processes," reprinted in *The Philosophy of Mind*, ed. by V. C. Chappell (Englewood Cliffs, N. J.: 1962), p. 161. [Reprinted in this volume, pp. 53–66. References below are to the occurrence in this volume.]

scrutiny and arrive at a precise assessment of its meaning and scope, we must begin by reawakening the basic experience of the world of which science is the second order expression. Science has not and never will have, by its very nature, the same significance *qua* form of being as the world which we perceive, for the simple reason that it is a rationale or explanation of that world. I am, not a 'living creature' nor even a 'man' nor again even 'a consciousness' endowed with all the characteristics which zoology, social anatomy or inductive psychology recognize in these various products of the natural or historical process—I am the absolute source, my existence does not stem from my antecedents, from my physical and social environment. . . . Scientific points of view, according to which my existence is a moment of the world's, are always both naive and at the same time dishonest, because they take for granted, without explicitly mentioning it, the other point of view, namely that of consciousness, through which from the outset a world forms itself round me and begins to exist for me.[2]

THE CHALLENGE

These two passages reflect opposing points of view about the significance of contemporary science for the study of man. The conflicts that these opposing positions generate have been with us ever since the rise of modern experimental and theoretical science and have origins that go back much further into the history of philosophy. On the one hand there have been philosophers who have maintained that it is science and only science that provides us with legitimate knowledge of what man is. Of course, we have all kinds of beliefs and opinions about the nature of man. But these beliefs could, in principle, be replaced or accounted for by scientific knowledge. But whenever such a position has been refined, articulated and defended, there have always been philosophers who find such a claim presumptuous, misguided and false. They have argued that no matter how highly developed, a scientific account of man, by its very *nature,* would not tell us the whole story of what man really is. At best, a scientific account provides us with a partial understanding of what man is; indeed what is distinctively human eludes the categories of science. And as Merleau-Ponty says, to understand the status of science itself, we must realize that it presupposes and takes for granted another point of view—that of consciousness itself.

The conflicts and oppositions that these differing points of view generate have become particularly acute in our time. Recently a good deal of philosophic passion and subtlety have been displayed by the

[2] *The Phenomenology of Perception,* trans. by Colin Smith (New York: 1962), viii

new defenders of scientific materialism; it is their arguments that I want to consider. I will try to show that they have failed to justify their position. And furthermore, in showing what is wrong here, there are some important consequences for the general issues concerning the relation of language to ontology. I do not want to claim that for once and for all it can be definitely shown that scientific materialism is mistaken. My own view of philosophic dialectic is that such definitive claims are always risky and never completely warranted—one must patiently try to show what is right and wrong with philosophic arguments and positions. It is in this respect that recent arguments for scientific materialism present us with a challenge.

But who is the scientific materialist and what precisely is he claiming? In using the term "scientific materialism" we want to distinguish this position from some varieties of classical materialism. Typically the classical materialist had a picture or model of what matter is—it consists of ultimate particles or atoms in motion. There are regularities of atoms in motion and it is the laws of motion that state what these regularities are. In part, especially in the early stages of the development of modern science, this sort of picture was based on what *seemed* to be the scientific results of the time. Scientific materialists are more sophisticated; they are sensitive to science as an ongoing process and of the dangers of stating *now* what the ultimate entities and laws of science will look like. Consequently we do not find an attempt to define explicitly what are the basic entities countenanced by science; this is a scientific matter. Indeed the very concept of matter is fraught with ambiguities. Instead we find a general and open characterization of what is physical—one which can be given specification only as science develops. As Feigl says, physical in the broad sense (what he calls physical$_1$) "may be defined as the sort of objects or processes which can be described (and possibly explained or predicted) in the concepts of a language with an intersubjective observation basis. This language or conceptual system is,—in *our* sort of world—characterized by its spatio-temporal-causal structure." [3] Such a characterization is deliberately open because the new scientific materialist or physicalist wants to counterance any sort of entity or process that is required for scientific description and explanation. His *philosophic* claim is that nothing else has to be recognized as real over and above what is needed for science. Playing on the classical formula, Sellars tells us "in the dimension of describing and explaining the world, science is the measure of all things, of what is that it is, and of what is not that it is not." [4]

[3] "The 'Mental' and the 'Physical'," *Minnesota Studies in the Philosophy of Science*, II, ed. by H. Feigl, M. Scriven, and G. Maxwell (Minneapolis: 1958), p. 421.
[4] Wilfrid Sellars, *Science Perception and Reality* (New York: 1963), p. 173.

Traditionally there have been three sorts of obstacles that stand in the way of the claim that man is *nothing but* a complex physical mechanism: the status of persons; the nature of thought and intentionality; and the nature of sensations and feelings.[5] For reasons that I do not want to explore here, the new scientific materialists have not focused on the concept of thought and persons. There is a conviction, which I do not believe is warranted, that these do not present serious obstacles to asserting scientific materialism. The issue that has presented the greatest challenge to them has been the status of sensations and feelings or what is sometimes technically called "raw feels." "Raw feels" is a term introduced to cover the sorts of things that I can non-inferentially report about myself which are non-conceptual in character, i.e. they lack the intentionality characteristic of thoughts. Pains, moods, sensations are typically considered to be candidates for "raw feels."[6] Prima facie, there seems to be all the difference in the world—a categorial difference—between a pain and a physical object or process. As Smart says in the passage that we quoted, sensations, states of consciousness do seem to be the sort of thing left out of the physicalist picture. But are they? This is just what the scientific materialist wants to deny. Positively speaking he wants to assert that "raw feels" are *identical*—strictly identical—with brain processes or aspects of brain processes. Or, as we shall see when we consider some of the more sophisticated versions of scientific materialism, he wants to *deny* that there are any such *mental* entities or events—there are no "raw feels."

THREE VERSIONS OF THE IDENTITY THEORY

This thesis has been labeled the "identity theory or thesis of mind and body," and we want to examine it in detail. We want to distinguish three types of identity theory—or, more accurately, three stages in the defense of an identity theory. These will be identified simply by the names of individuals who have defended these versions. They are the Feigl version, the Smart version and the Feyerabend-Rorty version. The first two have received a great deal of critical attention, but the third one has barely been discussed. Yet it is the most radical and challenging one, for it not only claims to overcome all the difficulties that have been presented against the first two versions, it challenges the very foundations of two of the most influential styles of philosophizing of our time, viz. conceptual analysis as practiced by many

---

[5] See Sellars, *op. cit.*, pp. 32ff.

[6] For a more complete characterization of the meaning of "raw feels," see Feigl, *op. cit.*, pp. 372ff., and Sellars, "The Identity Approach to the Mind-Body Problem," *Review of Metaphysics*, 18 (1965), 436.

Anglo-Saxon philosophers and the phenomenological analysis characteristic of Continental thinkers.

But before taking up the three versions of the identity thesis, a few preliminary remarks are necessary in order to clarify precisely what is the issue here. When the identity theorist tells us that "raw feels" or sensations[7] are identical with brain processes, he is not claiming that this is an analytic truth or that what we now mean by "sensations" is synonymous with the expression "brain processes." He is claiming that as a matter of fact, sensations will turn out to be identical with brain processes. Now this seems to be some sort of empirical hypothesis that would require empirical evidence for its confirmation. But where precisely is the philosophic issue? The philosophic issue is that the identity theorist wants to argue that it makes sense to claim that empirical inquiry will show that "sensations" are nothing but brain processes. For this is what his opponent challenges, accusing the identity theorist of making a category mistake or being involved in a fundamental conceptual confusion. The point has been perspicuously stated by Rorty when he says, the proponent of the Identity Theory is "one who thinks it is sensible to assert that empirical inquiry will discover that *sensations* . . . are identical with certain brain processes."[8] And he adds "a proponent of the Identity Theory is usually thought of as one who predicts that empirical inquiry *will* reach this result—but few philosophers in fact stick their necks out in this way. The issue is not the truth of the prediction, but whether such a prediction makes sense."

Secondly, strictly speaking, the identity theory is logically independent of the issue of scientific materialism. It is one thing to claim that "raw feels" or sensations and brain processes are identical, and quite another to claim that *what* is discovered to be identical turns out to be physical or material. Let us not forget that the claim of identity is just as fundamental to idealism as it is to materialism. And there have been philosophers who have claimed that *what* is identical is neither physical nor mental, but neutral. I mention this point here, because sometimes identity theorists argue as if once we show that it is sensible to assert the identity of sensations and brain processes, then materialism is secured, but this certainly doesn't follow.

The third point to keep in mind is what we mean by identity. Identity is not to be understood as correlation or even extentional equiv-

---

[7] Throughout this paper, I focus on "sensations," although the technical term "raw feels" has been introduced to cover all the sense modalities.

[8] Richard Rorty, "Mind-Body Identity, Privacy, and Categories," *Review of Metaphysics*, 18 (1965), 24. [Reprinted in this volume, p. 174. References below are to the occurrence in this volume.]

alence. If the identity theory amounted to the claim that when a specific sensation occurs, some specific brain process occurs, the thesis would be rather trivial. The identity theorist claims that there is a strict identity between sensations and brain processes. And he accepts the following formula for strict identity: $(x)(y)[(x = y) \supset (F)(Fx \equiv Fy)]$.

THE FEIGL AND SMART VERSIONS

With these preliminary remarks, we can briefly discuss the Feigl and Smart versions of the identity theory as a preliminary for encountering the Feyerabend-Rorty defense. Feigl tells us that:

> The identity thesis which I wish to clarify and defend asserts that states of direct experience which conscious human beings "live through," and those which we confidently ascribe to some higher animals, are identical with . . . aspects of neural processes in those organisms . . . what is *had-in-experience,* and (in the case of human beings) *knowable by acquaintance* is identical with the object of *knowledge by description* provided first by molar behavior theory and this in turn is identical with what the science of neurophysiology *describes*.[9]

Feigl himself characterizes this as a "double knowledge" theory. But let us analyze what Feigl is really claiming here. First, it is important to emphasize that Feigl does believe that we have two radically different forms of knowledge, knowledge by acquaintance and knowledge by description. When, for example, I report that I am in pain I am not necessarily uttering a non-cognitive cry of pain. I may be making a genuine report of what is "had-in-experience." As such, this report can be true or false, and if it is true, then I have genuine direct knowledge of my own states of consciousness. Furthermore, I can use a range of phenomenal predicates to describe my immediate experience, I can correctly describe a pain as dull or intense. The "verification" for this sort of knowledge by acquaintance differs from the way in which I verify knowledge by description because it is direct and immediate. Nevertheless *what* I know by acquaintance is, according to Feigl, identical with what the neurophysiologist refers to when he refers to certain configurational aspects of my cerebral processes. While these two sorts of knowledge differ, they are both knowledge. Feigl isn't saying that what I know by acquaintance is only appearance and what I know by description is reality. Both these

[9] *Op. cit.,* p. 446.

forms of knowledge, properly understood, are equally legitimate, and both are about what there really is. "The data of experience *are* the reality which a very narrow class of neurophysiological concepts denotes." [10] But while it may appear that what Feigl is claiming is relatively clear and what is needed is a justification of the thesis—the thesis itself is not at all free from difficulty and ambiguity.

In the first place, the statement of the thesis presupposes we are clear and satisfied with the philosophic distinction between knowledge by acquaintance and knowledge by description. But this is a distinction that has been severely, and in my opinion, devastatingly criticized.[11] Further, it is not at all clear in what sense, if any, we *verify* the type of first person reports that we make about what we supposedly know by acquaintance.[12] But let us pass by these thorny issues and ask how this form of the identity thesis is related to scientific materialism. If we interpret scientific materialism as the theory that denies that there are any such "entities" as sensations and feelings, then Feigl takes issue with scientific materialism. For he does not claim that "raw feels" do not exist. They do exist: it is just that they turn out to be identical with aspects of neurophysiological processes. But then what is the cash value of the claim that "raw feels" and some neurophysiological processes are identical? It is—to put the matter linguistically—that the referents of the expression "sensation" or "raw feels" are as a matter of fact, identical with the referents of appropriate expressions in neurophysiology. But is this sufficient to justify the identity thesis in any interesting or important sense? I suggest that it is not. For Feigl hasn't overcome the dualism that the identity theory is supposed to overcome; he has pushed the problem into the background. Formally, his "solution" is isomorphic with the type of dualism he is supposedly refuting. To see this, let us grant his major contention concerning the identity of the referents that we know by acquaintance and we know by description. Feigl is maintaining that we have two sorts of knowledge about one and the same thing, and indeed that the modes of verification of these two sorts of knowledge are different. Furthermore, these two sorts of knowledge are irreducible in the sense that even if the neurophysiologist of the future could completely describe and explain brain processes—what these *same* processes are "acquaintancewise" is left open. And no matter how complete and sensitive my phenomenological knowledge of my own "raw feels," the question of how these are to be described from a

[10] *Ibid.*, p. 453.

[11] For example, see Sellars' essay "Empiricism and the Philosophy of Mind," printed in *Science, Perception, and Reality*.

[12] See Jerome Shaffer, "Recent Work on the Mind-Body Problem," *American Philosophical Quarterly*, 2 (1965), 84.

neurophysiological point of view is an open matter. In short, instead of an ontological dualism between two types of entities, we are left with an epistemological dualism between two irreducibly different types of knowledge. In the spirit of the positivism from which Feigl emerges, we can ask what is the difference that makes a difference between saying that we are speaking of two different entities when we report our sensations and describe our neurophysiological processes, and saying that although we are *really* speaking about one entity, we have two radically different types of knowledge about it? This looks like a classic instance of what the positivists used to call a "pseudo-problem."

The basic difficulty with Feigl's statement and defense of the identity thesis results from his thinking that the cardinal issue is a matter of asserting an identity of reference for certain expressions in two independent forms of knowledge. But the tough problem for a strong version of the identity thesis concerns the status of characteristics, properties, or universals that we ascribe to "raw feels" and those which we ascribe to neurophysiological processes. To put the issue linguistically, we must confront the tangled issues of predication. Sellars locates the issue when he writes:

> In speaking of "raw feels" as identical with "brain states" [the identity theorist] does not simply mean that the very same logical subjects which have "raw feel" characteristics also have "brain state" characteristics, or that "raw feel" characteristics do not occur apart from "brain state" characteristics, but rather that the very characteristics are themselves identical. As Feigl puts it, "raw feel" universals are identical with certain "brain state" universals.[13]

But Feigl has not justified this claim, nor has he adequately clarified what it means to assert such an identity of universals or characteristics. Indeed his "double knowledge" theory appears to be incompatible with such a claim. For if the referents and the characteristics that we ascribe to these referents are identical in our knowledge by acquaintance and our knowledge by description, then it would seem that we do not really have two types of knowledge, but only one sort of knowledge.

It is misleading to label Feigl's position "materialism" (just as misleading as it would be to label it "idealism"), for he does not deny that "raw feels" exist. On the contrary, he categorically affirms their existence. But Smart in his defense of the identity thesis *and* scientific materialism does want to deny the existence of a class of events, entities, or features that are uniquely mental or psychical. Consequently

[13] "The Identity Approach to the Mind-Body Problem," p. 430.

he tries to meet the type of objection concerning properties that present so much trouble for Feigl's view. Examining how he tries to meet this objection will carry us further in appreciating the general difficulty with scientific materialism when it is defended along these lines.

Smart puts the objection as follows:

> It may be possible to get out of asserting the existence of irreducibly psychic processes, but not out of asserting the existence of irreducibly psychic *properties*. For suppose we identify the Morning Star with the Evening Star. Then there must be some properties which logically imply that of being the Morning Star, and quite distinct properties which entail that of being the Evening Star. Again there must be some properties (for example, that of being a yellow flash) which are logically distinct from those in the physicalist story.[14]

Now it is important to see why this is a difficulty for the proponent of scientific materialism. For he wants to admit that when I say something like "I see a yellowish-orange after image," I am (or can be) making a genuine report, something capable of being true or false. But he wants to deny that making of accurate reports of this type requires us to admit that there are irreducibly psychic processes or features. But we *now* identify sensations by a set of characteristics which are "logically distinct from those in the physicalist story." Indeed if this were not the case, the problem that sets the context for the assertion of the identity thesis would dissolve. So it *seems* as if the very statement of the identity thesis presupposes the existence of two different *types* of characteristics or features—those traditionally called "mental" and "physical."

How does Smart attempt to meet this objection? He suggests that "when a person says 'I see a yellowish-orange after image,' he is saying something like this: *'There is something going on which is like what is going on when* I have my eyes open, am awake, and there is an orange illuminated in good light in front of me, when I really see an orange.'"† But what is this proposed translation intended to achieve? Note that the second sentence does not contain any expressions that seem to commit us to saying that there are irreducible psychic properties. The words are what Smart calls "all quasi-logical or topic neutral" and this sort of claim is perfectly compatible with the claim that there are nothing but physical processes and qualities. If we accepted this sort of translation for our direct reports, then we would no longer have an obstacle to the defense of scientific materialism. But something funny is going on here, and when Smart originally put

---

[14] "Sensations and Brain Processes," p. 59.
† [*Ibid.*, p. 61.]

forth his answer to the objection he admitted that it is the "one which I am least confident of having satisfactorily met." [15]

Why is Smart so uneasy about his reply to the objection? The reason concerns what we are doing when we claim that when one utters the first sentence about a yellowish-orange after-image, "he is saying something like" the second sentence. If Smart's proposal is intended to mean that the second sentence has the same meaning as the first, or that we can translate the first sentence into the second as we might translate a Hebrew sentence into English, then his claim is clearly false. It can be shown that the second sentence does not have the same meaning as the first one and it has been argued that any so-called topic neutral sentence would fail to be an adequate translation of those sentences we use to make direct reports of our sensations and feelings.[16] Rorty locates the essential difficulty of this version of the identity theory—which he calls the "translation form"—when he writes

> I believe that an attempt to defend the translation form will inevitably get bogged down in controversy about the adequacy of the proposed topic-neutral translations of statements about sensations. There is obviously a sense of "adequate translation" in which the topic-neutrality of the purported translations *ipso facto* makes them inadequate. So the proponent of the translation form of the theory will have to fall back on a weaker sense of "adequate translation." But the weaker this sense becomes, the less impressive is the claim being made, and the less difference between the Identity Theory and the non-controversial thesis that certain brain-processes may be constantly correlated with certain sensations.[17]

We can sum up the difficulty with the identity theory as defended by Feigl and Smart in the form of a dilemma. The more one insists that there are two irreducible but equally legitimate types of knowledge of what is supposedly one and the same entity, the more innocuous the identity theory becomes because we shift the locus of the dualism and do not dissolve it, while the more one stresses that our non-inferential first person reports of sensations can be translated into a topic neutral language, the more it looks as if one is trying to resolve the apparent disparities between "sensation talk" and "physicalistic talk" by arbitrary stipulation.

The very statement of this dilemma points to a way of trying to slip through its horns. Roughly speaking, the scientific materialist gets into trouble because of the tension between wanting to claim that in

---

[15] *Ibid.*, p. 59.
[16] See James Cornman, "The Identity of Mind and Body," *Journal of Philosophy*, 59 (1962). [Reprinted in this volume, pp. 73–79.]
[17] *Op. cit.*, p. 78.

some sense there are two legitimate ways of knowing about what is supposed to be one and the same entity, and wanting to claim that, in some sense, one of these conceptual schemes could be replaced by the other. But why not take the idea of replacement or displacement seriously? Can we not imagine a situation where in principle at least, our sensation talk would disappear and be replaced by neurophysiological discourse in which we can better describe and explain everything that is to be described and explained. Recently, a number of philosophers including Feyerabend, Sellars, and Rorty have suggested that something like this might be the case, and that such a line of attack is the proper way of defending the core of scientific materialism. Before considering this position in detail, it is important to see how radical it is and how it does present a challenge to existing modes of philosophizing.

In what has been called "conceptual analysis" as well as in some varieties of phenomenological analysis, it is not uncommon to find philosophic arguments that run something like the following: There are certain basic categories, concepts, language forms, or modes of experience that we use in understanding and encountering the world. One of the main tasks of philosophy is to discover and lay bare the complex structure of our fundamental conceptual scheme(s). If a philosophic thesis is proposed and we can show that it is incompatible with our *basic* conceptual scheme or modes of experience, then this is sufficient to expose the absurdity of the thesis. Much of the strategy of the critics of the identity theory has been concerned with showing in detail how the theory is incompatible with the basic ways in which we now talk about, report and describe sensations, or what is sometimes called "the logic of sensation discourse." And defenders of the Feigl and Smart versions of the identity theory have tried to show how the theory is compatible with the ways in which we now talk about sensations. To illustrate my point about this type of criticism, consider the following statement of Malcolm in his related discussion of "thoughts":

> It might be objected that *as things are* the bodily location of thoughts is not a meaningful notion; but if massive correlations were discovered between thoughts and brain processes then we might *begin* to locate thoughts in the head. To this I must answer that our philosophical problem *is* about how things are. It is a question about our *present* concepts of thinking and thought, not about some conjectured future concepts.[18]

[18] Norman Malcolm, "Scientific Materialism and the Identity Theory," *Dialogue*, 3 (1963), 119.

Or consider the summation of an argument offered by Shaffer:

> As things now stand the Identity [of mental and physical events] cannot be maintained, since our language and conceptual scheme does not allow us to locate mental events in the brain. *So an Identity Theory in any of its variants cannot be accepted.*[19] (italics added)

THE RORTY AND FEYERABEND VERSIONS

The champions of what Rorty calls the "displacement" view claim that this sort of argument cuts absolutely no philosophic ice. They see it as an expression of the worst sort of philosophic conservatism. Suppose it is admitted that the basic ways in which we now report and describe sensations are not only different from, but *incompatible* with a physicalistic or materialistic conceptual scheme. What follows from this? Certainly not the conclusions of Malcolm and Shaffer. For an essential premise in their arguments is that there is something inviolable, indubitable, or unchallengeable about our present conceptual scheme. But one ought to consider the possibility that there may be good reasons for adopting a new conceptual scheme and abandoning our present one, no matter how deeply embedded it is. If the identity theory as we have interpreted it is a theory that defends the meaningfulness of a prediction (that we may discover that sensations are nothing but brain processes), then it certainly isn't sufficient to reject it on the basis of the ways in which we now talk or think. In differing ways, Feyerabend, Rorty, and Sellars have argued that even though there is a conceptual scheme deeply embedded in our present ways of thinking and speaking, such a scheme is not beyond radical criticism —the type of criticism that would suggest that our "manifest" ways of describing, explaining, and reporting do not tell us what there really is, but at best what we *believe* there is and what *appears* to us as real.[20] There are echoes of the past in these radical suggestions. Just as Plato challenged the absolute reality of what appears to us to be real, so these philosophers challenge the absolute reality of what appears to us to be most real. Of course, there is sharp disagreement

---

[19] *Op. cit.*, p. 98.

[20] See Rorty, "Mind-Body Identity, Privacy, and Categories"; Sellars, "The Identity Approach to the Mind-Body Problem," also chapters 1 and 3 of *Science, Perception, and Reality*; Feyerabend, "Explanation, Reduction, and Empiricism," *Minnesota Studies in the Philosophy of Science*, III, ed. by H. Feigl and G. Maxwell (Minneapolis: 1962), p. 90, also "Materialism and the Mind-Body Problem," *Review of Metaphysics*, 17 (1963), 49–67. [See also Feyerabend, "Mental Events and the Brain," reprinted in this volume, pp. 172–173.]

with Plato about what is taken to be the measure of the real. Since Rorty has presented the subtlest defense for the disappearance form of the identity theory, let us turn directly to an examination of his position.

The disappearance form of the identity theory holds that the relation between what we now call "sensations" and "certain brain processes"

> ... is not strict identity, but rather the sort of relation which obtains between, to put it crudely, existent entities and non-existent entities when reference to the latter once served (some of) the purposes presently served by reference to the former—the sort of relation that holds, e.g., between "quantity of caloric fluid" and "mean kinetic energy of molecules." There is an obvious sense of same in which what used to be called "a quantity of caloric fluid" is *the same thing* as what is now called a certain mean kinetic energy of molecules, but there is no reason to think that all features truly predicated of the one may be sensibly predicated of the other.[21]

Consequently, the disappearance form of the identity theory (if it can be justified) avoids the difficulties that plague the translation form because it "holds that it is unnecessary to show that suitable translations (into a 'topic neutral' language) of our talk about sensations can be given—as unnecessary as to show that statements about quantities of caloric fluid, when properly understood, may be seen to be topic-neutral statements." [22] Indeed the disappearance view dissolves the problem of "features" or "characteristics" which causes Feigl and Smart so much trouble because "from the point of view of this second form of the theory, it is a mistake to assume that 'X's are nothing but Y's' entails 'All attributes meaningfully predicable of X's are meaningfully predicated of Y's.'"

Consider how seductive this line of argument is, especially in light of recent investigations into the philosophy and history of science. If we isolated two different and competing theories from ongoing scientific inquiry such as the caloric theory and the kinetic theory of molecules and examined their logical structure, we could say that strictly speaking neither the entities referred to in each theory nor some of the predicates meaningfully used to describe these entities are identical. But what would the location and specification of these differences tell us about what there really is? Nothing. Because if we consider these theories in the context of scientific inquiry where dif-

[21] "Mind-Body Identity, Privacy, and Categories," p. 176.
[22] *Ibid.*, p. 177.

ficulties are noted about the caloric theory and where we can give a variety of good reasons for adopting the kinetic theory, we can say that we can now give a better explanation and description of what used to be called "a quantity of caloric fluid." We can say that what used to be called "a quantity of caloric fluid" turns out to be nothing but the mean kinetic energy of molecules, and we can add finally that there really is no such thing as "a quantity of caloric fluid."

Can we apply this sort of analogy to the case of sensation discourse and neurophysiological discourse? If we can, then we could say that even though the meaning and reference of such expressions as "sensations" differ from the meaning and reference of such expressions as "certain brain processes," and even though there are now attributes that we can now meaningfully predicate of sensations which are not meaningfully predicated of brain processes, we could, in principle, drop our present discourse about sensations and replace it with neurophysiological discourse without diminishing our ability to describe and predict. Or as Rorty says, "Elimination of the referring use of the expressions in question . . . from our language would leave our ability to describe and predict undiminished." [23] We could then say that what used to be called "sensations" are brain processes, or sensations are nothing but brain processes, and finally there are no sensations. In denying the existence of sensations, we would mean that there are no longer any good theoretical reasons (although there may be good practical reasons) for using a language in which we speak about sensations.

Rorty has defended this version of the identity theory with a number of ingenious arguments. He has even sketched a general theory of the conditions under which a term may cease to have a referring use without saying that those who originally made such a use held false beliefs. This last point is extremely important for understanding the plausibility of the disappearance theory. If it is really possible that neurophysiological discourse could, in principle, displace our present language for reporting and describing sensations, and if it is correct to say that there really are no sensations, it would seem that we have been talking nonsense all our lives. How can we make correct reports and give correct descriptions about our sensations—as we all think that we do—if there are no sensations? But Rorty tells us that the

> . . . absurdity of saying "Nobody has ever felt a pain" is no greater than that of saying that "Nobody has ever seen a demon," *if* we have a suitable answer to the question "What *was* I reporting when I said I felt a pain?" To this question, the science of the future may reply, "You

[23] *Ibid.,* pp. 180f.

were reporting the occurrence of a certain brain-process and it would make life simpler for us if you would, in the future *say* 'My C-fibers are firing' instead of saying 'I'm in pain'." [24]

Is Rorty right when he claims that this version of the identity theory overcomes the difficulties that we have encountered in exploring the other varieties of the identity theory? I do not think so. But to show this, we must pinpoint the crucial issue here and we can do this by distinguishing a weaker and a stronger thesis that his remarks suggest. Suppose we take seriously the suggestion that the scientist of the future may tell us I was really reporting the occurrence of a brain process when I said I felt a pain. We could accept this claim and still maintain that there is another legitimate way of knowing about and reporting this brain process in addition to the ways available to neurophysiology. There is nothing self-contradictory in saying, "My sensations may *really* be the brain processes studied by neurophysiology, but these 'brain processes' as *I* experience them, report them and describe them *have* the characteristics which I now ascribe to them." This is just the situation of the double knowledge theory that Feigl has advocated. And while we objected to Feigl's view *as an identity theory,* we did not rule out the possibility that we can describe and know one and the same thing in two radically different ways. But once again, if this is all that Rorty were saying there would be no advance beyond Feigl. We would be faced with an epistemological dualism rather than an ontological dualism. *Deciding what kind of entity, if any, is the referent for expressions like "sensations" is simply not sufficient to establish the identity theory in any important or interesting sense.*

It is clear, however, that there is something stronger that Rorty wants to hold, for he tells us that the identity theorist is justified in asserting that "at no greater cost than inconvenient linguistic reform, we *could* drop such terms [as 'sensation,' 'pain,' 'mental image']." [25] The situation that Rorty envisions is one where we could, in principle, drop our entire present language for reporting and describing sensations without diminishing our ability to describe and predict. The key concept here is that of "description" for I think that what Rorty is claiming turns out to be false, trivial, or radically unclear. "Description" like "experience" is what Dewey once called a weasel term and we must be extremely careful about how the concept of description is being used. I now have a rich vocabulary for describing my sensations, feelings, moods, etc. Whatever our ultimate conclusions about the significance of the phenomenological movement, I do think that it has shown us how multifarious and diverse our descriptions can be.

[24] *Ibid.,* p. 179f.
[25] *Ibid.,* p. 185.

Furthermore, we can make better and worse, more accurate and less accurate descriptions of what we now call sensations and feelings. The issue is not whether or not I can describe the same thing or event in neurophysiological discourse, but whether I can give the same *types* of descriptions and reports that I now give of my sensations and feelings in the new purified neurophysiological science. If I can't then there is a perfectly legitimate sense in which I can say that although for *scientific purposes* my ability to describe and predict is undiminished, nevertheless my ability to describe is diminished if I adopt the new neurophysiological discourse. Why? Because there would be no way of saying in this ideal language what I can now correctly say.[26] The point about description has its parallel in related discussions of motions and actions. Suppose a philosopher tells me that the same event that I describe as "Peter killed Paul with a kitchen knife" can be described as a series of complex motions. We might agree that there is a *sense* of "same event" whereby we are describing the same event, but it doesn't follow that we are giving the same type of description of the event nor that one type of description is replaceable by the other. Let us be careful. I don't want to deny that it is possible to envision a comprehensive language or conceptual scheme in which I can describe and predict neurophysiological processes and in which I can also make the sort of reports and descriptions that I can now make when I describe my sensations.[27] I may even be instructed to say "My C-fibers are firing" instead of saying "I'm in pain." Such a language might not be viewed as impoverishing my present discourse, but enriching it, for when related to neurophysiological theory the expression "My C-fibers are firing" meaning much more than my present expression "I'm in pain" means.

VALIDITY OF THE DISAPPEARANCE VERSION

But if this is the situation envisioned, then talk of reduction or dis-

[26] Norman Malcolm makes a related point concerning "explanation" and "thoughts" when he writes, "If a thought is identical with a brain process, it does not follow that to explain the occurrence of the brain process is to explain the occurrence of the thought. And in fact, an explanation of the one differs in *kind* from an explanation of the other." "Scientific Materialism and the Identity Theory," p. 124.

[27] This is precisely the type of "solution" that Sellars proposes when he says that "in the never-never land of ideal brain state theory the logical space of sense-impressions would, so to speak, be transposed into a new key and located in a new context." And it is because "raw feels will reappear transposed *but unreduced* in a theoretical framework adequate to the job of explaining what core persons can do," that he argues that the identity theory is "true but relatively uninteresting." "The Identity Approach to the Mind-Body Problem," pp. 447, 449, 430.

appearance of my present language for reporting and describing sensations is extremely misleading, for what disappears reappears in a new form in the comprehensive language.

If this is what the disappearance form of the identity theory comes to, then it is trivial. The point to keep in mind here is one that is so effectively made by Wittgenstein and which has been echoed in much of recent analytic philosophy as well as phenomenological analysis, viz. that there are many sorts of descriptions and many different types of statements that we take to be paradigms of *correct* descriptions. If one shows that for certain specified purposes, e.g. scientific explanation and prediction, we can disregard certain types of legitimate descriptions, this is not sufficient to show that the latter type of descriptions are illegitimate *überhaupt*.

It might be objected that I am being stubborn and perverse in failing to recognize the radicalness of the disappearance form of the identity theory. For I am insisting that any alternative conceptual scheme must enable me to give the same sorts of reports and descriptions that I now give of my sensations and feelings. But the point of the disappearance view is to expose the illegitimacy of this claim. What distinguishes my argument from the obstinate defender of the caloric theory who would reject the kinetic theory because, strictly speaking, one can't give the same sorts of descriptions that we can give in the caloric theory?

Or consider the analogy that Rorty presses between demons and sensations, for he says, "The Identity Theorist's claim is that sensations may be to the future progress of psycho-physiology as demons are to modern science." [28] The situation that Rorty has in mind is one where a primitive tribe believes that there are demons and that the presence of certain types of demons are the causes of different types of illnesses. If we encountered a witch doctor that defended the existence of demons, we would try to show him that modern science provides us with a better explanation and description of the causes of illnesses. If he persisted in claiming that there are demons because he has seen them, we would try to show him that these are hallucinations and we might do this by showing him that eating certain types of mushrooms also produces similar hallucinations. A sophisticated witch doctor might reply that "all modern science can do is to show (1) that the presence of demons is constantly correlated with that of germs, viruses, and the like, and (2) that eating certain mushrooms sometimes makes people think they see things that aren't really there. This is hardly sufficient to show that there are no demons." [29] But while we could

[28] Rorty, *op. cit.*, p. 179.
[29] *Ibid.*

tack on demon discourse to modern science, Rorty claims that it is precisely the simplicity of the type of account that we give in modern science that counts as an excellent reason for eliminating demon discourse. If the witch doctor challenges us by asking, what was I directly reporting when I reported the presence of a fat red demon, we would answer that he was reporting a hallucinatory experience. There are no demons.

How close and illuminating are the above analogies to the situation where sensation discourse is thought to be replaceable by neurophysiological discourse? The important feature of the above analogies is that they take place within the context of the scientific evaluation of competing or alternative *theories*. No matter how difficult it may be to state precisely what are the criteria that govern the evaluation of competing or alternative scientific theories, there is, or can be consensus about which theory is a better scientific theory. *If* we are dealing within the context of evaluating scientific theories, then it is certainly true that any theory can be displaced by a better theory. But if this awareness of the fallibility of scientific theories is to be helpful in understanding the displacement of sensation discourse, then it must be shown that the conceptual scheme in which I now report and describe my sensations is a scientific theory, or at least sufficiently like a scientific theory in respect to its possible displacement. And I do not see that the new scientific materialists have established this key premise. This failure is especially clear in Feyerabend's line of argument for he simply states that our ordinary ways of talking about and reporting our sensations is part of a theory which is seen as a rather poor scientific theory, and then goes on to argue correctly that any scientific theory can be replaced by a better one.[30] But by simply assuming that sensation discourse, especially in its reporting role, is a quasi-scientific theory, he begs the issue.

It might be thought that the demon analogy comes closer to doing the job of showing us how sensation discourse can be likened to a replaceable scientific theory. But if we examine the analogy closely, we see that it breaks down at the crucial point. The use that Rorty makes of the analogy consists of two parts, the explanatory and the reporting role of demon discourse. Insofar as demon discourse is used to explain and predict the occurrence of illnesses, it can be replaced by modern germ theory. But the recalcitrant feature of sensation discourse is my ability to give correct first person reports of my "sensations." If we are going to try to convince the sophisticated witch doctor to give up demon discourse, we have to be able to answer the question, what was he reporting when he reported the presence of a

[30] See "Materialism and the Mind-Body Problem."

demon. Our answer is that he was reporting a hallucinatory experience. But it is important to note that even if we restrict ourselves to the reporting role of demon discourse, there is no question here of *changing or dropping the predicates* and the types of descriptions used to describe these hallucinatory experiences. Imaginary demons can be short, red and fat just as real demons can. So the converted witch doctor might agree that germ theory is a better way of describing and explaining the occurrence of illnesses and that demons after all are only hallucinations. But he would add, I certainly perceive "something" when I think I see a demon and if I am to describe what I see then I must use physical predicates to describe it. So too, we might concede that neurophysiological discourse is a better way of scientifically explaining and describing the relevant phenomena and I may agree that "sensations" turn out to be brain processes. But if I am to describe these brain processes as *I experience* them then I must use phenomenal predicates to describe them or if I adopt a new language, the new expressions must at least express what I now express when I report and describe my "sensations." If Rorty is to make out the case for the disappearance view, he must show us that we could have good reasons for not only eliminating or changing the references of expressions like "sensations," but that we could have good reasons for dropping the type of predicates that we use in reporting and describing our "sensations." But the demon analogy fails to help us here. I will not describe the presence of demons differently after I discover that they are only hallucinations; I will continue to use the same sorts of predicates and descriptions in describing them, although I will be more cautious in drawing unwarranted ontological conclusions. But in the case of sensation discourse, I supposedly could eliminate the predicates that I now use to describe my "sensations." And it just isn't clear what would count as a good reason for doing so.

To underscore this last point, let us engage in a bit of philosophic science fiction. Suppose we imagine a creature who is not unlike ourselves insofar as he makes the same sorts of first person reports of his "sensations" that we do. He differs from us because of his ability and desire to do and say what in princple or theory can be done or said. "Linguistic inconvenience" and "practical difficulties" are no problems for him. Let us try to imagine what sorts of reasons might be offered by the future defender of an identity theory who claims that "empirical inquiry [has discovered] that *sensations* . . . are identical with brain processes." [31] He would presumably begin by showing all sorts of complex correlations between what our superhuman creature

[31] "Mind-Body Identity, Privacy, and Categories," p. 174.

reports as his sensations and brain processes. He would also lay bare his neurophysiological theory by which he can describe, explain and predict the occurrence of brain processes and what we have called "sensations." We would also expect a demonstration that the laws he has discovered are better able scientifically to explain what we now explain by our rough correlations in sensation discourse. And of course he would present the evidence in support of his theory. In short we would expect him to supply the types of reasons and evidence necessary for showing that his theory is the best scientific theory available. Would he have thereby given us or our superhuman creature good *theoretical reasons* for abandoning the ways in which we now report and describe our "sensations"? Not at all. At best he has shown that for scientific purposes there is no longer any need to employ our present sensation discourse. But this is not sufficient to show that there is something intrinsically wrong, illegitimate or superfluous about the way in which I now report and describe my sensations. We and our superhuman creature would reply that for the purposes of reporting and describing our sensations as we experience them, or—conceding that these "sensations" really are brain processes—for the purposes of reporting and describing these brain processes as they appear to us —our present sensation discourse enables us to make true reports and descriptions.

The above line of argument focuses on a basic tension in the disappearance version of the identity theory. On the one hand when Rorty makes claims like "Elimination of the referring use of the expression in question . . . from our language would leave our ability to describe and predict undiminished," he seems to be presupposing a metalanguage or metatheory in which we can evaluate different types of descriptive expressions and determine whether our ability to describe is or is not diminished. I have argued that it isn't clear what are the ground rules of such a metatheory. But on the other hand, Rorty sometimes writes as if the radical displacement of languages takes place without any inter-theoretical justification. Like Marx's concept of the state, one form of discourse withers away (in fact or in principle) when it no longer serves any function or purpose that isn't better performed by another form of discourse. Thus an entire mode of discourse including its *entire descriptive vocabulary* can be displaced. But then it is no longer clear what it means to say that our ability to describe is undiminished.

There is still another way in which the scientific materialist might try to meet our objections. He might claim that we have already conceded his major contention, viz., that sensations are (or may be) really brain processes. Of course, he might say there is a language in which we report and describe "sensations" and in itself there is nothing intrinsically wrong or nonsensical about such a language. But it is basically a language of appearance and not reality. It tells us how matters *appear* to us, not how they really are in themselves. There really are only brain processes, but they appear as sensations. To justify this sort of position, one would have to justify on *independent* grounds an ontological principle whereby science is the measure of what is that it is and of what is not that it is not. The point I want to emphasize in the context of the present discussion is that such a position is not really anti-dualistic: it presupposes some sort of dualism. It assesses this dualism differently. It categorizes one type of language as the language of reality and the other type of language as a language of appearance. Unless there were a fundamental difference between these two languags, it would be senseless to speak of appearance and reality.

In sum, I am claiming that Rorty's version of the disappearance form of the identity theory is loaded. It gains its rhetorical force because it presupposes that "ultimately" *the* legitimate form(s) of description is scientific description. And it presupposes that our present sensation discourse is sufficiently like a scientific theory so that it is intelligible to speak about its displacement in favor of a more adequate neurophysiological theory. If I am careless and claim that when reporting and describing sensations I am doing the same sort of thing that can better be done by science, then his argument has force. And if I argue that because I can now describe and report my sensations and that the structure of the language in which I do this is categorically different from the language of neurophysiological discourse, then I have a sufficient reason to claim that there are irreducible mental events or features, then Rorty is correct in exposing the fallacy of this line of reasoning. But if I claim that my present language for reporting and describing sensations is another, different, supplementary, legitimate mode of discourse for describing my experiences, I do not think that his arguments or any others that have been offered cut much philosophic ice.

We have been concerned with the technical details of the statement and defense of the versions of the identity theory, especially insofar as these have been used to defend scientific materialism. I suggested at the beginning of this paper that the entire discussion has consequences for the thorny issues of the relation of language and ontology. We can conclude with a brief indication of some of these.

It has been a fundamental bias, what Collingwood might have called an absolute presupposition of a good deal of contemporary analytic philosophy, that the new linguistic turn provides us with a technique for clarifying, resolving, and dissolving the tangle of ontological issues that have been inherited from philosophy's past. I think, however, that when the history of this contemporary discussion is written, we will see that linguistic discussions have generated as much confusion about ontological issues as they have clarification. It is an illusion to think that we have finally escaped from the complex issues of ontology. We can see this in the discussion of scientific materialism. Roughly speaking, most of the attention has been focused on the issue of reference with an attempt to show how we might plausibly identify the referents of such expressions as "sensations" and "certain brain processes," or to show how expressions that we may think refer to irreducible mental events do not necessarily refer to such events. The motivation behind this approach is the belief that the theory of reference is the key for telling us what there is, or more cautiously for telling us what are the ontic commitments of a given conceptual scheme. But focusing on the theory of reference can blind us to the important differences in our modes of description and predication, and the significance of these differences for ontology. It is not at all clear that we make much of a philosophic advance if we now speak of linguistic, conceptual, or epistemological differences where we once spoke of ontological differences. Indeed this shift tells us as much about one's biases concerning ontology as it does about the situation being analyzed. For the basic differences from this new perspective turn out to be no less fundamental than what were traditionally called "ontological" differences.

Furthermore, a good deal of modern analytic philosophy, especially those varieties influenced by logical positivism and atomism, have been conditioned by two basic biases. The first is nominalism and by "nominalism" I mean what Peirce meant when he used this term: it encompasses what contemporaries call realism or platonism. It is the belief that basically the only entities that are *real* are those which are fully determinate and "sharp edged"—the kind of entity that we supposedly discover when we discover the real referents of the basic expressions of our conceptual scheme. The indeterminate or vague is unreal, a sign of our ignorance or confusion, not of what there really is. Such a nominalism reinforces the conviction that the "real" ultimate referents of our basic vocabulary are what there is in the world. The second bias is the belief that, when all is said and done, it is science and only science that tells us what there is and that anything that cannot be accommodated to the paradigms of scientific explanation and description has some sort of secondary status.

It is Wittgenstein, perhaps more than any other contemporary philosopher who most deeply questioned and exposed the illegitimacy of these basic philosophic biases—perhaps because he was originally so profoundly affected by them. He has, or rather should have made us sensitive to the variety, complexity, and non-reductiveness of different perspectives, languages, and life forms, and of the constant danger of giving in to the basic urge to impose a single paradigm or standard on the complex web of human life and discourse. In this respect, I think there are significant family resemblances with what the Continental phenomenologists have been telling and showing us. For in their own idiom, they too have attempted to break us out of the reductive scientific mold that has shaped so much of modern thought and to make us alive again to the irreducible variety and tangle of experience and discourse.

There are dangers in the type of revolution that Wittgenstein was initiating, dangers more evident in some of his "followers" than in his own investigations. For we can too easily become mesmerized by the differences that we discover. In part, the new scientific materialists provide a healthy antidote to the excesses of a linguistic pluralism. It is not enough to describe the complex structure of our different languages and conceptual schemes. We want to understand how "things fit together." Nevertheless, both the spirit and letter of Wittgenstein and the Continental phenomenologists should reawaken us to an awareness that the consciousness of our own experiences or the language in which we report and describe our sensations and feelings is different from and no less legitimate than scientific discourse.

RICHARD RORTY

In Defense of
Eliminative Materialism

In this brief note, I should like to comment on two replies to my "Mind-Body Identity, Privacy, and Categories"[1]—one by James Cornman[2] and the other by Richard Bernstein.[3] I shall concentrate upon a single point which is made by both critics.

In my article, I attempted to work out an analogy between talking about demons and talking about sensations, urging that sensation-discourse might go the way of demon-discourse, given the proper neurological discoveries and resulting neurological ways of explaining behavior. More specifically, I argued that "sensation" might lose its reporting role as well as its explanatory role, just as "demon" had lost both its roles, and that both of these roles might be taken over by reference to brain-processes.

In response to this strategy, Cornman argues that

> Even if we grant that a pain is identical with a stimulation of C-fibers, it would seem that we still need sensation-terms to make the true descriptions of certain pains, or stimulation of C-fibers, as, for example, intense, sharp, and throbbing. No neurophysiological sentence is synonymous with "This pain (stimulation of C-fibers) is intense, sharp, and throbbing," and thus no neurophysiological sentence can be used to make the

Reprinted from *The Review of Metaphysics*, XXIV, 1 (September 1970), 112-121, by permission of the editor and Richard Rorty.

[1] *The Review of Metaphysics*, Vol. XIX (1965), pp. 24-54. [Reprinted in this volume, pp. 174-199].

[2] "On the Elimination of 'Sensations' and Sensations," *The Review of Metaphysics*, Vol. XXII (1968), pp. 15-35.

[3] "The Challenge of Scientific Materialism," *International Philosophical Quarterly*, Vol. VIII (1968), pp. 252-275. [Reprinted in this volume, pp. 200-222. References below are to the occurrence in this volume.]

same true description. Thus to eliminate the sensation-terms we apply to what we experience would seem to diminish our ability to describe considerably.[4]

My general line of reply to this point is to say that three neurological properties of the stimulation of C-fibers would correspond to "intense," "sharp," and "throbbing," and that terms signifying these properties would take over the roles of these latter terms just as "stimulation of C-fibers" took over the role of "pain." Cornman, however, anticipates this reply and attempts to rebut it as follows:

> Let us assume that "Jones' C-fibers are very stimulated" has acquired the descriptive role of "Jones' pain is intense," and that it also retains its theoretical role. Let us also grant that if this role change occurs, then "Jones' pain is intense" is no longer needed to make a true description of Jones because "Jones' C-fibers are very stimulated" gives us this description of Jones and more. . . . The objection is . . . that the reason we would no longer need "Jones' pain is intense" is that *what it states would be entailed by "Jones' C-fibers are very stimulated."* Consequently, we could no longer even make certain physiological claims about the brain without implying that there are sensations. . . . It is not important, then, which words we use now or ever. What matters is which descriptive roles they play. . . . Thus because "stimulation of C-fibers" taking on the descriptive role of "pain" accomplishes only the elimination of "pain" and not its role in true descriptions, such an elimination of sensation-terms fails to help the eliminative materialist. Indeed, if this is the only way sensation-terms can be eliminated, we should reject eliminative materialism, because we must either keep sensation-terms to make true descriptions or change physicalistic terms in such a way that using them descriptively implies that there are sensations. (Italics added)[5]

The same point is made by Bernstein:

> We might concede that neurophysiological discourse is a better way of scientifically explaining and describing the relevant phenomena and I may agree that "sensations" turn out to be brain processes. But if I am to describe these brain processes as *I experience* them then I must use phenomenal predicates to describe them or if I adopt a new language, the new expressions must at least *express what I now express* when I report and describe my "sensations." (Italics added)[6]

Both Bernstein and Cornman are claiming that if two terms play the same descriptive role, then sentences using the one must "entail"

[4] J. Cornman, *op. cit.*, p. 30.
[5] *Ibid.*, pp. 30–32.
[6] R. Bernstein, *op. cit.*, p. 218.

what is stated by the other (Cornman) or "express" what the latter sentences express (Bernstein). Both agree that our ability to describe would be diminished if we were no longer able to express what we expressed by words like "intense" and "throbbing," and both insist that the new language which I am suggesting we might use would either continue to express this or be deficient.

As a first attempt at getting around this objection, I can remark that the sentence

"I am having an hallucination of a fat red man-like shape"

which takes over the descriptive role of

"There is a fat red demon"

does not seem to entail the latter nor to express what the latter expresses. But this may seem a limp reply, since, as Bernstein points out, "there is no question here of changing or dropping the predicates and the types of descriptions used to describe these hallucinatory experiences. Imaginary demons can be short, red and fat just as real demons can."[7] Bernstein is quite right in noting that there is a disanalogy between the demons and the sensations, in that some of the predicates appropriate to demons are also appropriate for describing hallucinations, whereas I want to say that none of the predicates appropriate to sensations are appropriate to brain processes. Nevertheless, this disanalogy does not damage the point that a sentence about hallucinations does not seem to entail a sentence about demons. So why should "My C-fibers are very stimulated" entail "My pain is intense" (or perhaps "The stimulation of my C-fibers is very intense")? Granted that in the demon case the old-fashioned adjectives don't follow the old-fashioned referring expression into desuetude, why shouldn't they in the case of sensations? If referring expressions can go out of date, why not adjectives as well?

Since I assume that neither Cornman nor Bernstein really sees any great difference between nouns and adjectives here, are they saying that even when we admit that demons are only hallucinations or that sensations turn out to be brain processes we must still grant that "Here is an hallucination of a certain sort" entails (or "expresses what is expressed by") "Here is a demon" and "My C-fibers are stimulated" entails (or "expresses what is expressed by") "I am in pain"? But this seems paradoxical, for what does it mean to say "There are no demons" if not that the entailment does *not* hold? And if it doesn't hold in the

[7] *Ibid.*, p. 218.

demon case, why should it hold in the pain case? Why need we say that the employment of "My C-fibers are stimulated" to report immediate experience *changes the meaning of this expression* in such a way that it now entails "I am in pain"?

At this point in the argument, it seems to me, Cornman and Bernstein must either (a) find a way of squaring the claim that "I am having a certain sort of hallucination" entails (or "expresses what is expressed by") "There is a demon" with the fact that there are no demons, or (b) say that there is a further disanalogy between the demon case and the sensation case such that the entailment doesn't hold in the former but does in the latter. Since I see no way in which (a) can be followed up, and since there is evidence for (b), I shall focus on that alternative.

The evidence that Cornman and Bernstein see a further disanalogy between the two cases is that both devote attention to the difference between, as Bernstein says, "the context of the scientific evaluation of competing or alternative *theories*" and the case of replacing sensation-discourse. Bernstein thinks that it "begs the issue" to assume that "sensation-discourse, especially in its reporting role, is a quasi-scientific theory." [8] Cornman says that "sensation-terms are used to report phenomena we experience whether or not they have any explanatory function, and therefore we cannot justify their eliminability merely by eliminating their explanatory function." [9] Both remarks suggest that the principle being invoked to distinguish the sensation case from the demon case is something like the following:

(T) If a theory-laden term takes on the reporting role of a non-theory-laden term, then statements using the latter term are entailed by ("express what is expressed by") statements using the former, whereas if a theory-laden term takes on the reporting role of another theory-laden term, this is not the case.

The rationale for (T) might go something like this: the descriptive roles played by non-theory-laden terms (like "sensation" or "intense") are roles which must be played in any language which is adequate to describe what is experienced, whereas the descriptive roles played by theory-laden terms (like "demon" or "hallucination") may or may not be played, depending upon whether the explanatory theory which contains them is accepted. Both Cornman and Bernstein say things which suggest that they would accept a distinction between terms which are necessary to describe the objects-as-they-are-experienced and eliminable "theory-laden" terms—Bernstein in the passage quoted

[8] R. Bernstein, *op. cit.*, p. 217.
[9] J. Cornman, *op. cit.*, p. 23.

above about the need to describe brain processes "as I experience them" and Cornman in the following passage:

> It is most implausible to claim that a man's sensory phenomena have nothing like the features he experiences them to have, with the consequence that he has no special epistemological status even regarding those features he believes his sensory phenomena have.[10]

Furthermore, Cornman has devoted a separate article[11] to arguing that Quine's version of eliminative materialism will not work because "sensation," though a theoretical term, is a theoretico-reporting term. That is to say, it is used to refer to something that we are aware of, and therefore not to something postulated.[12] Cornman's assumption in this article is that "What we are aware of is not postulated,"[13] and only the postulated is eliminable; and this assumption seems to occur also in his reply to me in the form "What we are aware of must be expressed in any adequate language," whereas what we are not aware of need not be—or, in other words, "What we are aware of is not eliminable by changes in our ways of explaining things." † More specifically, it seems likely that Cornman would distinguish "demon" as a "theory-laden" theoretico-reporting term—because although we are aware of demons talking of demons entails talk about unobservable properties (e.g., those having to do with demonic intercourse with unobservable supernatural beings)—from "sensation" as a theoretico-reporting term which carries no commitment to unobservable properties.[14]

Now my answer to (T) is that what appears to us, or what we ex-

---

[10] *Ibid.*, p. 35.

[11] J. Cornman, "Mental Terms, Theoretical Terms, and Materialism," *Philosophy of Science*, Vol. XXXV (1968), pp. 45–63.

[12] *Ibid.*, p. 61.

[13] *Ibid.*, p. 61. Although this article is a reply to Quine, and in "On the Elimination . . ." Cornman regards me as taking a "new line" which goes beyond Quine's form of elimination and requires separate refutation, it seems to me that the basis of Cornman's objections to me and to Quine is the same. All my new line amounts to is the suggestion that the reporting role of sensation-discourse could be taken over by a neurological vocabulary. All that Cornman's reply to this new line comes to is that the new use of a neurological vocabulary will entail sentences phrased in the old vocabulary. But, if my comments so far have been sound, Cornman would not argue that such entailment holds if the entities referred to in the old vocabulary are *postulated* entities (like demons). So to both Quine and me Cornman is saying: your eliminative tactics will work only on what we are not aware of.

† [These last two quotations are Rorty's statement of what Cornman would say, and are not direct quotations.]

[14] See Cornman, "Mental Terms . . . ," p. 51 for a definition of "theory-laden term," and p. 61 for the claim that "sensation" is not such a term.

perience, or what we are aware of, is a function of the language we use. To say that "X's appear to us as F" is merely to say that "We customarily use 'F' in making non-inferential reports about X's." In other words, I would claim that if we got in the habit of using neurological terms in place of "intense," "sharp," and "throbbing," then our experience would be of things having those neurological properties, and not of anything, e.g., intense. It seems to me that Cornman and Bernstein are taking for granted that there is a sort of prelinguistic givenness about, e.g., pains which any language which is to be adequate must provide a means of expressing. This is why they claim that sentences using the neurological term in its reporting use would entail, or express what is expressed by, sentences using the "phenomenal" term. If it were the case that we experienced the same thing when we used the new vocabulary as when we used the old, then their point would be sound. But there is nothing to be this "same thing."

To see this point, let us imagine two sets of people, one raised to speak conventional English and the other raised to use only neurological predicates in the place of those conventionally used in introspective reports. Are these two groups experiencing the same things when they are simultaneously manipulated in various ways? Intuition perhaps suggests that they are. But what is this same thing, the intensity of the pain or the X-character of the brain process? Here, I think, intuition is baffled, and rightly so. Either answer would do equally well. On the Cornman-Bernstein view, however, we are forced to say either "both" or "something common to both." For if we want to claim that the neurologically-speaking people are using sentences which "entail what is stated by" or "express what is stated by" or "express what is expressed by" sentences used by the conventional English speakers, then we have to allow the claim in reverse also. If both sets of sentences are playing the same reporting role, then either "entails what is stated" by the other or "expresses what is expressed" by the other. So it will turn out that conventional speakers cannot speak of the intensity of a pain without implying the existence of certain neurons and their features, just as the neurologically-speaking people cannot use their language without implying the existence of something mental.

I suggest that rather than draw either of these consequences we should admit that there is nothing in common between the two experiences save that they are had under the same conditions—viz., the manipulation of the body in certain specified ways. That the "same descriptive role" is played is not a matter of the same feature or features being reported in either case, but simply a matter of the two sentences being used to answer the same question—viz., what do you experience under the following conditions? I suspect that Cornman and Bernstein think that changing from "intense" to "X-character" is a mere change of words without a change of descriptive role because they think of "descriptive role" as "role of referring to the same experiental feature." But they cannot, without begging the question, claim that "intense" refers to an experiential feature but "X-character" does not. They cannot make use of our intuition that the same feature is being experienced no matter which word is used in order to give the preference to "intense." For this intuition is neutral as between the two different languages.

To put the matter more generally, I think that the putative intuition that we will continue to have the same experiences no matter which words we use is in fact a remnant of what Sellars has called the Myth of the Given—the view that awareness comes first and language must follow along and be adequate to the initial awareness. The trouble with this view is that "adequate to" is an empty notion. There is no criterion for the adequacy of a bit of language to a bit of non-linguistic awareness. Indeed, the notion of a non-linguistic awareness is simply a version of the thing-in-itself—an unknowable whose only function is paradoxically enough, to be that which all knowledge is about. What *does* exist is the causal conditions of a non-inferential report being made. But there is no unique vocabulary for describing these causal conditions. There are as many vocabularies as there are ways of explaining human behavior.

I shall conclude this note by taking up a different but related topic. Both Cornman and Bernstein suggest that I am adopting, or for consistency must adopt, the view that, in Bernstein's words, " 'ultimately' *the* legitimate form(s) of description is scientific description." [15] Bernstein says that without this presupposition my arguments cut no ice against the view that "my present language for reporting and describing sensations is another, different, supplementary, legitimate mode of discourse for describing my experiences." Corman claims that "there is one last move an eliminative materialist might try"—viz., "an extreme version of scientific realism, one which holds that in all cases those pure theoretical terms of science that provide the best available explanations of behavior also provide the best available descriptions of the things whose behavior they explain." [16]

Against Bernstein, I can say that I am not in any sense claiming that the customary vocabulary of introspection is "illegitimate." Rather, I am merely claiming the same legitimacy for the neurological vocabulary—where "legitimacy" means the right to be considered a report of

[15] R. Bernstein, *op. cit.*, p. 220.
[16] J. Cornman, "On the Elimination . . . ," p. 34.

experience. My attitude is not that some vocabularies are "illegitimate," but rather we should let a thousand vocabularies bloom and then see which survive. The materialist predicts that the neurological vocabulary will triumph. He may be right, but if he is, it is not because of some special feature of this vocabulary which consists in its having originated in theoretical science. Given different cultural conditions, one can imagine the neurological vocabulary having been the ordinary familiar one and the mentalistic one the "scientific" alternative.

To make the same point in another context, I shall take up another of Bernstein's remarks:

> On the one hand when Rorty makes claims like "Elimination of the referring use of the expression in question . . . from our language would leave our ability to describe and predict undiminished," he seems to be presupposing a metalanguage or metatheory in which we can evaluate different types of descriptive expressions and determine whether our ability to describe is or is not diminished. But on the other hand, Rorty sometimes writes as if the radical displacement of languages takes place without any inter-theoretical justification. Like Marx's concept of the state, one form of discourse withers away (in fact or in principle) when it no longer serves any function or purpose that isn't better performed by another mode of discourse. Thus an entire mode of discourse including its *entire descriptive vocabulary* can be displaced. But then it is no longer clear what it means to say that our ability to describe is undiminished.[17]

To say that our ability to describe is undiminished is merely to say that by using some portion of language common to the competing vocabularies (e.g., "What do you experience when I do *that* to your arm?") we can isolate the questions to which alternative answers might be given and note that both vocabularies offer something to say in reply. No general metalanguage is needed, but merely some way of locating the place in the language-game which is to be filled by either of the alternative candidates. I quite agree with Bernstein's implicit suggestion that any general metalanguage or metatheory would be question-begging, and in particular any which always awarded the prize to the "scientific" alternative would be. Therefore I grasp the second ("withering away") horn of the dilemma he sketches. But I take no sides on the question of whether the materialist is right in his prediction that the ordinary ways of reporting on introspections will wither away. In my view, the truth of the prediction is of much less philosophical interest than the fact that the prediction is itself a coherent suggestion. (To back up the claim that it is coherent to suggest that "the entire descriptive vocabulary of a mode of discourse"

[17] R. Bernstein, *op. cit.*, p. 219.

might wither away while leaving our descriptive ability undiminished I can offer no better argument than the example of demons. I grant that in this case the adjectives used for describing demons persist. But, as I have said above, I do not think that the persistence of these adjectives counts against the force of the example.)

Turning now to Cornman's suggestion that I might fall back on an extreme form of scientific realism, I note that even this move will do me no good if (T) is true. For even if I claim that the "pure theoretical terms of science" provide the "best available descriptions," these best descriptions will still, according to (T), entail all the old-fashioned descriptions which scientific realism would wish to discard. So I construe Cornman as, in this passage, suggesting that extreme scientific realism could be used as the basis for a denial of (T). But on my view (T) is false whether one is a scientific realist or not. What defeats (T) is what defeats the Myth of the Given—not scientific realism, but an appreciation of the internal difficulties engendered in traditional empiricisms and rationalisms by the notion of a pre-linguistic item of awareness to which language must be adequate. To attack the Myth of the Given is to insist that predicates like "intense" are in principle replaceable. To adopt scientific realism is to say that they ought to be replaced, given the superior explanatory ability of neurological theory. I wish to take the first step—insisting on in-principle-replaceability—without taking the second.

Bibliography

The first, and major section of this bibliography is a fairly complete list of recent works directly concerned with the mind-body identity thesis. The second section lists works pertinent to seventeenth-century materialism; it is not intended to be complete, and it stresses contemporary discussions of classical views. The third section is a short selection of references useful for a general introductory background to contemporary philosophy of mind; more advanced works have been omitted. The final section is a sample of works in psychology, neurophysiology and computer science that are of interest in connection with mind-body materialism.

The following abbreviations are used for journals mentioned more than once: *A* (*Analysis*); *APQ* (*American Philosophical Quarterly*); *AJP* (*Australasian Journal of Philosophy*); *BJPS* (*The British Journal for the Philosophy of Science*); *D* (*Dialogue*); *JP* (*The Journal of Philosophy*); *M* (*Mind*); *PF* (*The Philosophical Forum*); *PQ* (*The Philosophical Quarterly*); *PR* (*The Philosophical Review*); *PS* (*Philosophical Studies*); *P* (*Philosophy*); *PPR* (*Philosophy and Phenomenological Research*); *PSci* (*Philosophy of Science*); *RM* (*The Review of Metaphysics*); *Th* (*Theoria*).

I. THE IDENTITY THESIS

Abelson, Raziel. "A Refutation of Mind-Body Identity," *PS*, XXI, 6 (December 1970), 85–90.

Armstrong, D. M. "The Headless Woman Illusion and the Defence of Materialism," *A*, XXIX, 2, New Series No. 128 (December 1968), 48–49.

———. *A Materialist Theory of the Mind*. New York: The Humanities Press, 1968.

Aune, Bruce. Comments on "Psychological Predicates" [appearing in this volume as "The Nature of Mental States"], by Hilary Putnam, in *Art,*

Mind, and Religion. Edited by W. H. Capitan and D. D. Merrill. Pittsburgh: University of Pittsburgh Press, 1967, 49–54.

Baier, Kurt. "Smart on Sensations," *AJP,* XL, 1 (May 1962), 57–68.

Bradley, M. C. Critical notice of *Philosophy and Scientific Realism,* by J. J. C. Smart, *AJP,* XLII, 2 (August 1964), 262–283.

———. "Sensations, Brain-Processes and Colours," *AJP,* XLI, 3 (December 1963), 385–393.

Brain and Mind: Modern Concepts of the Nature of Mind. Edited by J. R. Smythies. New York: The Humanities Press, 1965, especially J. Beloff, "The Identity Hypothesis: A Critique"; Lord Brain, F. R. S., "Some Aspects of the Brain-Mind Relationship"; and Anthony Quinton, "Mind and Matter."

Brandt, Richard and Jaegwon Kim. "The Logic of the Identity Theory," *JP,* LXIV, 17 (September 7, 1967), 515–537.

Budd, M. J. "Materialism and Immaterialism," *Proceedings of the Aristotelian Society,* New Series, LXX, 1969/70, 197–220.

Campbell, Keith. Critical notice of C. F. Presley (Ed.): *The Identity Theory of Mind, AJP,* XLVI, 2 (August 1968), 175–188.

Candlish, Stewart. "Mind, Brain and Identity," *M,* LXXIX, 316 (October 1970), 502–518.

Carnap, Rudolf. "Herbert Feigl on Physicalism," in *The Philosophy of Rudolf Carnap.* Edited by Paul Arthur Schilpp. La Salle, Illinois: Open Court, London: Cambridge University Press, 1963, 882–886.

Coburn, Robert C. "Shaffer on the Identity of Mental States and Physical Processes," *JP,* LX, 4 (February 14, 1963), 89–92.

Cooper, D. E. "Materialism and Perception," *PQ,* XX, 81 (October 1970), 334–346.

Cornman, James W. *Materialism and Sensations.* New Haven: Yale University Press, forthcoming.

———. "Mental Terms, Theoretical Terms, and Materialism," *PSci,* XXXV, 1 (March 1968), 45–63.

———. "On the Elimination of 'Sensations' and Sensations," *RM,* XXII, 1 (September 1968), 15–35.

———. "Sellars, Scientific Realism, and Sensa," *RM,* XXIII, 3 (March 1970), 417–451.

Davidson, Donald. "The Individuation of Events," in *Essays in Honor of Carl G. Hempel.* Edited by Nicholas Rescher, *et al.* New York: Humanities Press, Dordrecht-Holland: D. Reidel Publishing Company, 1970, 216–234, especially 228.

———. "Mental Events," in *Experience and Theory*. Edited by Lawrence Foster and J. W. Swanson. Amherst: University of Massachusetts Press, 1970, 79–101.

Dimensions of Mind. Edited by Sidney Hook. New York: Collier Books, London: Collier-Macmillan Ltd., 1961.

Economos, Judith J. *The Identity Thesis*. Unpublished Ph.D. dissertation, Department of Philosophy, University of California, Los Angeles. Ann Arbor: University Microfilms, Inc., 1967, catalogue number 67-12,220.

Ewin, R. E. "Actions, Brain Processes, and Determinism," *M*, LXXVII, 307 (July 1968), 417–419.

Feigl, Herbert. "The 'Mental' and the 'Physical'," in *Minnesota Studies in the Philosophy of Science*, II. Edited by Herbert Feigl, Michael Scriven and Grover Maxwell. Minneapolis: University of Minnesota Press, 1958, 370–497. Reprinted separately with a Postscript. Minneapolis: University of Minnesota Press, 1967.

———. "The Mind-Body Problem in the Development of Logical Empiricism," *Revue Internationale de Philosophie*, IV, 11 (January 1950), 64–83. Reprinted in *Readings in the Philosophy of Science*. Edited by Herbert Feigl and May Brodbeck. New York: Appleton-Century-Crofts, Inc., 1953, 612–626.

———. "Physicalism, Unity of Science and the Foundations of Psychology," in *The Philosophy of Rudolf Carnap*. Edited by Paul Arthur Schilpp. La Salle, Illinois: Open Court, London: Cambridge University Press, 1963, 227–267.

Feyerabend, Paul K. "Materialism and the Mind-Body Problem," *RM*, XVII, 1 (September 1963), 49–66.

Fleming, Noel. "Mind as the Cause of Motion," a review article of D. M. Armstrong, *A Materialist Theory of the Mind*, *AJP*, XLVII, 2 (August 1969), 220–242.

Fodor, Jerry A. "Explanations in Psychology," in *Philosophy in America*. Edited by Max Black. Ithaca: Cornell University Press, 1965, 161–179.

Foster, Lynn V. *Constructionalism and the Contemporary Mind-Body Debate*. Unpublished Ph.D. dissertation, Department of Philosophy, Brandeis University. Ann Arbor: University Microfilms, Inc., 1971.

Garnett, A. Campbell. "Body and Mind—the Identity Thesis," *AJP*, XLIII, 1 (May 1965), 77–81.

Goldberg, Bruce. "The Correspondence Hypothesis," *PR*, LXXVII, 4 (October 1968), 438–454.

Goldman, Alvin I. "The Compatibility of Mechanism and Purpose," *PR*, LXXVIII, 4 (October 1969), 468–482.

———. Review of D. M. Armstrong, *A Materialist Theory of the Mind*, JP, LXVI, 22 (November 20, 1969), 813–818.

Gustafson, Don F. "On the Identity Theory," *A*, XXIV, 2, New Series No. 98 (December 1963), 30–32.

Harris, Errol E. "The Neural Identity Theory and the Person," *International Philosophical Quarterly*, VI, 4 (December 1966), 515–537.

Hedman, Carl G. "On Correlating Brain States with Psychological States," *AJP*, XLVIII, 2 (August 1970), 247–251.

Heil, John. "Sensations, Experiences and Brain Processes," *P*, XLV, 173 (July 1970), 221–226.

Hinton, J. M. "Illusions and Identity," *A*, XXVII, 3, New Series No. 117 (January 1967), 65–76.

Hirst, R. J. "Mind and Brain: The Identity Hypothesis," in *Royal Institute of Philosophy Lectures, Volume I: The Human Agent*. London: Macmillan & Co. Ltd., New York: St. Martin's Press, 1968, 160–180.

Hochberg, Herbert. "Physicalism, Behavior, and Phenomena," *PSci*, XXVI, 2 (April 1959), 93–103.

Hocutt, Max. "In Defense of Materialism," *PPR*, XXVII, 3 (March 1967), 366–385.

Hoffman, Robert. *Language, Minds, and Knowledge*, chapter IV, "The Identity Theory." New York: Humanities Press, 1970, 91–113.

———. "Malcolm and Smart on Brain-Mind Identity," *P*, XLIII, 164 (April 1967), 128–136.

Hyslop, Alec. "The Identity Theory and Other Minds," *PF*, (New Series) II, 1 (Fall 1970), 152–153.

The Identity Theory of Mind. Edited by C. F. Presley. St. Lucia: University of Queensland Press, 1967.

Kane, R. H. "Minds, Causes, and Behavior," *RM*, XXIV, 2 (December 1970), 302–334.

———. "Turing Machines and Mental Reports," *AJP*, XLIV, 3 (December 1966), 344–352.

Kekes, John. "Theoretical Identity," *The Southern Journal of Philosophy*, VIII, 1 (Spring 1970), 25–36.

Kim, Jaegwon. "Psychophysical Laws and Theories of Mind," *Th*, XXXIII, Part 3 (1967), 198–210.

———. "Reduction, Correspondence and Identity," *The Monist*, LII, 3 (July 1968), 424–438.

Kneale, William. "Critical Notice of *A Materialist Theory of the Mind*," *M*, LXXVIII, 310 (April 1969), 292–301.

Kripke, Saul. "Identity and Necessity," in *Identity and Individuation*. Edited by Milton K. Munitz. New York: New York University Press, 1971.

———. "Naming and Necessity," three lectures delivered at Princeton University, January 20, 27 and 29, 1970, in *Semantics of Natural Language*. Edited by Donald Davidson and Gilbert H. Harman. New York: Humanities Press, Dordrecht-Holland: D. Reidel Publishing Company, 1971.

Landesman, Charles. Review of *The Identity Theory of Mind*, edited by C. F. Presley, *PR*, forthcoming.

Lewis, David. "Psychophysical and Theoretical Identifications," to appear in a volume edited by Professor Chung-ying Cheng, University of Hawaii.

———. Review of *Art, Mind, and Religion* [particularly of Hilary Putnam, "Psychological Predicates," appearing in this volume as "The Nature of Mental States"], *JP*, LXVI, 1 (January 16, 1969), 22-27 [particularly 23-25].

Luce, David Randall. "Mind-Body Identity and Psycho-Physical Correlation," *PS*, XVII, 1-2 (January-February 1966), 1-7.

Malcolm, Norman. "The Conceivability of Mechanism," *PR*, LXXVII, 1 (January 1968), 45-72.

———. "Rejoinder to Mr. Sosa," *D*, III, 4 (March 1965), 424-425.

———. "Scientific Materialism and the Identity Theory," *D*, III, 2 (September 1964), 115-125.

Margolis, Joseph. "Behaviorism, Materialism, Mentalism and Skepticism," *PF*, (New Series) II, 1 (Fall 1970), 15-23.

———. "Brain Processes and Sensations," *Th*, XXXI, Part II (1965), 133-138.

———. "Difficulties for Mind-Body Identity Theories," in *Identity and Individuation*. Edited by Milton K. Munitz. New York: New York University Press, 1971.

Maxwell, Grover. "Scientific Methodology and the Causal Theory of Perception." *Problems in the Philosophy of Science*. Edited by Imre Lakatos and Alan Musgrave. Amsterdam: North-Holland Publishing Company, 1968, 148-160. Cf. also discussion by W. V. Quine, K. R. Popper, A. J. Ayer, W. C. Kneale, and reply by G. Maxwell, 161-177.

Maxwell, Nicholas. "Physics and Common Sense," *BJPS*, XVI, 64 (February 1966), 295-311.

———. "Understanding Sensations," *AJP*, XLVI, 2 (August 1968), 127-145.

Medlin, Brian. "Materialism and the Argument from Distinct Existences," in *The Business of Reason*. Edited by J. J. MacIntosh and S. Coval. London: Routledge & Kegan Paul, New York: Humanities Press, 1969, 168-185.

Meehl, P. E., and Wilfrid Sellars. "The Concept of Emergence," in *Minnesota Studies in the Philosophy of Science*, I, edited by Herbert Feigl and Michael Scriven. Minneapolis: University of Minnesota Press, 1956, 239–252.

Mind, Matter, and Method: Essays in Philosophy and Science in Honor of Herbert Feigl. Edited by Paul K. Feyerabend and Grover Maxwell. Minneapolis: University of Minnesota Press, 1966, Part I, 17–233.

The Monist, LVI, 2 (April 1972), General Topic: Materialism Today, *passim*.

Munsat, Stanley. "Could Sensations Be Processes?", *M*, LXXVIII, 310 (April 1969), 247–251.

Nagel, Thomas. "Armstrong on the Mind," *PR*, LXXIX, 3 (July 1970), 394–403.

Noren, Stephen J. "Identity, Materialism, and the Problem of the Danglers," *Metaphilosophy*, I, 4 (October 1970), 318–334.

———. "Smart's Materialism: The Identity Thesis and Translation," *AJP*, XLVIII, 1 (May 1970), 54–66.

Norton, Rita. "On the Identity of Identity Theories," *A*, XXV, 1, New Series No. 103 (October 1964), 14–16.

Odegard, Douglas. "Disembodied Existence and Central State Materialism," *AJP*, XLVIII, 2 (August 1970), 256–260.

———. "Persons and Bodies," *PPR*, XXXI, 2 (December 1970), 225–242.

Pitcher, George and W. D. Joske. "Sensations and Brain Processes: A Reply to Professor Smart," *AJP*, XXXVIII, 2 (August 1960), 150–160.

Place, U. T. Comments on "Psychological Predicates" [appearing in this volume as "The Nature of Mental States"], by Hilary Putnam, in *Art, Mind, and Religion*. Edited by W. H. Capitan and D. D. Merrill. Pittsburgh: University of Pittsburgh Press, 1967, 55–68.

———. "Is Consciousness a Brain Process?", *British Journal of Psychology*, XLVII, Part 1 (February 1956), 44–50. Reprinted in *The Philosophy of Mind*. Edited by V. C. Chappell. Englewood Cliffs: Prentice-Hall, Inc., 1962, 101–109.

———. "Materialism as a Scientific Hypothesis," *PR*, LXIX, 1 (January 1960), 101–104.

Popper, Karl R. "Language and the Body-Mind Problem," *Actes du XIième Congrès Internationale de Philosophie*, Brussels, August 20–26, 1953, VII, 101–107.

Putnam, Hilary. "Brains and Behavior," in *Analytical Philosophy, Second Series*. Edited by R. J. Butler. Oxford: Basil Blackwell, 1965, 211–235.

———. "The Mental Life of Some Machines," in *Intentionality, Minds, and*

Perception. Edited by Hector-Neri Castañeda. Detroit: Wayne State University Press, 1967, 177–200.

———. "Minds and Machines," in *Dimensions of Mind.* Edited by Sidney Hook. New York: Collier Books, and London: Collier-Macmillan Ltd., 1960, 130–164. Reprinted in *Minds and Machines.* Edited by Alan Ross Anderson. Englewood Cliffs: Prentice-Hall, Inc., 1964, 72–97.

———. "On Properties," in *Essays in Honor of Carl G. Hempel.* Edited by Nicholas Rescher, et al. New York: Humanities Press, Dordrecht-Holland: D. Reidel Publishing Company, 1970, 235–254.

———. "Psychological Concepts, Explication and Ordinary Language," *JP,* LIV, 4 (February 14, 1957), 94–100.

———. "Robots: Machines or Artificially Created Life?", *JP,* LXI, 21 (November 12, 1964), 688–691. Reprinted in *Philosophy of Mind.* Edited by Stuart Hampshire. New York and London: Harper & Row, 1966, 63–91.

Quine, W. V. "On Mental Entities," *Proceedings of the American Academy of Arts and Sciences,* LXXX (1953), 198–203. Reprinted in *The Ways of Paradox and Other Essays.* New York: Random House, Inc., 1966, 208–214.

Raab, Francis V. "Of Minds and Molecules," *PSci,* XXXII, 1 (January 1965), 57–72.

Resnick, Lawrence. "Thinking and Corresponding," *PR,* LXXVIII, 4 (October 1969), 507–509.

Ripley, Charles. "The Identity Thesis and Scientific Hypotheses," *D,* VIII, 2 (September 1969), 308–310.

Rorty, Richard. "Incorrigibility as the Mark of the Mental," *JP,* LXVII, 12 (June 25, 1970), 399–424.

Routley, Richard and Valerie Macrae. "On the Identity of Sensations and Physiological Occurrences," *APQ,* III, 2 (April 1966), 87–110.

Ruddick, William. "Physical Equations or Identity Statements," in *Identity and Individuation.* Edited by Milton K. Munitz. New York: New York University Press, 1971.

Sellars, Wilfrid. "Empiricism and the Philosophy of Mind," in *Minnesota Studies in the Philosophy of Science,* I. Edited by Herbert Feigl and Michael Scriven. Minneapolis: University of Minnesota Press, 1956, 253–329. Reprinted with minor changes in Wilfrid Sellars. *Science, Perception and Reality.* London: Routledge & Kegan Paul Ltd., New York: The Humanities Press, 1963, 127–196.

———. "The Identity Approach to the Mind-Body Problem," *RM,* XVIII, 3 (March 1965), 430–451. Reprinted in *Boston Studies in the Philosophy of Science,* II, with comments by Israel Scheffler. Edited by Robert S. Cohen and Marx W. Wartofsky. New York: The Humanities Press,

1965, 55–76 and 77–80. Also reprinted in *Philosophy of Mind*. Edited by Stuart Hampshire. New York and London: Harper & Row, 1966, 7–30. Also reprinted in Wilfrid Sellars. *Philosophical Perspectives*. Springfield: Charles C. Thomas, 1967, 370–388.

———. "Phenomenalism," in *Science, Perception and Reality*. London: Routledge & Kegan Paul Ltd., New York: The Humanities Press, 1963, 60–105. Reprinted in *Intentionality, Minds, and Perception*, with Comments by Bruce Aune and Rejoinder by Wilfrid Sellars. Edited by Hector-Neri Castañeda. Detroit: Wayne State University Press, 1967, 215–274, 275–285 and 286–300.

———. "Science, Sense Impressions and Sensa: A Reply to Cornman," *RM*, XXIV, 3 (March 1971), 393ff.

Shaffer, Jerome. "Could Mental States Be Brain Processes?", *JP*, LVIII, 26 (December 21, 1961), 813–822.

———. "Persons and Their Bodies," *PR*, LXXV, 1 (January 1966), 59–77.

Sheridan, Gregory. "The Electroencephalogram Argument against Incorrigibility," *APQ*, VI, 1 (January 1969), 62–70.

Shope, Robert K. "Functional Equivalence and the Defense of Materialism," forthcoming.

Simon, Michael Arthur. "Materialism, Mental Language, and the Mind-Body Identity," *PPR*, XXX, 4 (June 1970), 514–532.

Smart, J. J. C. "Brain Processes and Incorrigibility," *AJP*, XL, 1 (May 1962), 68–70.

———. "Further Remarks on Sensations and Brain Processes," *PR*, LXX, 3 (July 1961), 406–407.

———. "The Identity Thesis—a Reply to Professor Garnett," *AJP*, XLIII, 1 (May 1965), 82–83.

———. "Materialism," *JP*, LX, 22 (October 24, 1963), 651–662.

———. *Philosophy and Scientific Realism*. London: Routledge & Kegan Paul Ltd., New York: The Humanities Press, 1963, especially chapters IV, V and VI.

———. "Ryle on Mechanism and Psychology," *PQ*, IX, 37 (October 1959), 349–355.

———. "Sensations and Brain Processes: A Rejoinder to Dr. Pitcher and Mr. Joske," *AJP*, XXXVIII, 3 (December 1960), 252–254.

Sosa, Ernest. "Professor Malcolm on 'Scientific Materialism and the Identity Theory,'" *D*, III, 4 (March 1965), 422–423.

Stevenson, J. T. "Sensations and Brain Processes: A Reply to J. J. C. Smart," *PR*, LXIX, 4 (October 1960), 505–510.

Strawson, P. F. "Persons," in *Minnesota Studies in the Philosophy of Science,* II. Edited by Herbert Feigl, Michael Scriven and Grover Maxwell. Minneapolis: University of Minnesota Press, 1958, 330–353. Reprinted in *The Philosophy of Mind.* Edited by V. C. Chappell. Englewood Cliffs: Prentice-Hall, Inc., 1962, 127–146. Incorporated in revised and expanded form as chapter III of P. F. Strawson, *Individuals.* London: Methuen & Co. Ltd., 1959.

Taylor, Charles. "Mind-Body Identity, a Side Issue?", *PR,* LXXVI, 2 (April 1967), 201–213.

———. "Two Issues about Materialism," a critical notice of *A Materialist Theory of the Mind,* by D. M. Armstrong, *PQ,* XIX, 74 (January 1969), 73–79.

Teichmann, Jenny. "The Contingent Identity of Minds and Brains," *M,* LXXVI, 303 (July 1967), 404–415.

Thompson, Dennis. "Can a Machine Be Conscious?", *BJPS,* XVI, 61 (May 1965), 33–43.

Thomson, Judith Jarvis. "The Identity Theory," in *Philosophy, Science, and Method: Essays in Honor of Ernest Nagel.* Edited by Sidney Morgenbesser, Patrick Suppes and Morton White. New York: St. Martin's Press, 1969.

Tomberlin, James E. "About the Identity Theory," *AJP,* XLIII, 3 (December 1965), 295–296.

Weissman, David. "A Note on the Identity Thesis," *M,* LXXIV, 296 (October 1965), 571–577.

Whitely, C. H. "The Mind-Brain Identity Hypothesis," *PQ,* XX, 80 (July 1970, 193–199.

Wolfe, Julian and George J. Nathan. "The Identity Thesis as a Scientific Hypothesis," *D,* VII, 3 (December 1968), 469–472.

Ziedins, Rudi. "Identification of Characteristics of Mental Events with Characteristics of Brain Events," *APQ,* VIII, 1 (January 1971), 13–23.

II. SEVENTEENTH-CENTURY MATERIALISM

Gunderson, Keith. "Descartes, La Mettrie, Language, and Machines," *P,* XXXIX, 149 (July 1964), 193–222.

Hampshire, Stuart. "A Kind of Materialism," *Proceedings and Addresses of the American Philosophical Association,* XLIII, forthcoming.

———. *Spinoza.* Baltimore: Penguin Books, revised edition, 1962.

Kenny, Anthony. *Descartes: A Study of His Philosophy.* New York: Random House, Inc., 1968.

La Mettrie, Julien Offray de. *Man a Machine.* Chicago: The Open Court Publishing Co., 1927.

Lange, Friedrich Albert. *The History of Materialism and Criticism of Its Present Importance*. Translated by Ernest Chester Thomas. 3rd Edition, with an introduction by Bertrand Russell. London: Kegan Paul, Trench, Trubner & Co., Ltd., New York: Harcourt, Brace & Company, Inc., 1925.

Peters, Richard. *Hobbes*. Baltimore: Penguin Books, 1956.

III. GENERAL PHILOSOPHY OF MIND

Aune, Bruce. *Knowledge, Mind, and Nature*. New York: Random House, Inc., 1967.

Cornman, James W. *Metaphysics, Reference and Language*. New Haven and London: Yale University Press, 1966, Part I, 3–79.

Geach, Peter. *Mental Acts*. London: Routledge & Kegan Paul, New York: Humanities Press, 1957.

Philosophy of Mind. Edited by Stuart Hampshire. New York and London: Harper & Row, 1966.

The Philosophy of Mind. Edited by V. C. Chappell. Englewood Cliffs: Prentice-Hall, Inc., 1962.

Ryle, Gilbert. *The Concept of Mind*. London: Hutchinson's University Library, New York: Barnes and Noble, Inc., 1949.

Shaffer, Jerome A. *Philosophy of Mind*. Englewood Cliffs: Prentice-Hall, Inc., 1968.

———. "Recent Work on the Mind-Body Problem," *APQ*, II, 2 (April 1965), 81–104.

Wittgenstein, THE PHILOSOPHICAL INVESTIGATIONS. Edited by George Pitcher. Garden City, New York: Doubleday & Company, Inc., 1966.

IV. PSYCHOLOGY, NEUROPHYSIOLOGY AND COMPUTER SCIENCE

Arbib, Michael A. *Brains, Machines and Mathematics*. New York: McGraw-Hill Book Company, 1965.

Brain and Conscious Experience. Edited by John C. Eccles. New York: Springer-Verlag, 1966, especially selections 7–14, 17 and 18.

Brain Mechanisms and Consciousness: A Symposium-Council for International Organizations of Medical Sciences. Edited by J. F. Delafresnage, with E. D. Adrian, F. Bremer and H. H. Jasper, consulting editors. Springfield: Charles C. Thomas, 1964.

Computers and Thought. Edited by Edward A. Feigenbaum and Julian Feldman. New York: McGraw-Hill Book Company, 1963.

George, F. H. *The Brain as a Computer*. Reading, Massachusetts: Addison-Wesley Publishing Company, Inc., 1962.

Gunderson, Keith. "Cybernetics and Mind-Body Problems," *Inquiry*, XII, 4 (Winter 1969), 406–419.

———. *Mentality and Machines*. Garden City, New York: Doubleday & Company, Inc., 1971.

———. "Robots, Consciousness, and Programmed Behaviour," *BJPS*, XIX, 2 (May 1968), 109–122.

Hayek, Friedrich. *The Sensory Order*. Chicago: University of Chicago Press, 1952.

Miller, George A., Eugene Galanter and Karl H. Pribram. *Plans and the Structure of Behavior*. New York: Holt, Rinehart and Winston, Inc., 1960.

Minds and Machines. Edited by Alan Ross Anderson. Englewood Cliffs: Prentice-Hall, Inc., 1964.

Nagel, Thomas. "Brain Bisection and the Unity of Consciousness," *Synthese*, forthcoming.

von Neumann, John. *The Computer and the Brain*. New Haven: Yale University Press, 1958.

The Neurophysiology of Lashley. Edited by Frank A. Beach, Donald O. Hebb, Clifford T. Morgan and Henry W. Nissen. New York: McGraw-Hill Book Company, Inc., 1960, especially essays 28–31.

Penfield, Wilder and Theodore Rasmussen. *The Cerebral Cortex of Man*. New York: Macmillan, 1950.

Rubinstein, Benjamin B. "Psychoanalytic Theory and the Mind-Body Problem," in *Psychoanalysis and Current Biological Thought*. Edited by N. Greenfield and W. Lewis. Madison: University of Wisconsin Press, 1965, 35–56.

"A Selected Designator-Indexed Bibliography to the Literature on Artificial Intelligence," in *Computers and Thought* [see above], 453–523. Compiled by Marvin Minsky.

Simon, Michael Arthur. "Could There Be a Conscious Automaton?" *APQ*, VI, 1 (January 1969), 71–78.

Sperry, R. W. "Neurology and the Mind-Body Problem," *American Scientist*, XL, 2 (April 1952), 291–312.

Wooldridge, Dean E. *The Machinery of the Brain*. New York: McGraw-Hill Book Company, 1963.

———. *Mechanical Man: The Physical Basis of Intelligent Life*. New York: McGraw-Hill Book Company, 1968.

FUNDERBURG LIBRARY
MANCHESTER COLLEGE

128.2
R727m

DATE DUE

WITHDRAWN
from
Funderburg Library